STRESS WITHOUT DISTRESS

Rx for Burnout

GEORGE MANNING

Professor of Psychology
Northern Kentucky University

KENT CURTIS

Professor of Industrial Technology and Education
Northern Kentucky University

U251
PUBLISHED BY
SOUTH-WESTERN PUBLISHING CO.
CINCINNATI, OH   WEST CHICAGO, IL   DALLAS, TX   LIVERMORE, CA

ISBN: 0-538-21251-9
Library of Congress Catalog Card Number: 86-62743

2 3 4 5 6 7 8 E 2 1 0 9

Printed in the United States of America

About The Authors

Dr. George Manning

Dr. Kent Curtis

George Manning is a professor of psychology and business at Northern Kentucky University. He is a consultant to business, industry, and government; his clients include AT&T, Sun Oil, IBM, Marriott Corporation, United Auto Workers, the Internal Revenue Service, and the National Institutes of Health. He lectures on economic and social issues including quality of work life, work force values, and business ethics. He serves as advisor to such diverse industries and professions as energy, transportation, justice, health, finance, labor, commerce, and the military.

He received graduation honors from George Williams College, the University of Cincinnati, and the University of Vienna. He was selected Professor of the Year at Northern Kentucky University, where his teaching areas include management and organization, organizational psychology, and personal adjustment. He maintains an active program of research and study in organizational psychology. His current studies and interests include the changing meaning of work, leadership development, and coping skills for personal and social change.

Kent Curtis has served as an administrator and faculty member at Northern Kentucky University since its inception in 1970. He is a professor in the departments of industrial technology and education. His teaching areas include supervisory development, human relations in business and industry, techniques of research design, counseling, and group dynamics.

He received a baccalaureate degree in biology from Centre College, a master's in counseling from Xavier University, and a doctorate in adult technical education from the University of Cincinnati. He has designed numerous employee and management training and development programs, which are presented to Fortune 500 companies, small businesses, and federal, state, and local government agencies.

Kent also presents open seminars and on-site programs in the areas of time and stress management, communication skills, and team building. His current studies and interests include developing effective "executive pairs" (secretary/manager teams); the manager as an effective teacher; and improving the quality of work life in organizations using employee involvement groups.

PREFACE

Each book in *The Human Side of Work* is special in its own way. *Stress Without Distress* is the one most helpful to the individual. One of life's developmental tasks is to learn to manage stress and prevent burnout. Everyone needs coping skills at some time, and this book teaches time-tested methods.

Our goal is for you to use this book to learn the causes and consequences of stress; to learn how stressful your world is at this point in time; to understand the role of personality in the stress equation; to learn coping skills to deal successfully with stress; and to develop a readiness plan in order to be prepared for life's inevitable stresses. The result should be a longer, fuller, and more satisfying life.

Specific topics, questions, and activities include:

- What are the telltale *signs of stress*? See pages 11–12.

- *How stressful is your world* and what does this mean for your health? See pages 19–27.

- Do you have a *stress-prone personality*? Are you a stress carrier? See pages 46–53.

- What *coping techniques* do successful people use? See pages 53–72.

- Learn the *1 × 3 × 7 = 21 plan* for dealing with stress. See pages 82–115.

- *How long will you live?* Add years to your life and life to your years. See pages 145–149.

- Avoid the *job burnout phenomenon.* Find out how to succeed at work and live to enjoy it. See pages 141–145.

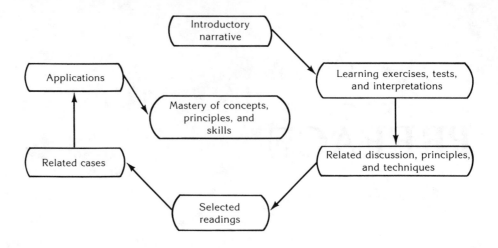

HOW TO USE THIS BOOK

This is a desk book for ready reference, a handbook for teaching others, and a workbook for personal development in the area of stress management. The material is arranged in a logical sequence for learning.

The best approach is to *interact* with the material. Read the narrative, take the tests and exercises, examine the interpretations, and review the principles and techniques — then ask: "How does this apply to me? How can I use this concept or information to improve?" Then take action. Also, use the related readings, cases, and applications to improve your stress-management knowledge and skills.

To increase interest and to improve your overall learning, try the following:

1. Use the learning objectives, discussion questions, and study quizzes included in each part of the book. This will focus your reading, improve comprehension, and increase retention of the material.

2. Share the results of your tests and exercises with family, friends, and co-workers. In this way, you can make tangible use of what you learn and may even help others.

3. Write in the book. Use the margins; underline; write your own ideas and personalize the material.

Good luck in your learning!

HOW TO TEACH FROM THIS BOOK

Personalize *Stress Without Distress* — for yourself and for the learner. Use the information, exercises, questions, activities, and tests to complement your own teaching style and resources; use any or all of the materials provided to suit the needs and goals of the group.

Steps

First, scan the material for topics and exercises. Second, outline a curriculum and lesson plan based on time frames and learning goals. Third, arrange learning aids, media, and other resources for smooth instruction. For assistance in this area, refer to the suggested readings, cases, applications, and films that accompany each part of the text. Also, see Appendix A for suggestions on teaching, testing, and grading as well as for information about other books in the *Human Side of Work* series.

Instruction

Multimedia, multimethod instruction usually works best. Each class period ideally would include a lecture to set the stage, learning exercises to personalize the subject, a discussion to interpret results, and use of related activities such as cases and readings to enhance knowledge and skills. A film, followed by group discussion and panel debate, is an ideal learning enhancer. See Appendix C for an annotated list of excellent films.

Final Note

Because this book is easy to read and covers the factual information needed by the learner, class periods should be used primarily for group involvement. Learning activities and group discussion will personalize the subject and promote maximum enjoyment and learning.

Stress Without Distress is intrinsically interesting. People relate naturally to such topics as stress in their world, the role of personality, personal coping skills, and the job burnout phenomenon. But they won't learn the material unless they get involved with it. As the instructor, the more practical you can make it for them, the better; the more personalized it is, the more helpful it will be. In this spirit, we conclude with a favorite proverb:

> I listen and I hear;
> I see and I remember;
> I do and I understand.
>
> *Confucius* (551–479 B.C.)

Good luck in your teaching!

Request: We want your suggestions. If you have questions or see a way to improve this book, please write. Thank you.

George Manning
Kent Curtis
Northern Kentucky University
Highland Heights, Ky. 41076

ACKNOWLEDGMENTS

The Human Side of Work is written by many people. It is the result of countless hours and endless effort from colleagues, students, and others who have helped in some important way. From initial draft to final form, many hands bring these books to life. To each we are grateful.

For this book, recognition is given to the following scientists and authors whose ideas and findings provide theoretical framework and important factual data:

Herbert Benson	Thomas Holmes	Hans Selye
Joseph Brady	Edmund Jacobson	Jay Weiss
Walter Cannon	Richard Lazarus	Harold Wolff
Kenneth Cooper	Richard Rahe	
Meyer Friedman	Ray Rosenman	

Appreciation goes to the following colleagues and supporters for substantive help in research, manuscript review, preparation, and advice:

Dan Alford	Michael Gray	Pam Ostendorf
Robert Caplon	David Hogan	Sandra Schlorman
Ken Carter	Sean Hogan	Arlie Schoepke
Grant Craig	Joyce Hungler	Vince Schulte
Gail DeMoss	Judith Kirkhorn	Betty Smith
Bill Dickens	Mary Ellen Long	Bill Stewart
Susan Dyrenforth	Walter Lovenberg	Laura Tesseneer
Grace Eddison	Kathy Lyon	Ralph Tesseneer
Alec Edge	Paul Maguire	Sam Vinci
Terrie Gabis	Steve McMillen	Sandra Ward
Charlotte Galloway	Diane Menendez	Mary Frances Warner
George Goedel	Heidi Neff	Susan Wehrmeyer

We want to thank J. Ellen Gerken for many of the figures, illustrations, and photographs.

George Manning
Kent Curtis

CONTENTS

Stress

stress (stres), noun, [OFr. estrece; L.L. estrictia L. strictus, strict; also, contr. of distress], **1.** strain; pressure; especially **a)** force exerted upon a body that tends to strain or depress its shape. **b)** the intensity of such force. **c)** the resistance or cohesiveness of a body resisting such force. **2.** tension; strained exertion: The stress of war affected all the people. **3.** physical and emotional wear and tear from pressure, conflict, and frustration. **4.** physical, emotional, and spiritual fatigue.

The job was getting to the ambulance attendant. He felt disturbed by the recurring tragedy, isolated by the long shifts. His marriage was in trouble. He was drinking too much.

One night it all blew up.

He rode in back that night. His partner drove.

Their first call was for a man whose leg had been cut off by a train. His screaming and agony was horrifying, but the second call was worse.

It was a child beating. As the attendant treated the youngster's bruised body and snapped bones, he thought of his own child. His fury grew.

Immediately after leaving the child at the hospital, the attendants were sent out to help a heart attack victim seen lying in a street.

When they arrived, however, they found not a cardiac patient but a drunk — a wino passed out.

As they lifted the man into the ambulance, their frustration and anger came to a head. They decided to give the wino a ride he would remember.

The ambulance vaulted over railroad tracks at high speed. The driver took the corners as fast as he could, flinging the wino from side to side in the back. To the attendants, it was a joke.

Suddenly, the man began having a real heart attack. The attendant in back leaned over the wino and started shouting.

"Die, you . . . ," he yelled. "Die."

He watched as the wino shuddered. He watched as the wino died.

By the time they reached the hospital, they had their stories straight. "Dead on arrival," they said. "Nothing we could do."

Source: Cincinnati Enquirer, *20 January 1980, sec. F, p. 10.*

PART ONE

Stress in Your World

Learning Objectives

After completing Part One, you will better understand:

1. the definition, causes, and consequences of stress;

2. the fight-or-flight syndrome as a biological response to stress;

3. the physical, psychological, and social signs of stress;

4. the importance of health habits and social relationships for managing stress;

5. the different types of stress;

6. the relationship between stressful events and personal health;

7. how stressful your world is, and what this means regarding your health;

8. how "little hassles" can affect your health;

9. the "critical balance" between the demands you face and your resources for coping.

INTRODUCTION

"The ambulance attendant" is a tragic story about stress, overload, and burnout. It is extreme but instructive, as it shows the value of understanding this important subject. Have you yourself ever been under stress? Have you ever felt there was too much of the world and not enough of you? If you have, you know firsthand the importance of managing stress in your life and your work.

If you do not cope with stress successfully, the price can be great. The following statements are not just meaningless sayings:

"That accident took ten years off my life."

"I was sick with worry."

"This job is killing me."

"He gives me a pain in the neck."

The stress caused by an accident can age you prematurely. The stress caused by emotional worry can make you physically sick. Your job can affect your health. And the stress from dealing with unpleasant people and situations can cause aches and pains in many parts of the body.[1]

Learning to manage stress effectively is one of life's developmental tasks. It is the secret to living a productive and satisfying life. For the typical working person, about half of the stress experienced is job related and about half relates to home and family. If things are bad at work, it helps to have a "port in the storm" at home; if there are problems on the home front, ideally there is "smooth sailing" on the job. The person who is fighting a two-front war — stress both on the job and in the home — has double trouble and is a candidate for what used to be called "breakdown" and is now popularly known as "burnout."

The purpose of this book is to help you understand the causes and consequences of stress and to teach coping skills to help you deal with life's inevitable problems. The concepts, principles, and techniques discussed will be of interest to both employee and manager and useful both on the job and in the home.

WHAT IS STRESS?

Stress is physical and emotional wear and tear resulting from real or imagined problems. Types of problems include:

- pressures, such as the effort required to raise a family and earn a living;

- conflicts, such as choosing between alternative careers, mates, and life-styles; and

• frustrations, such as wanting, but not having, good relations with someone you love, or wanting, but not being able to afford, a home of your own.

The human organism wears down with problems and age much the same as physical structures deteriorate from weather and time. Human problems may be self made or caused by others. They may occur at work or at home. They may be large or small. They may develop early in life or late. Yet each problem exacts a toll; each results in wear and tear on the person.

Hans Selye, a pioneer in stress research, defines stress as "the nonspecific response of the body to any demand." He formulated the concept of the "General Adaptation Syndrome" (G.A.S.). The G.A.S. is an automatic response to any physical or emotional threat to the well-being of an organism. This response occurs in three phases—the alarm reaction, the resistance stage, and the exhaustion stage.[2]

In the first phase, the *alarm reaction*, the body's resistance dips slightly below normal as preparation is made to fight the stressor. In the second phase, the stage of *resistance*, the body goes through a period of above-average and persistent resistance to stress. If stress continues, however, the final phase, the stage of *exhaustion*, may be reached. In this phase, the body's resources are depleted, breakdown occurs, and death may even result (see Figure 1.1).

FIGURE 1.1

The General Adaptation Syndrome

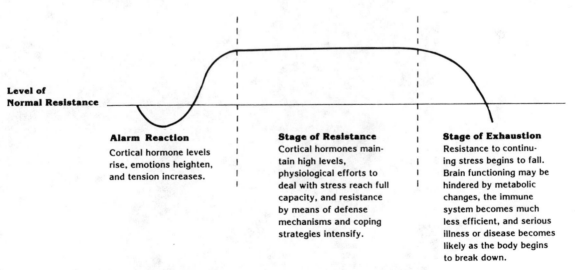

Level of Normal Resistance

Alarm Reaction
Cortical hormone levels rise, emotions heighten, and tension increases.

Stage of Resistance
Cortical hormones maintain high levels, physiological efforts to deal with stress reach full capacity, and resistance by means of defense mechanisms and coping strategies intensify.

Stage of Exhaustion
Resistance to continuing stress begins to fall. Brain functioning may be hindered by metabolic changes, the immune system becomes much less efficient, and serious illness or disease becomes likely as the body begins to break down.

Source: Hans Selye, The Stress of Life, *rev. ed. (New York: McGraw-Hill, Inc., 1976), 111-12, 163. Reprinted with permission. See also John P. Dworetzky,* Psychology *(St. Paul: West Publishing Co., 1982), 436.*

THE FIGHT-OR-FLIGHT SYNDROME

When a threat to well-being is perceived, a small area of the brain known as the hypothalamus is activated. The hypothalamus stimulates a number of physiological changes involving activity in both the endocrine system and the autonomic nervous system. You have probably felt the fight-or-flight response to stress — your heart beats faster, you feel an onset of energy, and you are mobilized to take protective action.

Specifically, the master gland of the endocrine system, the pituitary gland, sends large amounts of adrenocorticotrophic hormone (ACTH) into the bloodstream. ACTH activates the outer layer, or cortex, of the adrenal gland, and this results in the production of cortisol, a chemical that increases blood sugar and speeds up body metabolism.

Simultaneously, nerve impulses from the sympathetic branch of the autonomic nervous system reach the core of the adrenal glands, resulting in the release of adrenaline (also called epinephrine), which helps supply glucose to be used as fuel for increased muscle and nervous system activity, and noradrenaline (also called norepinephrine), which speeds up the heart rate and raises blood pressure. Within seconds, the entire organism is brought into an aroused physical state.

In addition, the individual experiences a state of general mental anxiety. No matter what you are consciously thinking, the endocrine system and autonomic nervous system have alerted and prepared your body to take action so that you can either combat the threat or run away. If you do fight or flee, the chemicals and hormones that have been generated are metabolized quickly. This biological response to stress, known as the

ILLUS. 1.1

The flight-or-fight syndrome began in prehistoric times.

Photo by Steve Castillo; Marine World/Africa USA on San Francisco Bay

fight-or-flight syndrome, was first described by Walter B. Cannon of Harvard Medical School around the turn of the twentieth century.[3]

For early men and women threatened by large predators, forest fires, and adverse climatic conditions, the fight-or-flight syndrome was an excellent aid for survival. When they rounded a bend and saw danger staring at them, a quick and automatic response prepared them to either fight or flee and thus cope with the problem. However, as explained by Selye in 1956, the fight-or-flight response can be hazardous for modern men and women. Times have changed, but human physiology has not.

Today, most of the threats we face are psychological instead of physical (a difficult boss, for example); fighting is inappropriate (it just makes a bad situation worse); and escape is not feasible (running away is usually not possible). Yet, our bodies react just as did our ancestors'—hormones and chemicals are automatically activated as a response to threat. Having been taught not to fight (civilized people are not supposed to use physical force), and being unable or unwilling to flee (this would be cowardly or irresponsible), we usually "sit tight." In this state, the level of metabolites in the bloodstream increases, and internal organs experience harmful wear and tear. Damage may result in a heart attack, stroke, ulcerative colitis, or some other harmful disease, depending on what heredity and history have predisposed for the individual.

Selye concludes that the fight-or-flight syndrome, so useful to our ancestors, can be a destructive force for people today unless it is managed properly. This is why stress has been called the dominant disease of modern times. Selye writes:

> . . . we are just beginning to see that many common diseases are largely due to errors in our adaptive response to stress, rather than to direct damage by germs, poisons, or life experience. In this sense, many nervous and emotional disturbances, high blood pressure, gastric and duodenal ulcers, and certain types of sexual, allergic, cardiovascular and renal derangements appear to be essentially diseases of adaptation.[4]

The primary purpose of this book is to show how to manage the fight-or-flight syndrome in today's world. The goal is to teach constructive, as opposed to maladaptive, responses to the stresses of life, both on the job and in the home.

COSTS OF STRESS—DISEASE AND AGING

During the 1930s, Harold Wolff of Cornell Medical College found that colds, flu, ulcers, arthritis, heart disease, and tuberculosis are stress related.[5] Physical and emotional wear and tear weaken the organism; fatigue results; and the person becomes susceptible to illness. In fact, according to one recent study, as many as 80 percent of doctors' visits in the United States are associated with stress.[6]

What disease a person may develop depends on both genetic makeup and environmental exposure, not on either factor alone. For example, cholera is rare in America today, but flu is common. Everyone has some idea of their own weakest area—for one, it may be the kidneys; for another, the heart; yet another may be susceptible to respiratory problems.

Aging is also stress related. Perhaps the best definition of the aging process is "the wearing down of the organism." This helps explain why one fifty-year-old may look sixty while another fifty-year-old may not even look forty. Selye explains:

> True age depends largely on the rate of wear and tear, on the speed of self-consumption; for life is essentially a process which gradually spends the given amount of adaptation energy that we inherited from our parents. Vitality is like a special kind of bank account which you can use up by withdrawals but cannot increase by deposits. Your only control over this most precious fortune is the rate at which you make your withdrawals. The solution is evidently not to stop withdrawing, for this would be death. Nor is it to withdraw just enough for survival, for this would permit only a vegetative life, worse than death. The intelligent thing to do is to withdraw and expend generously, but never wastefully for worthless efforts.
>
> Many people believe that after they have exposed themselves to very stressful activities, a rest can restore them to where they were before. This is false. Experiments on animals have clearly shown that each exposure leaves an indelible scar, in that it uses up reserves of adaptability which cannot be replaced. It is true that immediately after some harassing experience, rest can restore us almost to the original level of fitness by eliminating acute fatigue. But the emphasis is on the word almost. Since we constantly go through periods of stress and rest during life, even a minute deficit of adaptation energy every day adds up—it adds up to what we call aging.[7]

Three D's show the high costs of stress: disorders, drugs, and dollars.

Disorders

30 million Americans have some form of heart or blood-vessel disease.
1 million Americans have a heart attack every year.
25 million Americans have high blood pressure.
8 million Americans have ulcers.

Drugs

5 billion doses of tranquilizers are prescribed each year.
3 billion doses of amphetamines are prescribed each year.
5 billion doses of barbiturates are prescribed each year.

Dollars

$15.6 billion is lost each year by American industry because of alcoholism.
$700 million is spent each year to recruit replacements for executives with heart disease.

Although statistics such as these are staggering, they are somewhat impersonal. They do not communicate the suffering of the victims of stress and their loved ones.[8] True understanding comes from personal exposure to the costs of stress—premature aging and the three D's (disorders, drugs, and dollars).

To personalize the subject of stress, health, and aging—if you were to become ill, what would your illness probably be; what have history and heredity predisposed for you? What about the aging process? What is your true age, based on the amount of wear and tear you have experienced? Perhaps most importantly, are you spending your adaptive energy at the rate you wish and for the purposes you value?

PERSONAL SIGNS OF STRESS

People react to stress in different ways. Warning signals are varied and are unique to the individual. One person may have a nervous tic or may bite the fingernails when under stress. Another may crack the knuckles, bite a lip, or grind the teeth. Whatever your symptoms are, your body will usually tell you when you are experiencing too much stress, if you will only pay attention. Learn what your warning signals are; then, when you notice them, act to relieve the problem. Common physical, behavioral, and psychological signals of stress include:

- *Aches and pains.* When a person complains, "I have a headache," it may be caused by pressure, conflict, and frustration, resulting in body tension. Headaches, neck aches, backaches, and stomachaches are common signs of too much stress.

- *Sweating hands and paling or flushing of the face.* Many people experience these symptoms of too much stress. Such signs are especially disturbing to salespeople, politicians, and other public figures.

- *Inability to sleep or sleeping too much.* Some people toss and turn and cannot sleep because of too much stress. Still others wake up in the morning, look at the world, say "Oh, no!"—and go right back to sleep. Both insomnia and oversleeping are common signs of too much stress.

- *Inability to eat or eating too much.* Some people have upset stomachs and do not want to eat when they are under stress. Some of us have the opposite response—the refrigerator reaction: when we experience pressure, conflict, or frustration, we head right for the refrigerator. Often when we do so, we eat all one thing; we consume enormous amounts of candy, baked goods, salted snacks, or pizzas. Overeating is a common reaction to too much stress.

- *Skin disorders.* Can you remember junior high school or high school when you anxiously looked forward to your first date? About five o'clock on a Saturday afternoon, you went into the bathroom to get ready to go. You looked in the mirror, and right in the middle of your forehead . . . there was this big pimple. This may have been your sign of too much stress.

- *Mental and emotional blanks.* Your mind may go blank for short periods of time, or you may become temporarily numb to feelings because of stress. If continued over a long period of time, these mental and emotional blanks may result in a general lack of interest in people, ideas, and events in life.

- *Mistakes and accidents.* Have you ever forgotten something for no apparent reason? Have you ever had an accident for seemingly no cause at all? With severe or prolonged stress, objective thinking and problem-solving abilities decrease. Forgetfulness, errors, and accidents are common signs of too much stress.[9]

The preceding are physical, behavioral, and psychological signs of stress. Social problems such as spouse and child abuse, alcohol and drug abuse, and irritability with others can also be signs of too much stress.

When a situation becomes overly stressful, some people turn to alcohol and drugs for relief, and many become chemically dependent. Statistics in the United States show that approximately 10 million people have problems with alcohol consumption. This amounts to 1 out of every 20 Americans.[10]

When stress levels are high, some people displace their feelings onto close or safe targets. These are often the people they care about the most, such as family and friends. Perhaps you have kicked the dog, husband, wife, or child when you have been under stress. Whether you kick others physically or psychologically, the blow usually results in poor relations, personal guilt, and increased stress.

What are your symptoms of stress? What signals warn you of too many pressures, conflicts, and frustrations? Do you experience stress at a certain time of the day (morning, afternoon, evening); at a particular place (work, home); with certain people (family, co-workers, boss)? Helping you to know your signs of stress and to act to defuse stressful situations in a positive way is the purpose of this book. Figure 1.2 shows signs of stress at each stage of the General Adaption Syndrome.

THE IMPORTANCE OF HEALTH HABITS AND SOCIAL CONDITIONS

Health habits and social conditions are major factors that contribute to stress in your life. Although health and social problems are often unavoidable, many problems are self-induced and can be easily corrected.

Health Habits

Actuarial statistics and death records show that few people die of old age. Instead, they die because of poor health habits. Their hearts have been underdeveloped and overworked because of lack of exercise; their livers have been abused by too much alcohol; their lungs have been ruined by cigarette smoke; their blood vessels have been clogged by a poor diet;

FIGURE 1.2

Signs of Stress

STAGE 1—Alarm Reaction: The Stress-Arousal Stage (Includes the Following Symptoms)

Physical

High blood pressure
Heart palpitations
Unusual heart rhythms (skipped beats)
Sweating; cold chills
Headaches

Behavioral

Persistent irritability
Bruxism (grinding the teeth at
  night)
Insomnia

Psychological

Persistent anxiety
Forgetfulness
Inability to concentrate

STAGE 2—Stage of Resistance: The Energy-Conservation Stage (Includes the Following Symptoms)

Physical

Decreased sexual desire
Persistent tiredness

Behavioral

Lateness for work
Turning work in late
Increased alcohol consumption
Increased coffee, tea, or cola
  consumption

Psychological

Procrastination
Social withdrawal
Cynical attitude
Resentfulness
"I don't care" attitude

STAGE 3—Stage of Exhaustion: Breakdown Occurs (Includes the Following Symptoms)

Physical

Chronic stomach or bowel problems
Chronic physical fatigue
Chronic headaches

FIGURE 1.2 — continued

Behavioral	Psychological
Physical withdrawal from friends, work, and family	Chronic sadness or depression Chronic mental fatigue Desire to "drop out" Sense of hopelessness

Source: Based on the work of Daniel A. Girdano and George S. Everly, Jr., Controlling Stress and Tension, 2d ed. (Englewood Cliffs, N.J.: Prentice-Hall, Inc., 1986), 57.

or some other destructive health practice has resulted in accelerated wear and tear and contributed to their death.[11] Selye states:

> To die of old age would mean that all the organs of the body had worn out proportionately, merely by having been used too long. This is never the case. We invariably die because one vital part has worn out too early in proportion to the rest of the body. Life, the biologic chain that holds our parts together, is only as strong as its weakest vital link. When this breaks—no matter which vital link it is—our parts can no longer be held together as a single living being.[12]

The simple habits of exercising regularly, eating sensibly, obtaining needed rest, and avoiding drug and alcohol abuse are within the control of every person. If these practices are followed, increased longevity and better health can be expected. Test yourself to see if you engage in these healthy habits.

BE HEALTHY AND LIVE LONGER

Directions

The following habits increase your chances of living a long and healthy life. Indicate below whether or not you practice these health habits. Give yourself one point for each "yes" answer.

Health Habit	Yes	No	Explanation
No smoking	____	____	As the ads state, it's a matter of life and breath. Conclusive findings indicate that smoking harms your health and shortens your life. Nothing will add more years to your life than not smoking.
Moderate drinking	____	____	More than three drinks a day will take years off your life, but a drink on occasion may add a couple of years by reducing tension. Remember,

			though, it's *moderate* drinking—you can't save your "one a day" for 7 on Friday night.
Sufficient sleep	____	____	Although some people can exist on less, most adults require seven to eight hours of sleep to recharge their batteries. If you need less, OK; but check how you respond to stress if you sleep less.
Regular meals, no snacks	____	____	The best way to keep your weight down is to cut out snacks and keep a regular schedule for meals. Also, other problems may result from poor eating habits. For example, someone with normal weight but poor eating habits may develop diabetes.
Breakfast every morning	____	____	Although this sounds like a cereal commercial, we should live by the wise old adage "eat breakfast like a king/queen, lunch like a prince/princess, and dinner like a pauper." We need energy in that proportion throughout the day.
Normal weight	____	____	Excess weight puts strain on our internal organs, especially the cardiovascular system. Therefore, it is no mystery why being overweight shortens one's life.
Moderate, regular exercise	____	____	Note the words *moderate* and *regular*. Moderation by most doctors' standards means not increasing your heart rate beyond a safe level, depending on your age, exercise history, etc. Regular translates into three to five times a week. The weekend workout does little to increase health and longevity.
Totals	____	____	

Source: Based on the work of John Margolis, *"Key to Survival: Manage Stress Effectively,"* Management Review *(October 1977):6.*

SCORING AND INTERPRETATION

How did you do on the Be Healthy and Live Longer test? If you scored six or seven, be glad. Research shows that you may live up to 11.5 years past your normal life expectancy. Further, research indicates that the physical health of people over seventy-five years of age who follow these habits can be as good as, if not better than, thirty-five- to forty-four-year-olds who follow fewer than three of the habits. If you practice three or fewer of these habits, keep reading, and take special note of the $1 \times 3 \times 7 = 21$ plan presented later in this book.

Social Conditions

Social conditions help account for extra stress and too-rapid aging for many people. Boredom, forced retirement, and a lack of meaningful relationships are a few harmful social conditions. The following research emphasizes the importance of meaningful relationships, showing that "people need people":

> Nearly seven thousand adults were surveyed to determine health and health-related behaviors, as well as other background factors and the extent of their social relationships. Mortality (death rate) data were collected for a nine-year period on 96 percent of this original sample.
>
> A "social network index" was computed for each person consisting of the number and relative importance of social contacts. This index of social disconnection was significantly correlated with overall mortality rates as well as each specific cause of death.
>
> For every age group and both sexes, more people with minimal social contacts died than people with many social contacts. This effect was independent of health status at the time of the initial survey or of socioeconomic status. Furthermore, people who were socially isolated were more likely to engage in poor health behaviors (smoking, drinking, overeating, irregular eating, inadequate sleep, etc.).
>
> But the extent of one's social contacts still predicts mortality over and above the effects of any or all of these poor health practices. Thus, likelihood of death can be predicted better by knowing how isolated or connected a person is than by knowledge of the person's smoking history, even though smoking clearly increases mortality.
>
> The data warrant the researcher's conclusion that social and community ties [are] powerful determinants of consequent health status.[13]

Paul Rosch of the American Institute of Stress emphasizes the importance of social interaction: "The most significant observation is that widows die at rates 3 to 13 times as high as married women for every known major cause of death."[14]

The answer is to establish contact with people who are important to you and who give you pleasure; good friends and loved ones are helpful antidotes to too much stress. Also, relationships with animals can be important in the stress-management equation. Many people find that dogs, cats, horses, and other pets add happiness and meaning to their lives and help them cope with the pressures, conflicts, and frustrations they encounter.

TYPES OF STRESS

Stress is inevitable from the moment of birth. One definition of life is "the continual process of solving problems," and all problem solving involves pressure, conflict, and frustration — in other words, stress. Selye writes:

> No one can live without experiencing some degree of stress all the time. You may think that only serious disease or intensive physical or mental injury can cause stress. This is false. Crossing a busy intersection, exposure to a draft, or even sheer joy are enough to activate the body's

stress mechanism to some extent. Stress is not even necessarily bad for you; it is also the spice of life, for any emotion, any activity, causes stress.[15]

Selye goes on to explain that there is a difference between good stress and bad stress, or distress, and that the mind is aware of the difference but the body is not and will experience wear and tear in any case. For example, if being in love, winning a sports event, or realizing significant achievement in your work are meaningful and satisfying, these experiences represent good stress, but also wear and tear. On the other hand, if boredom, sickness, or war are undesirable experiences, these represent distress—also wear and tear.

In the case of either good stress or distress, the wear and tear will be the same because even though the mind knows the difference and may choose good experiences over bad, the body reacts in the same way. Heart rate and blood pressure go up; brain activity is altered; and stress hormones, particularly epinephrine, norepinephrine, and ACTH appear in the bloodstream.

The question is, if problems are unavoidable and wear and tear is inevitable, what should be your goal? How should you cope? What should your philosophy be toward stress? The answer is to maximize good-stress experiences up to, but not beyond, the point at which they become harmful to others or yourself and to minimize distress whenever possible.

An analogy makes this point. Imagine an empty cup that represents your life. It is sitting between two pitchers—a pitcher of good stress, full of satisfying experiences and pleasurable events, and a pitcher of distress, full of unhappy experiences and unpleasant events. You must strive to pour from the good-stress pitcher into your life's cup. Fill it as full as possible, but not to the point of overflowing. Remember, too much of even

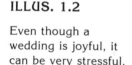

ILLUS. 1.2

Even though a wedding is joyful, it can be very stressful.

a good thing can be harmful. Remember also, a half-full cup represents a half-full life, and too little stress is undesirable as well. And never, if at all possible, pour from the distress pitcher.

Consider the following experiment:

> One group of infant rats was given mild electric shocks every day for three weeks. A second group was split up and each rat put into a small compartment for a few minutes each day. And a third group was simply left in the nest and not handled at all. It was expected that the early traumatic experience of the first group would result in symptoms of emotional disorder in adulthood, but suprisingly, the nonstimulated rats were the ones who showed deviations in both behavior and development.

> From this and other investigations it was discovered that: (1) the shocked and manipulated rats matured more rapidly; (2) both groups of stimulated rats showed a more normal and adaptive stress response in adulthood, whereas the nonstimulated rats showed a more sluggish stress response; and (3) the nonstimulated rats showed a stress response in unfamiliar but otherwise neutral situations.[16]

Another analogy shows the importance of experiencing optimum good stress and minimizing distress.

In this picture, stress is the wind that propels life forward. Too much wind may break the mast, and an ill wind may capsize the boat. You

Good stress, too much stress, and distress

are the captain, who must sail your life to go the farthest on the most beautiful seas.

The difference between good stress and distress is detailed in the two stress cycles illustrated in Figure 1.3. One is positive, resulting in a full and satisfying life; the other is negative, resulting in decreased happiness and reduced effectiveness.

In summary, the proper amount of stress keeps you alert and interested in what you are doing. It helps you to be both healthy and satisfied. Indeed, some of your best moments in life are accompanied by stress. Think of a wedding, birth, or some special feat you have performed. Finally, remember Selye's words: "Stress . . . is also the spice of life," and "Complete freedom from stress is death."[17]

PEOPLE IN A WORLD OF CHANGE

Alvin Toffler, author of *Future Shock*, writes that change is descending upon people today at such a rate and volume that breakdown may result. He defines future shock (breakdown) as "the distress, both physical and psychological, that arises from an overload of the human organism's physical adaptive systems and its decision-making processes."[18]

The following, from a young father and businessman, personalizes the subject of stress and overload: "The job of managing a career isn't too bad. Deadlines, travel, and all the meetings aren't that bad. I can handle being a father to two boys and a new baby girl. Being a husband and spending time with my wife is good. The work of keeping up a home and yard is fine. It's doing all of these things at the same time that's killing me. I hope I can keep it up."

Stress is caused by life changes — events that somehow require you to adapt or cope. The idea that people can be victims of too many life changes, and can get sick as a result, began with Adolf Meyer of Johns Hopkins University around 1900. Meyer kept detailed life charts on his patients that indicated that many illnesses occurred when people experienced clusters of major events in their lives.[19]

Beginning in 1949, Thomas Holmes of the University of Washington School of Medicine applied Meyer's concept of life charts to the case histories of over 5,000 patients. He identified 43 common changes that occurred over and over in the lives of these patients. He found that these life changes tended to take place shortly before the onset of major illness. Some of the changes were desirable, such as marriage and vacations, while others were undesirable, such as the death of a spouse or loss of employment. Holmes assigned an arbitrary number (50) to marriage to represent the amount of readjustment required for this life change, and based on a survey of a cross section of the adult population, the readjustment values of the other 42 items were determined. In 1967, Holmes and Richard Rahe published "The Social Readjustment Rating Scale," an evaluation instrument based on this research. In 1976, Holmes developed

FIGURE 1.3

Two Stress Cycles

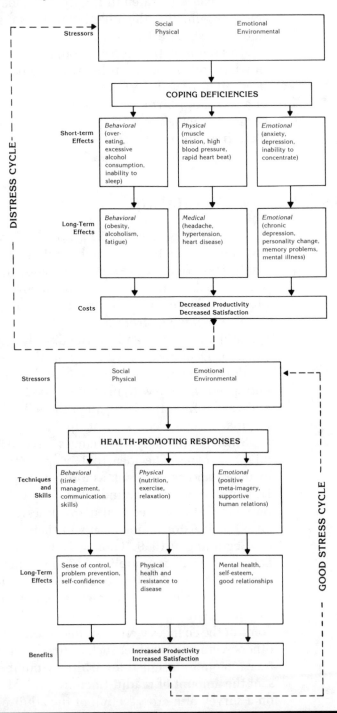

Source: Based on the work of Edward A. Charlesworth and Ronald G. Nathan, Stress Management: A Comprehensive Guide to Wellness *(Houston: Biobehavioral Publishers and Distributors, Inc., 1982), 22–23.*

an updated version of "The Social Readjustment Rating Scale" entitled "Schedule of Recent Experiences."

In order to determine how stressful your world is, complete the following questionnaire.

HOW STRESSFUL IS YOUR WORLD?
SCHEDULE OF RECENT EXPERIENCES

All of the events in your life, both good and bad, exact a penalty in the form of stress. The amount of stress you experience could affect your health. This test was developed to help predict (and prevent) physical problems that can come from too much change and stress in your life.

Directions

Under Number of Occurrences, indicate how many times in the past year each of the events has occurred.

Multiply the number under Stress Value by the number of occurrences of each event, and place the answer under Your Score.

Add the figures under Your Score to find your total for the past year.

Life Event	Number of Occurrences	Stress Value	Your Score
1. Death of spouse	_____	100	_____
2. Divorce	_____	73	_____
3. Marital separation	_____	65	_____
4. Detention in jail or other institution	_____	63	_____
5. Death of a close family member	_____	63	_____
6. Major personal injury or illness	_____	53	_____
7. Marriage	_____	50	_____
8. Loss of job	_____	47	_____
9. Marital reconciliation	_____	45	_____
10. Retirement from work	_____	45	_____
11. Major change in the health or behavior of a family member	_____	44	_____
12. Pregnancy	_____	40	_____
13. Sexual difficulties	_____	39	_____

Life Event	Number of Occurrences	Stress Value	Your Score
14. Gaining a new family member (e.g., through birth, adoption, relative moving in, etc.)	_____	39	_____
15. Major business readjustment (e.g., merger, reorganization, bankruptcy, etc.)	_____	39	_____
16. Major change in financial state (e.g., a lot worse off or a lot better off than usual)	_____	38	_____
17. Death of a close friend	_____	37	_____
18. Changing to a different line of work	_____	36	_____
19. Major change in the number of arguments with spouse (e.g., either a lot more or a lot fewer than usual regarding child rearing, personal habits, etc.)	_____	35	_____
20. Taking on a mortgage or loan for a major purchase (e.g., purchasing a home, business, etc.)	_____	31	_____
21. Foreclosure on a mortgage or loan	_____	30	_____
22. Major change in responsibilities at work (e.g., promotion, demotion, lateral transfer)	_____	29	_____
23. Son or daughter leaving home (e.g., marriage, attending college, etc.)	_____	29	_____
24. In-law troubles	_____	29	_____
25. Outstanding personal achievement	_____	28	_____
26. Spouse beginning or ceasing work outside the home	_____	26	_____
27. Beginning or ceasing formal schooling	_____	26	_____
28. Major change in living conditions (e.g, building a new home, remodeling, deterioration of home or neighborhood)	_____	25	_____
29. Revision of personal habits (dress, manners, associations, etc.)	_____	24	_____
30. Troubles with the boss	_____	23	_____
31. Major change in working hours or conditions	_____	20	_____

Life Event	Number of Occurrences	Stress Value	Your Score
32. Change in residence	_____	20	_____
33. Changing to a new school	_____	20	_____
34. Major change in usual type and/or amount of recreation	_____	19	_____
35. Major change in church activities (e.g., a lot more or a lot less than usual)	_____	19	_____
36. Major change in social activities (e.g., clubs, dancing, movies, visiting, etc.)	_____	18	_____
37. Taking on a mortgage or loan for a lesser purchase (e.g., purchasing a car, RV, freezer, etc.)	_____	17	_____
38. Major change in sleeping habits (a lot more or a lot less sleep or change in part of day when asleep)	_____	16	_____
39. Major change in number of family get-togethers (e.g., a lot more or a lot fewer than usual)	_____	15	_____
40. Major change in eating habits (a lot more or a lot less food intake, or very different meal hours or surroundings)	_____	15	_____
41. Vacation	_____	13	_____
42. Christmas	_____	12	_____
43. Minor violations of the law (e.g., traffic tickets, jaywalking, disturbing the peace, etc.)	_____	11	_____

This is your total life change score for the past year _____

Source: Reprinted with permission from T. H. Holmes and R. H. Rahe, "The Social Readjustment Rating Scale," Journal of Psychosomatic Research 11 (1967):213–18. Copyright © 1967, Pergamon Press, Ltd.

SCORING AND INTERPRETATION

If your total score on the Schedule of Recent Experiences is 149 or below, you are on fairly safe ground. Life events and changes in your world are not causing undue stress. On the other hand, a score between 150 and 199 indicates mild life changes, with a 37 percent chance that you will feel the impact of stress through physical symptoms. Scores from 200 to 299 represent moderate stress in your world, with a 51 percent chance that you will experience stress-related illness in the near future. Finally, a score of over 300 points represents a serious threat to your well-being, with a 79 percent chance of sickness in the near future unless you take corrective action.

If you had a high score, you may wonder what this means in terms of illness. What kind of illness? How serious? Holmes and his associates researched the answer to this question. They studied patients who had been inflicted with 42 different diseases. The results were startling.

A list showing 16 major disorders appears in Figure 1.4. Column 1 identifies the disorder; column 2 shows its relative seriousness; and column 3 lists the accumulated scores on the Schedule of Recent Experiences during the two years prior to onset of the illness.

The higher the score, the more serious the problems. Not only does a person with an average score of over 300 on the Schedule of Recent Experiences have a 79 percent chance of falling ill, it is also probable that the type of disorder will be serious as well. People with the highest scores were more likely to suffer chronic illness — cancer or heart disease. In contrast, those with lower scores tended to have minor disorders that are acute and short in duration — headaches and skin disorders.

DISCUSSION

There are eight major points to remember about the Schedule of Recent Experiences:

- The purpose of the questionnaire is to heighten your awareness of the relationship between life events, stress, and physical problems. You should share your results with your family and friends — those who influence you and who are influenced by your life changes, stress levels, and health.

- If your score alarms you, do something about it. For example, if you have a high score because you have recently graduated from school, moved to a new residence, taken a new job, married, lost a loved one, and changed your eating and sleeping habits, and you are now considering pregnancy, you may decide to postpone such an important decision. Allow time to pass so the fatigue of previous adjustments can wear off and your body can rest before you add more stress to your world. Your cup may already be overflowing,

FIGURE 1.4

Life Changes and Disorders

Column 1 Illness	Column 2 Seriousness of Illness (Units in Parentheses)	Column 3 Average Life Changes (Two Years Preceding the Illness)
Headache	(88)	209
Psoriasis	(174)	317
Eczema	(204)	231
Bronchitis	(210)	322
Anemia	(312)	325
Anxiety reaction	(315)	482
Gallstones	(454)	563
Peptic ulcer	(500)	603
High blood pressure	(520)	405
Chest pain	(609)	638
Diabetes	(621)	599
Alcoholism	(688)	688
Manic-depressive psychosis	(766)	753
Schizophrenia	(785)	609
Heart failure	(824)	772
Cancer	(1020)	777

Source: A.R. Wyler, M. Masada, and T.H. Holmes, "Magnitude of Life Events and Seriousness of Illness," *Psychosomatic Medicine* 33 (1971), 115–122; Walter H. Gmelch, *Beyond Stress to Effective Management.* Copyright © 1982, John Wiley & Sons, Inc.

and the additional stress of a new event, no matter how satisfying, may result in physical problems.

• On the other hand, you may have a low score on the questionnaire, which may reflect a half-full cup. In such a case, perhaps you should proceed with the room addition you have been considering, accept the challenge of leading a Boy Scout troop, or go back to school to complete your education, if these activities would be satisfying. Lack of stimulation can be boring and can lead to the distress of stagnation and depression. Remember, your goal is to pour from the pitcher of good-stress experiences into your life's cup up to, but not beyond, the point of overflowing.

- Recognize that some stress is self made and some stress is made for you. You may not have asked for some of your life changes; forces beyond your control may have caused them. In any case, you must cope with the stress. It is the total score and its impact on your health that counts, not who causes it.

- Both good and bad events wear a person down, cause fatigue, and increase susceptibility to physical disorders. For example, marital reconciliation (45 points) and gaining a new family member (39 points) are both positive events that take a great deal of adaptive energy. It is interesting to note that of the 43 stressful events included in the questionnaire, only 13 are clearly negative, 6 are positive, and the other 24 are essentially neutral.

- Although everyone experiences some amount of stress, not everyone reacts to stress in the same way. Some people will get headaches, others backaches. In some people, stress and ulcers go together. The kind of disorder a person develops depends on both the individual and the environment. Regarding the individual, heredity may predispose one person to arthritis and another to ulcers. Regarding environment, the chance of anyone getting bubonic plague today is low, but respiratory ailments are not unusual. It is important to note that change itself does not cause illness. As Holmes emphasizes, "it takes a germ."[20]

- Perception plays an important part in stress management. Some people perceive life changes as negative and more stressful; others welcome new experiences and challenges. This quality can be called hardiness. It should be noted that even the most hardy individual has physical and emotional limits and should consider the health effects of continual and major life changes.

- The items, scores, and probabilities of the Schedule of Recent Experiences are based on a cross section of the population and may not apply for a particular individual. For example, some people are "turtles" by temperament. Imagine someone like Albert Einstein — deliberate, contemplative, and unhurried. The following reflects his humble and relaxed temperament: "Before God we are all equally wise and equally foolish," and "I never think of the future. It comes soon enough."

  On the other hand, some people are "racehorses" by temperament. Consider Thomas Alva Edison, who, at the age of sixty-seven, connected the camera and the phonograph to produce "talking pictures," which he hoped to use for educational purposes. Full of energy and eagerness, Edison wrote: "Genius is one percent inspiration and

ILLUS. 1.3

Some people react to stress in ways that are physically harmful.

99 percent perspiration," and "Show me a satisfied man, and I will show you a failure."

Individual temperament has little to do with hardiness, and each temperament (the turtle and the racehorse) can be equally happy, productive, wise, and healthy. But if we try to speed up the turtle, it will be distressful; and it is likely that a person like this could tolerate fewer life changes than could the average person. Similarly, if we try to slow down the racehorse, it will be distressful. Racehorses love variety and action and thrive on more life change than does the average person. Before you say: "Aha! That explains my high stress score. I am a racehorse!," you should realize that most people fall somewhere between the extreme turtle and extreme racehorse temperaments. Therefore, the foregoing scores and predictions would apply.

LITTLE HASSLES MEAN A LOT

Besides the stress of life events, "little hassles" make a difference in the amount of physical and emotional wear and tear we experience. This was the conclusion of a study done by Richard Lazarus and his associates at the University of California at Berkeley. Lazarus reports:

> In short, we found that major events do have some long-term effects, but in the short term, hassles seem to have a much stronger impact on mental and physical health. . . . In sum, it is not the large, dramatic events that make the difference, but what happens day in and day out, whether provoked by major events or not.[21]

Figure 1.5 is a summary of the most common sources of hassles and uplifts for the average adult.

FIGURE 1.5

The Top Ten Hassles and Uplifts

What are the most common sources of pleasures and hassles in life? It all depends on who you are.

When my colleagues and I asked 100 white, middle-class, middle-aged men and women to keep track of their hassles and uplifts over a one-year period, we got one set of candidates for the Top Ten annoyances and joys. When we asked a group of college students, we got another. Canadian health professionals gave us still another list.

The ten most frequent hassles and uplifts in the middle-aged group were, in order of frequency:

Hassles	Uplifts
1. Concern about weight	1. Relating well with spouse or lover
2. Health of a family member	2. Relating well with friends
3. Rising prices of consumer goods	3. Completing a task
4. Home maintenance	4. Feeling healthy
5. Too many things to do	5. Getting enough sleep
6. Misplacing or losing things	6. Eating out
7. Yard work or outside home maintenance	7. Meeting responsibilities
8. Property, investment, or taxes	8. Visiting, phoning, or writing someone
9. Crime	9. Spending time with family

| 10. Physical appearance | 10. Pleasing home atmosphere |

People differ widely in the problems and pleasures typical of their lives. Only three hassle items—and not a single uplift—rated among the top ten for all three groups. The big three: misplacing or losing things, physical appearance, and too many things to do.

Each group had certain hassles common to its station in life. For the middle-aged, middle-class group, the predominant theme was economic concern—worries about investments and rising prices. The Canadian health professionals tended to check off hassles that reflect the anxieties and pressures of their careers: too much to do, not enough time to do it all, too many responsibilities, and trouble relaxing. Students were most hassled by anxiety over wasting time, meeting high standards, and being lonely.

As for pleasures, there again the groups diverged. The uplifts of the middle-aged are the joys of a home-body: being in good health; enjoying hearth, home, and kin. Students, on the other hand, tend to be more hedonistic; their uplifts include having fun, laughing, and entertainment. The only two uplifts shared by young and middle-aged alike were completing a task, and having good times with friends.

Source: Reprinted with permission from Psychology Today *magazine. Copyright © 1981 American Psychological Association.*

ILLUS. 1.4

Among the top ten hassles, misplacing or losing things ranks sixth as stress-producing.

For a measure of your hassle level, complete the following questionnaire.

WHAT IS YOUR HASSLE QUOTIENT?

Directions

For each statement, circle Y if it is true or mostly true, and circle N if it is false or mostly false.

	Y (Yes)	N (No)
1. I am concerned about my weight (either too heavy or too light).	Y	N
2. I have a good relationship with a spouse or lover.	Y	N
3. The rising cost of living bothers me.	Y	N
4. I have a sense of accomplishment.	Y	N
5. I have a lot to do to maintain my home.	Y	N
6. I have good friends.	Y	N
7. Misplacing or losing things is a problem for me.	Y	N
8. I am in good health.	Y	N
9. I have too much to do and too little time to do it.	Y	N
10. I get enough sleep.	Y	N
11. I am not satisfied with my physical appearance.	Y	N
12. I spend a lot of time with the people who are important to me.	Y	N
13. Managing finances and keeping records take a lot of my time.	Y	N
14. My home is pleasant.	Y	N
15. Someone close to me is in poor health.	Y	N
16. I eat out (in) often enough.	Y	N

Source: Adapted from Bethesda Hospitals: Stress Management Program (St. Louis, Mo.: Department of Health Promotion, St. Louis University Medical Center).

SCORING AND INTERPRETATION

Count the odd-numbered statements on the Hassle Quotient test for which you have circled Y (Yes). This is your hassle score. _____

Count the even-numbered statements for which you have circled N (No). This is your uplift score. _____

Your hassle quotient is high if your hassle score is either greater than four or greater than your uplift score. In this case, life's little hassles are causing you extra pressure, conflict, and frustration, with corresponding physical and emotional wear and tear.

It is difficult to determine which stressors are more important, life changes or little hassles, because they often happen at the same time. Indeed, life changes can cause little hassles, and vice versa. Divorce, for example, may result in many little hassles such as loneliness, reduced income, and too many things to do. Similarly, joblessness often interferes with family relations, feelings of self-worth, and personal health. Harvey Brenner of Johns Hopkins University has found that the stress of job loss is particularly serious. During a period of approximately 25 years after 1940, for every 1 percent increase in national unemployment, there was a 1.9 percent increase in deaths from heart disease and cirrhosis, a 4.1 percent increase in suicides, and an increase in first-time admissions to state mental institutions (4.3 percent for men and 2.3 percent for women).[22]

THE CRITICAL BALANCE

How you handle stress depends on the demands you face — life changes and hassles — and your resources for meeting these demands, not on any one factor alone. Just as your physical health depends partly on the number and strength of the germs you are exposed to and partly on your body's ability to resist these invaders, your psychological health depends to some degree on the people and problems in your life and partly on your mental and emotional strength. If you have strong physical, psychological, and spiritual resources, you can deal with tremendous amounts of life change and many little hassles. Figure 1.6 shows the relationship between the demands you face and your resources for coping.

Selye describes the critical balance as a process of adaptation:

> Life is largely a process of adaptation to the circumstances in which we exist. A perennial give-and-take has been going on between living matter and its inanimate surroundings, between one living being and another, ever since the dawn of life in the prehistoric oceans. The secret of health and happiness lies in successful adjustment to the ever-changing conditions . . . the penalties for failure in this great process of adaptation are disease and unhappiness.[23]

An important point in the "demands-resources" equation is the need for renewal. The person who expends resources (time, energy, and emotion) without replenishment ultimately experiences burnout. Physical, psychological, and spiritual fatigue occurs. The secret is to reach a balance.

FIGURE 1.6

The Critical Balance

Demands We Face —
Events, Hassles, and Handicaps

Low status

Unhappy marriage

Sexual problems   Boredom

Unrealistic goals   Job problems

Quarrels with
associates

Debts,
money trouble

Inadequate   Inferiority
competencies   feelings

Loss of
Loved ones

Physical   Sickness
handicaps

War

Unsatisfactory living conditions,
(e.g. food, shelter)

Resources for Coping —
Physical, Psychological, and Economic Assets

TLC

Happy marriage

Close friends   Self-confidence

Adequate income   Mental health   Physical fitness

Realistic frame
of reference

Satisfactory
status

Adequate
competencies

Satisfactory living
conditions
(e.g. housing, food)

Satisfying job

Source: Data from James C. Coleman, Personality Dynamics and Effective Behavior (Glenview, Ill.: Scott, Foresman & Company, 1960), 183. Reprinted with permission.

A cherry tree needs sun and rain, and a person must receive to give. In your own life, what are you doing both to meet demands and to replenish your resources?

The following exercise will provide you with an estimate of your critical balance at this point in time.

WHO'S ON TOP – THE WORLD OR YOU?

Directions

For an estimate of your critical balance, see the demands you face in the left column and your resources for coping in the right. Circle the number between each pair that reflects conditions as they are now.

Demands		Resources
Low self-esteem	1 2 3 4 5 6 7 8 9 10	Positive self-image
Negative attitude	1 2 3 4 5 6 7 8 9 10	Positive outlook
Loneliness	1 2 3 4 5 6 7 8 9 10	Close friends
Job problems	1 2 3 4 5 6 7 8 9 10	Job success
Unhappy marriage (relationship)	1 2 3 4 5 6 7 8 9 10	Happy marriage (relationship)
Debts, money troubles	1 2 3 4 5 6 7 8 9 10	Financial security
Poor health	1 2 3 4 5 6 7 8 9 10	Good health
Boredom	1 2 3 4 5 6 7 8 9 10	Excitement
Inner turmoil	1 2 3 4 5 6 7 8 9 10	Peace of mind
Sexual problems	1 2 3 4 5 6 7 8 9 10	Sexual satisfaction
Low social status	1 2 3 4 5 6 7 8 9 10	High social status
Quarrels and conflict	1 2 3 4 5 6 7 8 9 10	Smooth relationships
Physical problems	1 2 3 4 5 6 7 8 9 10	Physical fitness
Inferiority feelings	1 2 3 4 5 6 7 8 9 10	Self-confidence
Too much work	1 2 3 4 5 6 7 8 9 10	Acceptable work load
Too little rest	1 2 3 4 5 6 7 8 9 10	Sufficient rest
Poor eating habits	1 2 3 4 5 6 7 8 9 10	Good eating habits
Feeling out of control	1 2 3 4 5 6 7 8 9 10	Sense of control

| Confusion, lack of goals | 1 2 3 4 5 6 7 8 9 10 | Clear goal direction |

| Unsatisfactory living conditions (food, shelter, etc.) | 1 2 3 4 5 6 7 8 9 10 | Satisfactory living conditions (food, shelter, etc.) |

SCORING AND INTERPRETATION

Everyone faces demands, and everyone has resources for coping. Also, times and conditions change for everyone. Based on your answers to the Who's on Top test at this point in time:

If Your Score Is:	Your Balance Is:
20–60	Poor; major resources and coping skills are needed.
61–100	Negative to average; additional resources and coping skills are required.
101–160	Average to positive; you are doing well, but should continue to improve.
161–200	Excellent; your critical balance is in your favor.

RECOMMENDED RESOURCES

The following reading, case, and films are suggested for greater insight into the material in Part One:

Reading — Anatomy of an Illness as Perceived by the Patient

Case — The Price of Success

Films — Future Shock
Learn to Live with Stress; Programming the Body for Health
Stress, Health and You

REFERENCE NOTES

1 Hans Selye, *The Stress of Life*, rev. ed. (New York: McGraw-Hill, Inc., 1976), 173–78.

2 Selye, *The Stress of Life*, 1.

3 Linda Standke, "The Advantages of Training People to Handle Stress," *Training/HDR* 16 (February 1979): 23–26; Walter B. Cannon, *The Wisdom of the Body* (New York: W.W. Norton & Co., Inc., 1932), 228.

4 Selye, *The Stress of Life*, xvi–xvii.

5 Thomas H. Holmes and Minoru Masuda, "Psychosomatic Syndrome: When Mothers-in-Law or Other Disasters Visit, A Person Can Develop A Bad, Bad Cold. Or Worse," *Psychology Today*, 5 (April 1972): 71.

6 Matthew J. Culligan and Keith Sedlacek, *How to Kill Stress Before It Kills You* (New York: Grosset & Dunlap, Inc., 1976), 75.

7 Selye, *The Stress of Life*, 428–29.

8 Edward A. Charlesworth and Ronald G. Nathan, *Stress Management: A Comprehensive Guide to Wellness* (Houston: Biobehavioral Publishers and Distributors, Inc., 1982), 10.

9 Selye, *The Stress of Life*, 173–78.

10 *The New Awareness: The Caring Community Series No. 1* (Center City, Minn.: Hazeldon Foundation Inc., 1975), 9–11.

11 Selye, *The Stress of Life*, 432.

12 Selye, *The Stress of Life*, 432.

13 L.F. Berkman, "Psychological Resources, Health Behavior and Mortality: A Nine Year Follow-Up Study" (paper presented at the annual meeting of the American Public Health Association, Washington, D.C., October, 1977), 7, as found in Philip G. Zimbardo, *Essentials of Psychology and Life*, 10th ed. (Glenview, Ill.: Scott, Foresman Co., 1980), 364.

14 Claudia Wallis, Ruth Mehrtens Galvin, and Dick Thompson, "Stress: Can We Cope?" *Time* 121, no. 23 (June 1983): 48–53.

15 Selye, *The Stress of Life*, xv.

16 Based on the work of Seymour Levine, "Stimulation in Infancy," *Scientific American* 202, no. 5 (May 1960): 80–86.

17 Selye, *The Stress of Life*, xv; Hans Selye, *Stress Without Distress* (Philadelphia: J. B. Lippincott Company, 1974), 32.

18 Alvin Toffler, *Future Shock* (New York: Random House, Inc., 1970), 290.

19   Thomas H. Holmes and T. Stephenson Holmes, "How Change Can Make Us Ill," *A Report from Your Blue Cross Plan: Stress* 25, no. 1 (1974), 66–75.

20   Wallis, "Stress: Can We Cope?", 49.

21   Richard S. Lazarus, "Little Hassles Can Be Hazardous to Health," *Psychology Today* 15 (July 1981): 58–62.

22   Wallis, "Stress: Can We Cope?", 50.

23   Selye, *The Stress of Life*, xv–xvi.

STUDY QUIZ

As a test of your understanding and the extent to which you have achieved the objectives in Part One, complete the following questions. See Appendix F for the answer key.

1. According to Selye, the body's response to stress is:
   a. type A behavior
   b. withdrawal
   c. type B behavior
   d. the General Adaptation Syndrome
   e. frustration

2. According to Selye, the first stage of the G.A.S. is the:
   a. alarm reaction
   b. exhaustion stage
   c. resistance stage
   d. refractory period
   e. reaction formation

3. If the body is mobilized and the stressor is not removed, you enter the:
   a. alarm reaction
   b. exhaustion stage
   c. resistance stage
   d. refractory period
   e. reaction formation

4. The final stage of the G.A.S. is the:
   a. alarm reaction
   b. exhaustion stage
   c. resistance stage
   d. refractory period
   e. reaction formation

5. Continued stress, after the body has reached the exhaustion stage, leads to:
   a. diseases of adaptation
   b. an "alpha state"
   c. a second alarm reaction
   d. reaction formation
   e. type B behavior

6. According to Holmes, stress is caused by:
   a. unrealistic expectations
   b. irrational beliefs

    c. life changes

    d. boredom

    e. an internal locus of control

7. According to the Schedule of Recent Experiences, which is the most stressful for the average person?

    a. Death of spouse

    b. Jail term

    c. Change in personal habits

    d. Being fired at work

    e. Divorce

8. If your score on the Schedule of Recent Experiences is above 300 in one year, your chances of becoming ill are:

    a. 99%

    b. 46%

    c. 79%

    d. 29%

9. "Little hassles" can result in:

    a. stress

    b. job satisfaction

    c. good relationships

10. Having an argument at home can be a:

    a. pressure stressor

    b. conflict stressor

    c. frustration stressor

    d. work stressor

    e. a, b, and c

11. People today are faced with threats that are primarily:

    a. immediate and physical

    b. psychological and social

    c. genetic and long term

12. The fight-or-flight response was generally adaptive for _____ man, but it is often unnecessary and harmful for _____ man.

    a. modern; prehistoric

    b. prehistoric; modern

    c. none of the above

13. Inappropriate fight-or-flight reactions can lead to stress disorders such as:

    a. high blood pressure

    b. tension and migraine headaches

c. ulcers
d. all of the above

14. Two of the top ten hassles in life are:
    a. health of family member/eating out
    b. misplacing or losing things/too many things to do
    c. crime/sickness
    d. feeling healthy/physical appearance

15. Two of the top ten uplifts in life are relating well with your spouse or lover and feeling healthy.
    a. True
    b. False

16. How you handle stress depends on the balance between the demands you face and your resources for coping.
    a. True
    b. False

17. Which of the following would appear on a list of behavioral signs of stress?
    a. Overeating
    b. Inability to sleep
    c. Arguments and quarrels
    d. All of the above

18. People who are "racehorses" love variety and thrive on changes in life, while those who are "turtles" will never be happy because they find it difficult to keep up with life.
    a. True
    b. False

19. Both good and bad stress can cause physical illness.
    a. True
    b. False

20. In the critical balance between the demands you face and your resources for coping, personality plays an important part.
    a. True
    b. False

21. Statistics show that death from "old age" actually is primarily a result of poor health habits.
    a. True
    b. False

22. The philosophy toward good and bad stress recommended in the text is to:

    a. strive for good stress, but remember that too much of a good thing can be harmful
    b. maximize good stress and minimize bad stress
    c. pour as much good stress as possible into your pitcher of life
    d. all of the above

23. A major point to remember about the Schedule of Recent Experiences:

    a. if your score is high, consider postponing new life changes
    b. if your score is high, it is your own fault
    c. if your score is high, stress in your life is beyond your control

24. Psychological health depends to some degree on the people and problems you face and partly on your _____ and _____ strength.

    a. mental; emotional
    b. financial; political
    c. power; physical

25. Stress is defined as physical and emotional wear and tear on a person resulting from real or imagined problems.

    a. True
    b. False

26. _____ and _____ are two important factors that contribute to stress in our lives.

    a. Health; social relationships
    b. Height; weight
    c. Truth; beauty
    d. None of the above

27. Relationships with animals do nothing to help people cope with the pressures, conflicts, and frustrations they encounter.

    a. True
    b. False

28. _____ and _____ are two social conditions that help account for extra stress and rapid aging for many people.

    a. Boredom; lack of a meaningful relationship
    b. Large families; high income
    c. Social gatherings; travel

29. The text describes aging as:

    a. the wearing down of the organism
    b. the price of life
    c. an unalterable process

30. According to Selye, true age depends on the rate of wear and tear the body experiences.

    a. True
    b. False

31. Types of problems associated with stress include:

    a. pressures, such as raising a family and earning a living
    b. conflicts, such as choosing between alternative careers, mates, and life-styles
    c. frustrations, such as wanting but not having good relationships with family and friends
    d. all of the above

32. The fight-or-flight syndrome is a(n):

    a. emotional disease
    b. biological response to stress
    c. cultural response to stress
    d. athletic maneuver

33. Social problems associated with stress include:

    a. spouse and child abuse
    b. alcohol and drug abuse
    c. irritability with others
    d. all of the above

34. Stress has been called the dominant disease of _____.

    a. modern times
    b. younger men
    c. rich people
    d. new relationships

35. Stress can result from real or imagined problems.

    a. True
    b. False

DISCUSSION QUESTIONS AND ACTIVITIES

The following questions and activities help personalize the subject. They are appropriate for classroom exercises and homework assignments.

1. What are the stressors you face at this point in time?

   Pressures? _____

   Conflicts? _____

   Frustrations? _____

2. What are your personal signs of stress?

   Physical? _____

   Psychological? _____

   Social? _____

3. Is your stress *good* stress or *distress*?

   _____

   _____

   _____

4. How stressful is your world? Is your cup overflowing, or not yet full?

   _____

   _____

   _____

5. What "little hassles" do you have to deal with? How do you cope?

   _____

   _____

   _____

6. Who's on top—the world or you? Are your resources for coping keeping up with the demands you face?

   _____

   _____

   _____

7. Discuss in small groups: (a) sources of good stress in group members' lives; (b) sources of distress; and (c) the concept of overload and underload.

8. Use small-group discussion to consider the concept of "critical balance." What are the demands faced and resources for coping for various group members?

9. Discuss in small groups the role of stress in health and aging. What are the "health habits" and "aging influences" of members of the group? Are there certain health practices the group would endorse?

10. When faced with a stressor, do you tend to avoid confrontation (flight) or confront the stressor (fight); or do you avoid confrontation until cornered, and then fight?

———————————

PART TWO

Personality and Stress

Learning Objectives

After completing Part Two, you will better understand:

1. how personality traits can make you susceptible to stress;

2. the fourteen coping behaviors for dealing with stress;

3. how susceptible you are to stress, based on your personality type.

PERSONALITY PLAYS A PART

Are you the type of person who takes a low stress level and makes it into a mountain? Or are you the type who can handle many little hassles and many life changes while keeping them in perspective?

In the critical balance between demands and resources, personality plays an important part in determining a person's susceptibility to stress and stress-related problems. Some people are "hard going" and process their life events and small problems in a way that increases wear and tear unnecessarily. Others are easygoing, and their approach to life and problems helps them in the process of adaptation. Whether a person is a "turtle" or a "racehorse" by temperament, certain personality traits and living habits, formed largely through the influence of culture, correlate positively with heart disease. That these traits and habits can and should be changed is the central point of *Type A Behavior and Your Heart* by Meyer Friedman and Ray Rosenman.

Friedman and Rosenman, two cardiologists in private practice in San Francisco during the 1970s, became interested in the connection between personality types and heart disease almost by accident. Needing the chairs in their waiting room reupholstered, they scheduled the work to be done. As the upholsterer left, he asked the doctors what line of work they were in. They answered that they were heart specialists. He said, "I was just wondering, because it is so strange that only the front edges of your chair seats are worn out"—patients had been sitting on the edges of their chairs.

The doctors were initially puzzled by this, but after reflecting on the many diagnostic sessions they had conducted with their patients and the patients' families, they thought they understood the reason. Time after time, they could remember having a conversation something like this: "Doctor, I know your tests tell you this, and your instruments tell you that, but if you want to know my Jim's problem, it is. . . ." In almost every case, the family would go on to describe an almost identical constellation of behaviors and personality characteristics that they believed had caused the heart disease.[1]

Friedman and Rosenman label high-stress behaviors as type A and their opposites as type B. Included in the list of type A, coronary-prone behaviors are the following:[2]

- *An intense drive to advance oneself or one's causes and to "beat the competition."* Whatever the occupation, trade, or profession, the type A's mental set is to be "number one." The goal may be related to work, family, or personal life, but in any case, the type A person is intensely driven to succeed.

- *An adversarial and competitive manner in interpersonal relations.* Opinionated and often rigid, the type A person is not easy-going, seemingly likes to argue, talks "at" others instead of "with" them, and is subject to vocal outbursts. There is a general, free-floating hostility, as the type A is irritated easily by little things. Type A people always seem to be in a struggle against time, other people, or events.

- *Continuous involvement in a wide variety of activities at several levels of demand.* The type A person has a history of simultaneous work on big-picture, middle-picture, and little-picture matters, with little or no rest in between. The type A is like an octopus, wishing to have ten arms in order to get more things accomplished. As a rule, lengthy books, repetitious chores, and routine work are avoided by the type A person.

- *A quick pace in walking, eating, speaking, and gesturing.* The type A person has a habitual sense of urgency. Such a person moves through the day as if always in a hurry. It might be said that type

ILLUS. 2.1

The type A personality always appears to struggle against time.

A people have the "hurry-up disease." They seem to be in mortal conflict with Father Time; yet, in the battle against impossible deadlines and time constraints, type A's will lose. The type A person tries to accomplish too many things in too little time.

- *Physical and mental alertness.* The type A person is characteristically tense and poised for action. Although extreme alertness may have been necessary in primitive times (as a defense against panthers and pythons), constant excitement of the body—a high level of hormonal and chemical activity—without constructive physical release becomes self-destructive in modern society.

- *Impatience in human dealings.* Type A's are extremely demanding in human relationships (especially with the people they care about). Expecting perfection from others, who rarely match up, type A's become critical and are prone to argument. They have a reputation for shouting, and have been known to throw things. Although their colorful personalities may attract others and people may care for them, the type A's intolerance for the imperfections of others often harms their relationships.

- *Inability to relax.* Type A's are subject to a condition known as "Sunday neurosis," an inability to relax without feeling guilty. When type A's find themselves with a day of rest, they quickly become restless, feeling that they are wasting time. Type A's have a strong need to be doing something useful and do not equate free time and relaxation with being useful.

- *Dislike for waiting.* Type A's hate waiting in lines. If they have to wait in a line, such as at the store, bank, or theater, they become irritated. If forced to wait in a traffic jam, type A's will typically experience increased blood pressure as they dwell on the lost time and productivity caused by the delay. It is common to see type A people honking the horn, leaning out of the window, chainsmoking, and talking to themselves.

   This behavior contrasts with that of type B people, who consider that if they want to get to their destinations, they must wait; there is no alternative. They cannot get out of their cars and throw the others out of the way, so they avoid thinking about the delay. Instead, the type B uses forced waiting time to do something constructive, which might even involve relaxation.

In summary, type A people tend to be success oriented, driven by internal forces to accomplish more and more in less and less time. When this urge is out of control, they become workaholics. Often, type A's have poor human relationships because they seem to have little or no time or patience for people, or their aggressive behavior upsets others. Also, type A's may have trouble winding down from the tense state at which they operate; muscle tension, aches and pains, and insomnia are common. Finally, type A's rarely pause to enjoy the moment, as they are typically in a hurry; their mental focus is usually on the next task, the next mountain to climb.

The primary significance of Friedman and Rosenman's work was their finding that type B personalities experience less stress (physical and emotional wear and tear) and have a lower incidence of cardiovascular disease, while type A's experience greater stress and have a higher incidence of heart disease. Further, they discovered that heart disease in type A people is often exhibited early in life, sometimes when they are in their thirties and forties. Friedman and Rosenman maintain that coronary heart disease almost never occurs before seventy years of age in type B people, even if they smoke, eat fatty foods, and don't exercise.[3]

It is not a new observation that some people are more prone to heart disease than others. Sir William Osler lived long ago, but he wrote a clear description of the type A person: "It is not the delicate, neurotic person who is prone to angina, but the robust, the vigorous in mind and body, the keen and ambitious man, whose engine is always at 'full speed ahead' . . . the well set man of from forty-five to fifty-five years of age, with military bearing, iron gray hair, and florid complexion."[4]

A direct, causative relationship has not been established between personality type, stress levels, and heart disease (only a correlational relationship has been established). But you should be aware whether you are a type A or type B person. Consider that at present, 20 percent of all American males have heart attacks before the age of sixty; 5,000 to 10,000 Americans have heart attacks daily; and 20 percent of these victims die within the first hour of the attack. These statistics alone should encourage you to do everything you can to reduce your chances of being one of the stricken.[5]

The following is a questionnaire to help you determine your personality type.

THE STRESS BAROMETER—
TYPE A, TYPE B BEHAVIOR TEST

Directions

What am I like? The following is a list of personality traits and behavior patterns. After each trait, check the answer that best describes you. Sometimes you will feel that you belong somewhere between the columns. This is to be expected.

	Column A	Column B
I become impatient when events move slowly	____ often	____ rarely
I work overtime or bring work home	____ often	____ rarely
I feel guilty when I relax and do nothing	____ often	____ rarely
I find myself talking "at" people instead of "with" people	____ often	____ rarely
I speak, eat, and move at a quick pace	____ often	____ rarely
I can't stand waiting in lines	____ often	____ rarely
I do things to extremes	____ often	____ rarely
I have a strong need for perfection	____ often	____ rarely
I become angry easily	____ often	____ rarely
I have disagreements with others	____ often	____ rarely
I try to think about or do two or more things at once	____ often	____ rarely
I am number oriented (I like to count my accomplishments and possessions)	____ often	____ rarely
I overschedule myself	____ often	____ rarely
I take little notice of my physical surroundings	____ often	____ rarely
I worry more than I should	____ often	____ rarely
I become impatient with people	____ often	____ rarely
I hurry the ends of sentences, or do not speak them at all	____ often	____ rarely
I feel driven to accomplish my goals	____ often	____ rarely

| I am tense | _____ often | _____ rarely |
| I am subject to vocal outbursts | _____ often | _____ rarely |

Source: *Based on Meyer Friedman and Ray H. Rosenman,* Type A Behavior and Your Heart *(New York: Alfred A. Knopf, Inc., 1974), 80–88;* Stress!, *created and developed by Curriculum Concepts, Inc., New York, N.Y. (Chicago: American Hospital Association, 1977), 11.*

SCORING AND INTERPRETATION

Give yourself one point for each check mark in column B in the Stress Barometer test, and circle the total on the following chart. Your score is an indication of whether you are a type A or type B person and indicates your corresponding susceptibility to stress and stress-related illness. See Figure 2.1 for a reading.

DISCUSSION

There are four major points to remember about the Stress Barometer test:

- The purpose of the test is to increase your awareness of the relationship between behavior traits and health.

- There are three elements of the type A personality — speed/impulse, aggression/competition, and anger/hostility. Of these, anger/hostility is usually the biggest problem. Acceptable outlets are often found for speed/impulse and aggression/competition in the areas of hobbies, sports, and business. Anger and hostility are not as personally or socially acceptable. Thus, their effects are often experienced internally, resulting in harmful physical wear and tear.

- Scores reveal levels of susceptibility for groups of people, and these may or may not be accurate for you as an individual because (1) there is no certainty that all type A personalities (scores 1 through 8) will have heart disease; and (2) there is no assurance that if you are a type B personality (scores 13 through 20), you will not have heart disease. What is assured is that if you do, it will not be the fault of your personality.

- Type A and type B behaviors are determined largely by cultural influence; societies help create type A and type B people. Compare American culture with Polynesian; or compare two cultures with the same roots — Germany and Austria. Note the contrast between America and Germany (type A) and Polynesia and Austria (type B).

Right now you may be thinking, "But wait a minute; it seems that the societies that have achieved great advances in all the fields — business, engineering, medicine, transportation, etc. — are type A societies, and these accomplishments are to be valued." This is true. In a world of competition and struggle, type A behavior may help get you to the top — over other people's bodies, perhaps — however, four important points should be noted:

- Although type A behavior may help you get to the top, it could be damaging your health, and you may not live to enjoy the results of your efforts unless you become more B-like somewhere along the way. The obituaries of every town newspaper tell the story of young and talented people who die because of type A behavior. Their legacy

---

FIGURE 2.1

The Stress Barometer

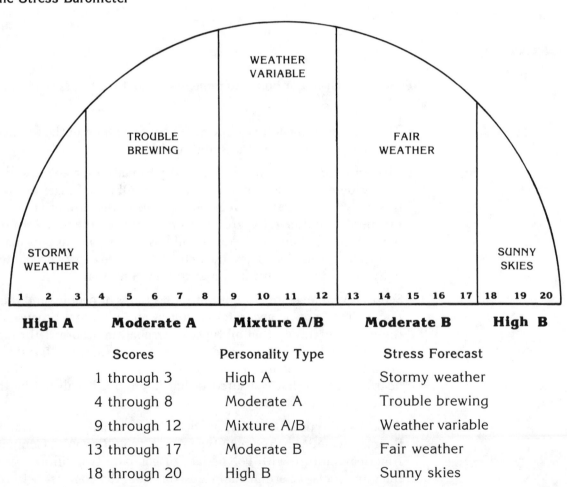

Scores	Personality Type	Stress Forecast
1 through 3	High A	Stormy weather
4 through 8	Moderate A	Trouble brewing
9 through 12	Mixture A/B	Weather variable
13 through 17	Moderate B	Fair weather
18 through 20	High B	Sunny skies

---

remains — but they are gone. Often, they are only thirty, forty, fifty, or sixty years of age.

- Just because our world has been one of competition and struggle in the past, it does not mean that this must be the world of the future. People, more than all other creatures, create their world. Thus, there can be peace instead of war, and cooperation as opposed to competition, if people want these and have sufficient will to attain them. People can create families, organizations, and societies supportive of type B behavior. Imagine a family that teaches love over hate, or a company that encourages employee cooperation over competition.

- Recent studies show that as many type B as type A individuals actually obtain high levels of accomplishment. This may be due to the fact that positive A qualities, such as ambition and persistent hard work, are offset by negative A traits, such as impatience in decision making and argumentativeness in human relations. Indeed, there is evidence that type A's are not as good at performing some executive functions — examining alternatives, setting priorities, and enlisting the aid of co-workers and subordinates — as are their type B counterparts.[6]

- An individual or society can be B-like without being lazy or unproductive. It is possible to achieve great feats by working efficiently and to enjoy these accomplishments by living intelligently. It is possible to be successful and live to enjoy it.

COPING BEHAVIORS — HOW TO BE A "B"

In 1923, a group of the world's most successful businessmen met in a Chicago hotel. Present were:

- the president of the country's largest independent steel company;
- the president of the country's largest utility company;
- the president of the New York Stock Exchange;
- the biggest "bear" on Wall Street;
- the head of the world's greatest monopoly.

These individuals controlled nearly as much wealth as there was in the United States Treasury at the time. Newspapers and magazines printed their stories; young people were urged to follow their example. Twenty-five years later, the results were in:

- the president of the country's largest independent steel company — Charles Schwab — died bankrupt, living on borrowed money for five years before his death;

- the president of the country's largest utility company—Samuel Insull—died a fugitive from justice and penniless in a foreign land;

- the president of the New York Stock Exchange—Richard Whitney— served time in Sing Sing Prison;

- the biggest "bear" on Wall Street—Jessie Livermore—died from suicide;

- the head of the world's greatest monopoly—Ivan Kruegar—died from suicide.[7]

It is important to succeed in what you do. But it is also important to live to enjoy the fruits of your labor. This is the point of being a "B." Whether you are a businessperson, homemaker, parent, or student, the following principles can help you cope with the inevitable stresses of life and work. These principles apply to turtles, racehorses, and all temperaments in between. They will help you to become a "B".

Don't Worry; Take Action

Many people are "worry warts." If they don't have something to worry about, they make up something. You must stop worrying and start doing. Being concerned is normal, but worrying never solves any problem. If you can solve a problem, do so; but don't sit around worrying about what you cannot change, no matter how important it might be. Starvation in Cambodia, human rights in China, and a traffic jam you are caught in may be beyond your ability to solve. Nor should you worry about unimportant things such as a ticking clock, a barking dog, or your mate's idiosyncrasies.

If something upsets you, do what you can to improve things, but avoid worrying. This only makes a bad situation worse. Try following the advice of St. Francis of Assisi, which was later popularized in the following prayer: ". . . give us serenity to accept what cannot be changed, courage to change what should be changed, and wisdom to distinguish one from the other." Another saying, author unknown, makes the same point: "Of all the troubles mankind's got, some can be solved and some cannot. If there is a cure, find it; if not, never mind it."

Besides worry, two other emotions are particularly distressful. These are resentment over the past and anger in the present. A useful technique to help cope with these negative emotions is to accept unpleasant realities. Sample realities:

- you cannot change the past;

- some things are beyond your control;

- not everyone is going to agree with you;

- you are going to make mistakes.

The act of accepting unpleasant realities helps reduce nonproductive resentment and anger.

Set Priorities

People can handle enormous amounts of pressure, conflict, and frustration as long as they feel in control. It is only when events seem to be spinning on, out of control, that accelerated wear and tear (stress) occurs. Studies show that stress illness happens most to people who are under the greatest pressure but have the least power to influence results.

Have you ever felt out of control? Have you ever felt you had too many problems and too little time? The loss of control can be a major distressor. Setting priorities can help avoid this problem.

When setting priorities, you should be aware of the 80/20 rule: 80 percent of the value of anything comes from 20 percent of its elements.[8] For example, salespeople usually receive 80 percent of their business from 20 percent of their customers. Similarly, supervisors usually obtain 80 percent of their productivity from 20 percent of their subordinates (and 80 percent of their problems from another 20 percent). Finally, in the typical family, 80 percent of the trouble is caused by 20 percent of the members.

Knowing and following the 80/20 rule is an important stress-coping technique. Realizing that 80 percent of what you value usually comes from 20 percent of what you do, you should prioritize your activities and work on the top 20 percent first. You should write these down and check them off as you complete them. Doing this will help you feel in control of situations, increase satisfaction, provide a feeling of progress, and alleviate unnecessary stress.

When setting priorities, you should consider your personal needs and goals in life. Ask yourself, "What is important—family, work, hobbies?", and then prioritize your activities accordingly. Otherwise, you will become frustrated and feel unfulfilled, always working on things that are relatively unimportant to you.

In the work setting, meetings are one of the biggest sources of stress. Although meetings can be essential, they can also be a waste of valuable time and effort. To ensure that your meetings are in line with your priorities, consider a technique used during World War II to conserve gasoline. In each car, there was a sign affixed: "Is this trip necessary?" You may want to begin to ask: "Is this meeting necessary? Does this meeting support my critical 20 percent?"

Follow the Principle of Moderation

Stress not only is inevitable, it is desirable. Creative tension usually accompanies great achievement, and the desire to succeed is necessary to overcome many of life's obstacles. The goal is not to reduce all stress, but to experience stimulation and work in your life that is satisfying without being destructive.

The following story shows the value of avoiding extremes:

> In "How Much Land Does a Man Require," Tolstoy wrote about Pakhom, a greedy man who was offered, by the Starshima of the Bashkirs, all the land he could cover by foot in a single day, from sunrise to sunset.

Lured by the fantastic offer, Pakhom set out at the crack of dawn and walked on hour after hour. It seemed as though the farther he went, the better the land became. At midday, he looked up and saw the sun overhead. It was a sign that he should turn back and head for the starting point. But then he thought of how much more land he could acquire, and the thought compelled him to keep on going.

Hour after hour passed. Now, surely, Pakhom would have to turn around and go back if he were to reach the starting point before sunset. Finally, he turned toward the starting point. But before long, he realized he had waited too long. He had been too greedy.

His heart pounded fiercely as he began to run. Soon, his breath grew shorter and shorter. Still he forced himself to run faster and faster, even though his legs were numb.

At last, Pakhom could see the Starshima and a small group of Bashkirs at the starting point awaiting his return. With his last ounce of strength, he reached the group, fell to the ground in complete exhaustion, and died.

The people buried him, saying, "This is how much land a man requires."[9]

Besides avoiding excesses such as Pakhom's, you should strive for balance in your life. You should have balance between rest and work and thus avoid laziness or becoming a workaholic. You should recognize that you are both a public and private person and thus enjoy others but take pleasure in solitude as well. Daily, you should do something for each dimension of your being—spirit, mind, and body.

Aristotle's prescription "moderation, moderation, all things in moderation" is a good rule to live by regarding both excesses and balance. To the romantic, this may sound unattractive. But the fact is, if your goal in life is to experience the greatest satisfaction over the longest duration, you must avoid excesses, live a balanced life, and strive for "stress without distress."

Moderation is especially important when you are sick. Sometimes, no matter what steps you take, the flu or a cold temporarily defeats your immune system's defenses. Slow down. You can't expect your body to cope with a high activity level and combat disease simultaneously. You will get well faster if you give your body a needed break and rest.

Enjoy the Little Things in Life

There are many small pleasures available to us, while the great successes of life are few and far between. Consider how often you are able to buy a home, be promoted, or have a baby, as opposed to how often you could enjoy your small child, read a good book, take a walk with your mate, or enjoy a quiet thought all alone.

The following story shows how it helps to focus on the positive and natural things in life, however small:

The historian Will Durant described how he looked for happiness in knowledge, and found only disillusionment. He then sought happiness in travel, and found weariness; in wealth, he found discord and worry. He looked for happiness in his writing, and was only fatigued.

One day he saw a woman waiting in a tiny car with a sleeping child in her arms. A man descended from a train and came over and gently kissed the woman, and then the baby, very softly, so as not to waken him.

The family drove off and left Durant with a stunning realization of the true nature of happiness. He relaxed and discovered, "every normal function of life holds some delight."[10]

When asked for advice, it is not unusual for those who have survived heart attacks or learned they have only a short time to live to say, "Take pleasure from the little things in life."

Sometimes very small things right under our noses can give us pleasure. Gary Schwartz, professor of psychology at Yale University, uses the healing power of scent in the treatment of anxiety, hypertension, and other stress-related disorders. It is interesting to note that a spicy apple scent reminiscent of cider seems to work best.

Finding something that gives you pleasure may require a change in your environment. If so, take steps to make your work and living area pleasant and satisfying. Try to surround yourself with people who give you happiness, and strive to do the activities that give you peace of mind.[11]

Go Easy with Criticism

There are two kinds of criticism — of self and of others; go easy on both.

With regard to self-criticism, you may be too demanding, expecting perfection in all you do. Because you tend to find fault, you have trouble feeling good about yourself and your accomplishments. For example, you

ILLUS. 2.2

By enjoying the little things in life, one can better cope with stress.

may do ten tasks; if eight turn out well and two do not, you may focus enormous attention on the two unsuccessful outcomes. This results in lowered self-esteem. In this way, self-criticism is a form of self-punishment.

One answer to too much self-criticism is to avoid the "must not" syndrome, a tendency to think in absolutes (I must not fail; I must not cry; I must not be afraid). By replacing must nots with should nots, you preserve high goals, while experiencing less guilt and shame if you happen to fall short.

With regard to criticism of others, you may expect other people to be perfect and then feel disappointed, angry, and frustrated when they fail to measure up. You should remember that everyone, including yourself, has both good and bad characteristics; nobody is perfect.

If you want to be honest in your relationships and enjoy others as well, and if you would like to shape their behavior a little too, you should state your preferences honestly and openly—but don't concentrate on the negative. The following is a guide for healthy relations with others:

- State what you do and do not like. You may have to repeat what you do not like several times, because people are often poor listeners and usually hear only what they want to hear. But be careful not to nag the other person.

- Recognize the strengths of other people. Tell them. This will reinforce their good qualities, as most people want to be recognized and appreciated for what they do.

- Ignore inappropriate behavior. If the behavior is not part of the person's basic "nature," it will go away (extinguish). If it is part of the "personhood" (an essential element of personality), it is almost impossible to change. At this point, you have two choices—either ignore the behavior, or avoid the person.

In behavior modification, therapists prefer to use positive reinforcement, rather than punishment, to change behavior. To eliminate undesirable behavior, reinforcement is withheld, usually in the form of ignoring bad conduct. Imagine an emotionally handicapped person whose behavior is appropriate until attention is given to someone else. The person may react by having a temper tantrum that includes stomping around the room and shouting. This inappropriate behavior would be ignored, while good behavior would be recognized, rewarded, and thus reinforced.[12]

Type B's realize the importance of going easy on criticism and typically take a live-and-let-live attitude. Type A's often do not. They are prone to "psychosclerosis," or hardening of the attitudes. As such, they are closed to new ideas and experiences and regularly go on campaigns to change other people's behavior. Usually, these are losing campaigns that lead to ulcers, poor relationships, or both. Think about it; could someone change your behavior if you did not want to change?

Don't Try to Be Superwoman or Superman

Everyone has limitations of some sort—physical, emotional, or financial. To reduce unnecessary stress, decide what is important to you and put your time and effort into those activities. Tolerate some imperfections, and don't try to be all things to all people. Avoid overpromising, overscheduling, and overcommitting.

To understand the "superperson syndrome," look at the business and social calendar of the typical type A. There is probably more scheduled than can ever be accomplished. The type A person commonly tries to do more, ever more, until breakdown occurs. Breakdown may take the form of failure to meet commitments, or it may mean physical and emotional exhaustion.

Learning when, how, and why to say no helps. When—as early as possible; as soon as you realize that saying yes would be a mistake. Otherwise, others will be counting on you when they should not. How—with tact and compassion, because the other person's request is probably important to that individual. Why—because if you do not say no, something you have already promised to do will suffer, or you, yourself, will break down, bringing more harm to others than the consequences of the no response.

Saying no can be difficult. You may fear disapproval or rejection from others. Sometimes, too, it may be hard to say no because you do not want to disappoint others. If you have a difficult time saying no, you might try saying: "I would like to say yes, but other things I have promised to do will suffer. You must wait until these obligations are finished." This approach should not upset the other person. Reasonable people will understand, and friends will accept it.

Some people who have trouble saying no have a closet at home. Every morning, as they start their day, they reach in and pull out a big red cape; they must think they are from the planet Krypton. The following story makes the point that no one is Superwoman or Superman:

> The famous boxer Muhammad Ali was on a plane trip from Chicago to Las Vegas when the stewardess asked everyone to please fasten their seat belts. Of course, everyone did, except Muhammad Ali. When she leaned over to ask him to please buckle his seat belt, Ali said, "Superman don't need no seat belt." The stewardess thought and sweetly said, "Yes, and Superman don't need no airplane either."[13]

The fact is, the average person can handle a maximum of four major commitments at any one time and do them well. Imagine an individual with four responsibilities: (1) home and family; (2) work; (3) education; and (4) community service. Another major commitment, no matter how worthy, could be the "straw that breaks the camel's back."

Every well has a bottom, and every person has limitations. For the person with a turtle temperament, the tolerance point may be three major commitments, while the breaking point for the person with a racehorse temperament may be as high as six.

An effective way to avoid the superperson syndrome is to share the pain; delegate duties. When you are overloaded, gaining the help of others can result in three important benefits: (1) other people develop; (2) personal health improves; and (3) overall performance is better. Figure 2.2 shows that delegation is not a new idea.

Because we all have limits, we must make choices and concentrate our energies on doing high-priority activities well, while postponing or avoiding others. In this spirit, Salvador de Madariaga, the Spanish essayist, wrote:

> Our eyes must be idealistic and our feet realistic. We must walk in the right direction, but we must walk step by step. Our tasks are to define what is desirable; to decide what is possible at any time within the scheme of what is desirable; to carry out what is possible in the spirit of what is desirable.[14]

Take a Break

Begin to think of yourself as a balanced person who can work hard and relax as well. You may need to move, speak, and eat more slowly. Also, you should avoid scheduling your life so that you are always in a hurry, rushing from place to place, never having time for a rest pause. Of course, you should try to accomplish as much as you can in life, but leave room for needed breaks.

When things are going badly, it often helps to escape for a while—take a walk, read a book, work in the garden, or take a nap. Changing your activity long enough to recover breath and balance is a good coping technique. The fact is that the average workday is not eight hours of uninterrupted labor. In order to combat fatigue and remain productive, people need breaks and will take them whether they are scheduled or not.[15]

An often overlooked form of "taking a break" is the emotional release that tears can bring. Women have used this well, and with recent changes in society's attitudes, more and more men are discovering the relief crying can bring when they are truly upset. Imagine the comfort tears can provide for one who has lost a child or experienced some other tragedy.

Individuals, families, organizations, indeed whole nations, have the need to escape for a while. During World War II, immediately after the battle of Dunkirk, England was on the brink of defeat. If ever a country needed to produce, England at that time did. However, consider the following. Prior to Dunkirk, the average work week was 56 hours. After Dunkirk, the prime minister announced an increase to 69.5 hours for all workers in war-related industries. What actually resulted was a work week of barely 51 hours.[16] The nation simply was fatigued and could produce no more; and had America not entered the war, relief might have been impossible and defeat probably would have resulted.

The coffee break, the day of rest, the emotional release, and the annual vacation are pauses that refresh in the world of work. These breaks are useful antidotes to physical and emotional stress, and you must not feel guilty when you take one. It is interesting to note that for medium-heavy

FIGURE 2.2

The Need to Delegate

Lack of Delegation

Perhaps the earliest recognition of the importance of delegation is found in the Bible. The Book of Exodus, Chapter 18, tells how "Moses sat to judge the people; and the people stood before Moses from the morning unto the evening." Moses' father-in-law, Jethro, saw this and told him: "The thing thou doest is not good. Thou wilt surely wear away, both thou, and this people that is with thee: for the thing is too heavy for thee; thou art not able to perform it alone." At that time the Israeli organization chart was as follows:

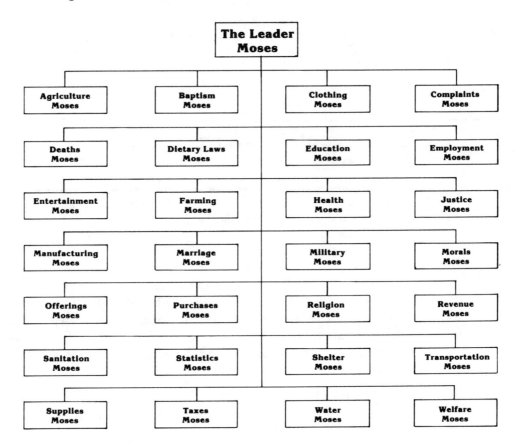

Delegation

The subordinate rulers, Jethro advised, could judge "every small matter" and bring the great matters to Moses. Up to this point, the Israelites had spent 39 years on a journey that had taken them only about halfway to the Promised Land. After delegation took place, they completed the remaining half of the journey in less than a year. The new organization chart looked like this:

FIGURE 2.2—*continued*

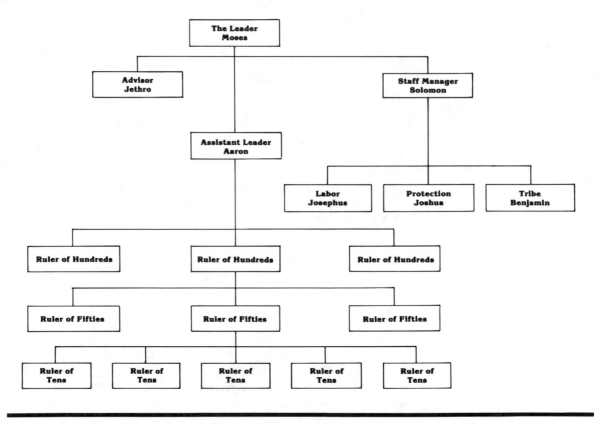

Source: Reprinted with permission from Ernest Dale, Management: Theory and Practice, *3d ed. (New York: McGraw-Hill, Inc., 1973), 193–94.*

work, the optimum work week for volume produced (over an extended period of time) is 48 hours. After 48 hours, the average person is affected by fatigue and would be better off going home. Otherwise, mistakes are made, sickness is experienced, and complaints are increased, all of which reduce overall productivity.[17]

The following are tips to consider when you escape for a while on vacation:

- Plan ahead for smooth sailing. Knowing ahead of time where you want to go and what you want to do saves valuable vacation time.

- Give yourself time to leave your work world behind you. A day to run errands, pack, and close the house or apartment would not be unreasonable.

- Leave yourself a lineup before you depart. List the things you have to do when you return. This saves trying to remember where you left off.

- Relax. You are on vacation to unwind, change your pace, and enjoy yourself. Forget the compulsion to be in control and to produce.

A break in the day allows one to gain a sense of perspective.

Trust in Time

Many of life's events can be painful; sometimes it may seem as though the anguish will never end. Although time may not heal all wounds, it often helps.

If you suffer a loss in your personal life or career and you feel your world has collapsed, there is a good possibility that within a year or two, the pain will be gone and you may even be stronger for the experience. As Dickens expressed so well in *David Copperfield*, "The best metal has been through the fire." And as Milton wrote in *Paradise Lost*, "Our torments, also, in length of time become our elements." Finally, Ecclesiastes 3 says: "To everything there is a season, and a time to every purpose under the heaven: A time to be born, and a time to die; a time to sow seed, and a time to pluck up that which is planted; . . ."

Sometimes, our only choice in a stressful period is to "trust in time."

Talk with Others

When things bother you, talk them out with a level-headed person you can trust. This helps relieve tension, adds perspective, and helps you figure out what to do. The word "catharsis" — from the Greek *kathairein*, to purge — means "cleansing." This is what happens in the talking-out process.

Talking it out is difficult for some people. Because of temperament or social conditioning, they are quiet and introverted, and talking about their problems can be uncomfortable. Other people are extroverted and find it easy to express their feelings and problems. Everyone needs to talk over their troubles with someone at times. Otherwise, tension builds up inside a person until the inevitable explosion occurs. Then everyone asks, "What in the world happened to Bill?" Typically, the more isolated you become, the more desperate your situation may seem.

Talking it out requires trust that the other person will not use what you say against you or be judgmental in a negative way. There is an old saying that you must be careful with whom you talk, because 70 percent of the people you may talk to don't care about your problems and 20 percent are glad you have them. Only 10 percent truly care and want to help.

Those people in the 10 percent might be your spouse, parents, or a friend or two. You may have been in someone else's 10 percent. In any case, whether you are the listener or the talker, you should remember that the good ideas, moods, and advice of others can have a relaxing and comforting effect that can help you to cope with stress. Family and friends can be important allies against the negative effects of stress.

People often turn to authority figures to talk out their problems. It is common for both the professional counselor and the work-group supervisor to hear people's problems. Whether or not the counselor or the supervisor is helpful depends on his or her willingness to listen and personal integrity. This counselor must be worthy of the subordinate's trust, that is, unwilling to take advantage of the subordinate's problems and frailties.

Avoid Self-Medication

Do you happen to have your pharmacology Ph.D.? Most people do not. But you wouldn't know it when you consider the self-prescribed medication used today. In 1983 alone, $73.2 billion was spent in the United States on just tobacco and alcohol. This is an average of $475 per person. The amount spent on other drugs and chemicals (legal and illegal) is incalculable.[18]

Most people know that cigarette smoking is an extremely dangerous habit. It is estimated that most cases of lung cancer could be prevented if people did not smoke. Cigarettes also contribute to heart disease. The addictive agent in tobacco is nicotine, which causes adrenalin to be released, triggering a small fight-or-flight response that raises blood pressure.

It helps to understand why nicotine is so addictive. Cigarette smoking causes the release of endorphins, natural body substances chemically similar to opiates such as morphine and other painkillers. When endorphin levels increase, you feel more pain free, at ease, and euphoric. Since each time you have a cigarette you release a dose of endorphins, you tend to want to continue having cigarettes.

The key is to substitute some other, healthful habit that achieves the same effect. Vigorous aerobic exercise seems to do this best. Thus, an exercise program provides an excellent complement to a smoke-ending program.

Figure 2.3 shows the negative effects of cigarette smoking, a major form of drug abuse. The graph compares the death rates for male and female smokers and nonsmokers.

Figure 2.4 shows the effects of alcoholism, another form of drug abuse, on job performance over a period of time.

The questions in Figure 2.5 were prepared by Alcoholics Anonymous as guidelines for evaluating drinking habits. If you answer yes to four or more questions, says AA, "the chances are you have a serious drinking problem or may have one in the future."

Besides tobacco and alcohol abuse, you should strive for freedom from the chemical tyranny of tranquilizers, sleeping pills, headache medicine, and other central nervous system depressants. You should also avoid dependency on medicines such as antacids, laxatives, and cold remedies and use natural relaxation techniques to normalize body functions.[19]

You should avoid self-medication because too many chemicals of the wrong type in the body usually make a poor situation worse, causing stress to become distress. If conditions are serious enough to require medication,

FIGURE 2.3

Death Rates for Smokers and Nonsmokers

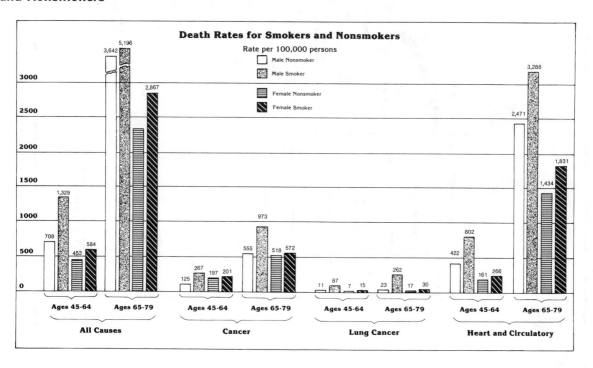

Source: Smoking, Tobacco, and Health: A Fact Book *(Washington, D.C.: U.S. Department of Health and Human Services, 1981), 30.*

FIGURE 2.4

How an Alcoholic Employee Behaves

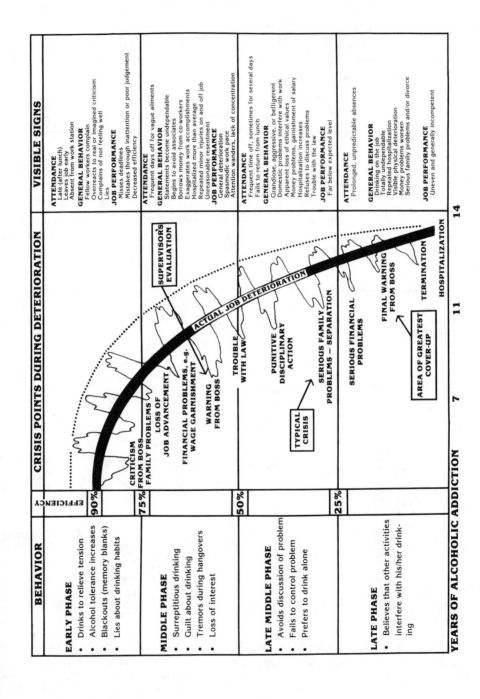

Source: *Excerpted from Administrative Management, copyright © 1969, by Dalton Communications, Inc., New York. Reprinted with permission.*

FIGURE 2.5

Are You Drinking Too Much?

1. Have you ever tried to stop drinking for a week or longer, only to fall short of your goal?

2. Do you resent the advice of others who try to get you to stop drinking?

3. Have you ever tried to control your drinking by switching from one alcoholic beverage to another?

4. Have you ever taken a morning drink during the past year?

5. Do you envy people who drink without getting into trouble?

6. Has your drinking problem become progressively more serious during the past year?

7. Has your drinking created problems at home?

8. At social affairs where drinking is limited, do you try to obtain extra drinks?

9. Despite evidence to the contrary, have you continued to assert that you can stop drinking on your own whenever you wish?

10. During the past year, have you missed time from work as a result of drinking?

11. Have you ever blacked out during your drinking?

12. Have you ever felt you could do more with your life if you did not drink?

Source: "What Industry Is Doing About 10 Million Alcoholic Workers," U.S. News and World Report *80, no. 2 (January 12, 1976), 66–67. Reprinted with permission.*

by all means seek professional help and obtain the correct medication. Otherwise, avoid the ravages of tobacco, alcohol, and drugs. Remember the old adage "two wrongs do not make a right." Go natural.

See Figure 2.6 for a summary of commonly used drugs in the United States today. Included are usual short- and long-term effects and potential for dependency.

Improve Job Proficiency

Developing technical knowledge, increasing practical experience, and learning human-relations skills (most people work with and through others) are excellent ways to reduce inappropriate stress at work and even to prevent stress in the first place. Important skills that help reduce stress on the job are communications and effective time-management skills for all

FIGURE 2.6

Use and Abuse of Common Drugs

Type of Drug	Examples and Comments	Slang Names	Usual Forms*	Medical Use	Potential for Excessive Use to Lead to Physical (Ph) and Psychological (Ps) Dependence	Common Effects at Peak of Drug Response	Long-term Symptoms	Possible in Overdoses
Depressants "Downers"	Barbiturates (seconal, amytal, luminal), Methaqualone (quaalude), glutethimide (doriden), and others. Any drug used to calm or sedate could be in this category.	Barbs, dolls, blue devils, candy, red devils, phennies, ludes, 714's, sopors.	Legitimate looking tablets and capsules.	Treatment of insomnia and tension.	High for both Ph and Ps; varies somewhat between drugs. Ph withdrawal effects can be life threatening.	Anxiety reduction, mild euphoria, impaired judgment.	Addiction, toxic psychosis, possible convulsions.	Death from depression of breathing and from dangerous behavior under influence.
Alcohol	Sedative-hypnotic (whiskey, gin, beer, wine, and others).	Booze, juice.	Alcoholic beverages.	Rare; antiseptic.	High for both Ph and Ps. Ph withdrawal effects can be life threatening.	Loss of inhibitions; impaired speech and judgment; lethargy.	Neurological damage, cirrhosis, toxic psychosis, addiction.	Death from depression of breathing and from dangerous behavior under influence.
Opiates**	Narcotic sedatives — heroin, morphine, dilaudid, codeine, methadone, opium, and others; derived from the seed pods of the poppy plant. Exerts effects by depressing central nervous system.	Horse, H, smack.	Injection; legitimate looking tablets and capsules; powders (white, brown, or gray); smoking.	Treatment of severe pain, diarrhea, and cough; analgesic effects.	High for both Ph and Ps; varies somewhat between drugs. Ph withdrawal effects uncomfortable, but rarely life threatening.	Initially may vomit, then become calm and euphoric; impaired intellectual functioning and coordination; respiratory depression.	Addiction, constipation, loss of appetite, temporary impotency.	Death from depression of breathing; cardiovascular collapse.
Tranquilizers	Drugs, used for calming effect — Valium, Librium, Serax, and others.		Pills, capsules.	Anxiety/tension psychological disorders.	Low for Ph; some Ps.	Relaxation, relief of anxiety and tension, improved functioning.	Drowsiness, blurred vision, skin rash, tremors.	Death possible with abuse or overdose.
Stimulants** "Uppers"	Amphetamines — benzedrine, methedrine, dexedrine; "speed" (methamphetamine); "ripoff speed" (drugs made to look like prescription diet drugs but containing caffeine and other legal stimulants); cocaine (rock, flake, powder forms) — derived from cocoa leaves.	Pep pills, bennies, speed, coke, flake, snow, crack.	Legitimate looking tablets and capsules; crystals or powders (usually white); injection; inhalation.	Amphetamines — control of appetite, mild depression, narcolepsy. Cocaine — local anesthetic.	Ph unlikely but Ps yes; severe depression can occur on withdrawal and lead to suicide.	Alertness, "high" feeling, talkativeness; may become irritable, paranoid, and aggressive.	Loss of appetite, anxiety, delusions, panic reaction, aggression, depression.	Amphetamine — chest pain, unconsciousness paralysis; cocaine - death from heart rhythm defects and/or convulsions.
Caffeine	Stimulant found in coffee, tea, cola beverages, chocolate, cocoa, and some over-the-counter drugs such as aspirin and No-Doz.	Java.	Liquid, capsules.	Treatment of migraine headaches, some forms of coma.	Ph no; Ps yes.	Increased alertness; reduction of fatigue.	Insomnia, gastric irritation, habituation.	Severe toxic effects unlikely.
Tobacco "Nicotine"	Cigarettes, cigars - stimulant	Fag, coffin nail.	Smoking.	None.	Ph high, Ps high.	Alertness, calmness, sociability.	Cardiovascular damage, emphysema, lung cancer, mouth	At least 1200 toxic chemicals identified as products of

						and throat cancer, habituation.	tobacco smoke. Death from cancer or cardiovascular disease common.
Hallucinogens	LSD, mescaline (peyote), psilocybin, DMT, STP, and others. These drugs alter perception of reality.	Acid, window pane, blotter, blue stars, sugar.	Tablets, capsules, liquid, or impregnated on blotters, stamps, or pieces of clear gelatin.	None.	No Ph; extent of Ps unknown, probably low.	Loss of coordination, hallucinations, changes in space and time perception, may make irrational verbal statements and movements.	Can produce panic reaction, intensify already existing phychosis.	Severe toxic effects unlikely; death can occur from dangerous behavior while under influence.
Delirients "dissociative anesthetic"	Phencyclidine hydrochloride (PCP) and any drug with actions like belladonna (such as Jimson Weed). Produce hallucinations & delirium at doses causing significant toxic effects.	PCP, angel dust.	Smoking, tablets, capsules, powder, seeds; may be mixed with other drugs.	None - human; Animal - immobilizing agent.	Low for Ph; moderate to high for Ps.	"Blank stare", confusion, disturbed speech, agitation, hostile behavior, gross incoordination, "floating" sensation.	Violent psychotic behavior, impaired judgment, emotional dependence, coma, or stupor.	Death from heart and breathing system effects or dangerous behavior.
Inhalants: A. Gasoline & Solvents	Almost any vaporous liquid or aerosol may be inhaled for a temporary "high".		Nitrous oxide is usually found in small (2 inch) metal "bullets"; nitrites are strong smelling solutions generally in small brown bottles.	None, except nitrous oxide as anesthetic.	Ph and Ps varies greatly with agent and patterns of use.	Inebriation, impairment of judgment and coordination, delirium.	Varied — some substances can damage body organs such as liver and kidneys.	Death possible with overdose or long-term use; cause varies with agent.
B. Nitrous Oxide	"Laughing Gas", "Whippets" — intended for use in charging whipped cream canisters.					Laughing episodes and euphoria.		
C. Amyl or butyl Nitrite	Rush, "poppers", "amyl", etc.					Sudden lowering then rising of blood pressure and heart rate, suffocating sensation, flushed "prickly heat" feeling.		
Marijuana	Derived from the flowers and top leaves of the female cannabis sativa plant, a weed of the hemp family; concentrated preps of resin are known as hashish and hash oil. Tetrahydrocannibinol (THC) is the active ingredient in marijuana and hashish causing psychogenic reactions.	Grass, joint, reefer, pot, Texas tea, rope.	Generally as dark green or brown plant particles; often in plastic bags or as cigarettes.	Treatment of glaucoma, asthma, and those who suffer from nausea and vomiting from cancer therapy.	Ph unlikely: Ps low for most users, moderate to high for a few.	Mild stimulation, followed by relaxed euphoric feeling; red eyes; interference with thinking, judgment, and recent memory.	Possible lung cancer and chronic respiratory disorders, acute panic reactions, habituation.	Death from dangerous behavior while under influence.

*Fake look-alikes exist for many street drugs. No one can be absolutely certain of the quality of any street drug without analysis.

**People who inject drugs under non-sterile conditions run a high risk of contracting hepatitis, abscesses, or circulatory disorders.

Source: Adapted from Dennis Coon, Essentials of Psychology (St. Paul: West Publishing Co., 1985), 142–43; Spencer A. Rathus, Essentials of Psychology (New York: Holt, Rinehart & Winston, 1986), 335–42; Benjamin B. Lahey, Psychology (Dubuque, Iowa: Wm. C. Brown Group, 1986), 156–66; and James McConnell, Understanding Human Behavior, 5th ed. (New York: Holt, Rinehart & Winston, 1986), 71–82.

workers and leadership and effective delegation skills for supervisory personnel.

One major stressor on the job and in some homes is the environment. Glare from lights, noise from radios, drifting smoke, poor temperature control, and distractions from people talking are all stressors that can usually be reduced with a little effort.

Use a Decompression Chamber Technique

It is important to leave the pressures, conflicts, and frustrations of one arena of life behind you when you enter another arena. In other words, leave home problems at home and work problems at work as much as possible. This is hard to do unless you use a decompression chamber technique.

The decompression chamber is the private, peaceful time and space you carve out between work and home. It is the personal period and place you reserve to mentally unwind, physically relax, and spiritually renew yourself. Typically, the person in the decompression chamber applies the three R's — review the day's events, rehearse the evening's activities, and relax.

Examples of decompression chamber techniques include:

- the businessperson who uses the ride between work and home to forget one world and prepare for the next;

- the homemaker who sets aside personal time between daytime household chores and nighttime family activities.

Most busy people can benefit from the decompression chamber technique as a coping mechanism.

Keep a Sense of Humor

Humor and laughter are natural diversions from too much stress, and they are always available. You simply cannot be distressed while you are laughing. A lively sense of humor and a good laugh a few times a day are excellent preventatives and restoratives against pressures, conflicts, and frustrations, since laughter puts a healthy distance between you and life's problems. Remember, laughter is like jelly — when you spread it around, you can't help getting some on yourself. Also, when you smile you will relax, and this will relax others as well.[20]

The story of Norman Cousins, well-known writer and editor, shows the importance of humor. Cousins was diagnosed as having a serious disease of the connective tissues of the body. He was in severe pain and was informed that he had only a 1 in 500 chance for full recovery. He entered treatment that involved many drugs and hospital care. But Cousins was not improving at all; his condition remained poor.

With his doctor's permission, Cousins totally changed the approach. He checked out of the hospital and into a nearby hotel. He substituted large doses of vitamin C for the drugs he had been taking, and he began watching comedies and old television reruns of "I Love Lucy" and "Candid Camera."

Despite the pain, Cousins started laughing. Then he realized that something strange was going on. The more he laughed, the less pain he noticed. "Ten minutes of good laughter gave me an hour of pain-free sleep. . . . The more I laughed, the better I got." For more information on the importance of humor, see the excerpt from *Anatomy of an Illness as Perceived by the Patient* in the readings section of this part.

Accentuate the Positive

Perception plays a role in the stress equation. To a degree, stress is determined by mental attitude. Two people can suffer setbacks. One may become stronger and wiser for the experience; the other may never recover and may actually worsen. The difference may be that one focuses on the positive and the other on the negative.

Do not close your eyes to the truth, but avoid negative thinking; emphasize the positive things in life. A positive mental attitude helps you tolerate life's ups and downs and gives you strength to overcome problems. Optimism and positive thinking are contagious. Your good attitude will rub off on others; so smile—it will help others too.

The Chinese have a symbol for "crisis" consisting of two characters, each with a separate meaning (see Figure 2.7). The upper character

FIGURE 2.7

Crisis: Opportunity Within Danger

represents danger, and the lower character stands for opportunity. The "B" view accentuates opportunity, as opposed to danger, in a crisis.

To review, the fourteen principles for being a "B" are:

- don't worry; take action;
- set priorities, following the 80/20 rule in your life and your work;
- follow the principle "moderation, moderation, all things in moderation";
- enjoy the little things in life;
- go easy with criticism;
- don't try to be Superwoman or Superman;
- take a break;
- trust in time;
- talk with others;
- avoid self-medication;
- improve job proficiency;
- use a decompression chamber technique;
- keep a sense of humor;
- accentuate the positive.[21]

Notice that none of these principles says, "Be lazy," or "Don't achieve great things in life." Great achievements make life worthwhile, and most accomplishments require hard work (good stress). The point of following the fourteen principles is not only to succeed, but to live to enjoy success. In this regard, when you consider the meaning of success, remember Cervantes' advice in *Don Quixote*: "The road is always better than the inn."

To personalize the principles for becoming a "B," which of these coping techniques do *you* need to try? Worry less and do more. Work smarter, not necessarily harder. Introduce more balance and moderation into your life. Slow down and enjoy the little things of life. Be less critical and more accepting, both of yourself and of others. Learn when, how, and why to say no. Escape for a while. Let time be a healer. Share feelings, reduce tension, and talk it out. Go "natural" and avoid self-medication. Develop skills to help you reduce job stress. Make the decompression chamber technique work for you. Enjoy a good laugh frequently. Emphasize the positive in your life.

Most people can benefit by following these fourteen coping behaviors. They are time-tested techniques that can help you deal with the stresses of life.

ILLUS. 2.4

Taking relaxed time with a friend is suggestive of the "B" personality.

RECOMMENDED RESOURCES

The following reading, case, and film are suggested for greater insight into the material in Part Two:

Reading — Mr. A and the Stranger: A Parable

Case — How Do You Handle a Stress Carrier?

Film — The Time of Your Life

REFERENCE NOTES

1 Meyer Friedman and Ray H. Rosenman, *Type A Behavior and Your Heart* (New York: Alfred A. Knopf, Inc., 1974), 55, 67–70, 193–95.

2 Friedman and Rosenman, *Type A Behavior and Your Heart*, 51–79.

3 Friedman and Rosenman, *Type A Behavior and Your Heart*, 70–86.

4 Walter McQuade, "What Stress Can Do to You," *Fortune* 85 (January 1972): 102–7.

5 *Manage Your Stress: Participant's Workbook* (New York: McGraw-Hill, Inc., 1980), 6.

6 *Manage Your Stress: Participant's Workbook*, 3.

7 Saul I. Teplitz, *Life Is for Living*, in Will Forpe and John C. McCollister, *The Sunshine Book: Expressions of Love, Hope and Inspiration* (Middle Village, NY: David Publishers, Inc. 1979), 102.

8   Alan Lakein, *How to Get Control of Your Time and Your Life* (New York: Peter H. Wyden, Inc., 1973), 83–86.

9   Adapted from L. Tolstoy, *Master and Man* (London: J. M. Dent and Sons, Ltd., 1910), 65–83.

10 June Callwood, "The One Sure Way to Happiness,' *Reader's Digest* 1105, no. 630 (October 1974), 137–40, as condensed from June Callwood, *Love, Hate, Fear, Anger, and the Other Lively Emotions* (Hollywood: Newcastle Publishing Co. Inc., 1964).

11 *Manage Your Stress: Participant's Workbook*, 33–35.

12 Gary S. Belkin, *Practical Counseling in the Schools*, 2d ed. (Dubuque, Iowa: Wm. C. Brown Group, 1981), 85–111.

13 As heard on the Paul Harvey News on the ABC Radio Network. Used with permission.

14 T. V. Smith and Edward R. Lindeman, *Democratic Way of Life* (New York: New American Library of World Literature, Inc., 1951), 123.

15 Norman R. F. Maier, *Psychology in Industrial Organizations*, 4th ed. (Boston: Houghton-Mifflin Company, 1973), 406–9.

16 Maier, *Psychology in Industrial Organizations*, 406–9.

17 Maier, *Psychology in Industrial Organizations*, 406–9.

18 *Smoking, Tobacco, and Health: A Fact Book* (Washington, D.C.: U.S. Department of Health and Human Services, 1981), 30; *1984 U.S. Industrial Outlook* (Washington, D.C.: U.S. Department of Commerce: Bureau of Industrial Economics, 1984), 38:25, 39:1; *1980 Census of Population: Age, Sex, Race, and Spanish Origin of the Population by Regions, Divisions, and States: 1980* (Washington, D.C.: U.S. Department of Commerce: Bureau of the Census, May 1981), 3.

19 *Manage Your Stress: Participant's Workbook*, 10–21; Charles Kuntzleman, *Your Active Way to Weight Control*, 1980, 8–9 (Box 8644, Clinton, Iowa).

20 Gmelch, *Beyond Stress to Effective Management*, 102.

21 Adapted in part from Ellen Brown, "Tackling Your Tensions," *Cincinnati Post*, 21 May 1979, 12.

STUDY QUIZ

As a test of your understanding and the extent to which you have achieved the objectives in Part Two, complete the following questions. See Appendix F for the answer key.

1. People who are aggressive, competitive, rushed, impatient, angry, and hostile are termed:

    a. hyperencephalic
    b. type A
    c. hypoencephalic
    d. type B
    e. externalizers

2. Living a balanced life means that you do not focus on just one person, thing, or goal. You get involved in:

    a. work
    b. play
    c. both of the above

3. Friedman and Rosenman found that type A men had _____ incidence of coronary heart disease than type B men.

    a. greater
    b. less
    c. the same

4. All of the following behaviors are typical of the type A personality except:

    a. walking, eating, and talking rapidly
    b. aggressive competition
    c. irritability
    d. relaxing with others

5. Type A behavior is often inefficient because when you rush you can:

    a. make mistakes
    b. become less rigid and try the same thing again and again
    c. become less creative in problem solving
    d. all of the above

6. Aristotle's prescription "moderation, moderation, all things in moderation" refers to:

    a. working long hours
    b. free time
    c. striving for "stress without distress"

7. Type A behavior includes which of the following?

   a. Inability to advance oneself
   b. Inability to compete
   c. Inability to relax

8. Feeling out of control is a major cause of stress.

   a. True
   b. False

9. You should not try to be Superman or Superwoman because the average person can only handle a maximum of four major commitments at any one time. Everyone has physical, financial, and emotional limits.

   a. True
   b. False

10. One way to cope with stress is to keep a sense of humor.

    a. True
    b. False

11. The major finding of the type A/type B studies is that type B personalities experience less stress and have a lower incidence of cardiovascular disease than do type A people.

    a. True
    b. False

12. Of the following, which is not a type B coping behavior?

    a. Enjoying the little things in life
    b. Going easy with criticism
    c. Trusting in time
    d. Talking it out with others
    e. Avoiding self-medication
    f. Keeping a sense of humor
    g. Denying that problems exist

13. Newspaper obituaries tell about middle-aged people who die because of:

    a. type A behavior
    b. type B behavior
    c. type C behavior
    d. both B and C

14. A _____ relationship has been established between personality type and heart disease.

    a. causative
    b. correlational
    c. scientific
    d. experimental

15. All of the following are steps to take in becoming a type B personality except:

    a. not worrying; taking action
    b. following the "principle of moderation"
    c. setting priorities following the 80/20 rule
    d. increasing the amount of commitments you make to family and friends

16. Included in the list of type A behaviors are all of the following *except*:

    a. an intense drive to advance oneself
    b. a quick pace of walking, eating, speaking, and gesturing
    c. inability to relax
    d. smooth human relations

DISCUSSION QUESTIONS AND ACTIVITIES

The following questions and activities help personalize the subject. They are appropriate for classroom exercises and homework assignments.

1. At this point in time, are you a type A or a type B, or are you somewhere in between? What forces have caused you to be this way?

_____

_____

_____

2. Of the fourteen coping behaviors to be a "B," which ones appeal to you?

_____

_____

_____

3. Divide into groups to discuss type A/type B personality traits. Are there additional techniques for being a "B" that group members recommend?

4. For various group members, discuss factors that encourage type A/type B behavior traits—parents, school, jobs, etc. Discuss problems and possibilities for becoming a "B."

PART THREE

Stress Prevention

Learning Objectives

After completing Part Three, you will better understand:

1. the elements and importance of the $1 \times 3 \times 7 = 21$ plan in preparing for stress;

2. the importance of tender loving care (TLC) in managing stress.

THE 1 × 3 × 7 = 21 PLAN

A readiness plan is needed to prepare for inevitable stress. One good system is the 1 × 3 × 7 = 21 plan presented in the following pages. If this weekly plan is followed, you will be better prepared to deal with pressure, conflict, and frustration. This will reduce physical and emotional wear and tear and will help reduce disease and aging. Note that you should consult your physician before changing health habits, particularly in the areas of exercise and nutrition.

When you talk with your doctor, blood pressure will be discussed. Your blood pressure is simply the measurement of the pressure your circulating blood exerts on the walls of your blood vessels. In order to travel through the miles of blood vessels throughout your body, blood must be under pressure.

A problem arises if you have high blood pressure (hypertension). Hypertension means that your heart is having to work too hard to pump blood through the body to nourish tissues and sustain life.

Your blood pressure may be high because your heart is sending out an increased amount of blood with each pump. This may happen if salt (sodium) overload causes you to retain extra fluids, resulting in more blood for your heart to pump. Another common cause is blockage of the arteries by fatty debris (plaque) that clings to the arterial walls and narrows the openings that the blood must pass through. This buildup is called atherosclerosis. Atherosclerosis also involves fibrosis, which is a buildup of scar tissue in the arterial walls themselves.

Blood pressure is recorded as two numbers, such as 120/80. The first number represents your systolic pressure, the pressure in your arteries when your heart is in its pumping phase. The second number represents the diastolic, or resting pressure.

Although a reading of 120/80 is considered normal for adults, the first number (systolic pressure) may range 20 points in either direction (from 100 to 140). The second number (diastolic pressure) may range 10 points (from 80 to 90). A blood pressure reading of 140/90 is considered to indicate mild hypertension.

Although hypertension can be caused by genetic factors, most cases can be controlled by changes in living habits. If detected, high blood pressure is fairly easy to control. However, if unnoticed and untreated, hypertension is highly damaging and will cut years off your life.[1]

What is the good news? You can take positive steps to solve the problem. Following the $1 \times 3 \times 7 = 21$ plan is an excellent way to deal with stress and prevent and control hypertension.

The following is a breakdown of the $1 \times 3 \times 7 = 21$ plan.

1: Meta-imagery

At least one time a day, use meta-imagery. Shakespeare wrote, "There is nothing either good or bad, but thinking makes it so." The physical basis for Shakespeare's observation is the fact that the autonomic nervous system cannot differentiate between real and imagined experiences. It acts the same in either case, and this is the reason why voodoo, hypnosis, and other forms of "mind over body" work. To fantasize pleasure on a paradise island is more healthful than to fantasize a pitched battle. If you have ever been chased by a panther in your sleep or awakened in the morning having just fought World War III, you know the harmful effects of thinking negative thoughts.

The following is an account of what can happen when a man believes he has been cursed by an enemy and that he will die. It is an example of negative meta-imagery:

> He stands aghast, with his eyes staring at the treacherous pointers, and with his hands lifted as though to ward off the lethal medium, which he imagines is pouring into his body. His cheeks blanch and his eyes become glassy, and the expression of his face becomes horribly distorted. . . . He sways backwards and falls to the ground, and after a short time, appears to be in a swoon. . . . From this time onwards, he sickens and frets, refusing to eat and keeping aloof from the daily affairs of the tribe. Unless help is forthcoming in the shape of a countercharm, death is only a matter of a comparatively short time.[2]

Walter Cannon studied a large number of voodoo deaths and concluded that these deaths result from changes in the body that accompany strong and prolonged emotion. The victim who has been cursed believes he will die and therefore becomes terrified. The fear may be so intense that it results in a heart attack or other bodily disorders, including even death.[3]

More recently, the laboratory findings of Hans Selye have helped explain why meta-imagery and other forms of mental conditioning work. Selye identified distinct chemicals and hormones, called *catatoxins*, that are produced by the body when a person is in a negative emotional state— angry, worried, resentful; and different chemicals and hormones, called *syntoxins*, that are released when one is in a positive emotional state— happy, confident, satisfied. Selye found that catatoxins are associated with disease and poor health, while syntoxins are invigorating and health provoking.[4]

The following is a dramatic example of the power and consequences of negative meta-imagery:

> There was a railway employee in Russia who accidentally locked himself in a refrigerator car. He was unable to escape and couldn't attract the attention of those outside, and so he resigned himself to his fate. As

he felt his body becoming numb, he recorded the story of his approaching death in sentences scribbled on the wall of the car. "I am becoming colder," he wrote. "Still colder, now. Nothing to do but wait. . . . I am slowly freezing to death . . . half asleep now, I can hardly write. . . ." Finally, "These may be my last words." And they were, for when at length the car was opened, they found him dead. And yet the temperature of the car was only 56 degrees. The freezing apparatus was and had been out of order. There was no physical reason for his death. There was plenty of air; he hadn't suffocated. He was the victim of his own illusion. His conclusions were all wrong. He was so sure he knew.[5]

Because thoughts and emotional states can have a powerful influence on physical health, at least once every day you should pause for a few minutes to think about and appreciate the good things in your life — your family, health, job, and friends. You may have had so many problems and bad experiences that you have fallen into the habit of negative thinking.

Some people are especially prone to negative thinking. You may know a person who always seems to look on the dark side of things. If a cup is half full, it is seen as half empty; if the weather is partly sunny, there are complaints about the clouds. Such a person not only produces catatoxins that damage his or her own health but can create a cloud of gloom that is detrimental to everyone's health and happiness.

You should use pleasant thoughts to counteract negative feelings. The following shows the benefits of positive meta-imagery:

> A youthful looking, graying lady was asked what she used to preserve her attractive appearance. Her reply was, "I use for the lips, truth; for the voice, sweet words; for the eyes, appreciation; for the hand, charity; for the figure, uprightness; and for the heart, I use love."[6]

As you evaluate yourself, are you in the habit of negative thinking? If so, begin today, and at least once every day, use positive meta-imagery to increase the level of syntoxins in your body and good stress in your life.

× 3: Exercise

Have at least three good physical workouts a week. As a minimum, you should exercise three times a week for approximately 40 minutes, including warm-up and cool-down activities. This is true for both men and women, regardless of age. Although muscle strength, endurance, flexibility, and body composition (a healthful balance between fat and muscle) are important fitness goals, cardiovascular fitness is the primary goal of these workouts. Thus, fast walking, jogging, cycling, and swimming are good exercises, as they raise the heart rate high enough to help your cardiovascular system. These types of exercises are called *aerobic* exercises. For best results, you should work harder than what is comfortable for you, but stop short of total exertion.

A general guide for the average person is to exercise regularly, starting slowly and building up to three to five sessions per week that double the heart rate for at least 20 minutes.[7] Fewer than three exercise sessions are insufficient, and more than five are unnecessary for optimum benefit to the average person.[8] The following presents a more specific guide for determining the correct heart rate for cardiovascular fitness:[9]

Target Training Rate
for Cardiovascular
Fitness

What is an appropriate level of exercise? There is an intensity of activity that is sufficient to develop cardiovascular fitness, but not strenuous enough to exceed safe limits. This is called the "target training rate," measured in beats per minute by the heart (BPM). Your target training rate is between 60 and 85 percent of your maximal aerobic power. Below 60 percent of this capacity, you achieve little cardiovascular benefit, and above 85 percent, there is little benefit from the extra intensity.

The concept of maximal aerobic power is merely the technical name for the point at which, despite your best efforts, your heart and circulatory system cannot deliver any more oxygen to your tissues. Exhaustion soon follows. Almost simultaneously, the heart becomes unable to beat any faster. This constitutes your maximal attainable heart rate.

A sophisticated way to determine maximal attainable heart rate is to take an exercise stress test. If this is impractical, you can roughly approximate your maximal attainable heart rate by subtracting your age from 220. This figure is used to calculate your training heart rate.

To obtain the proper target training rate, you should first determine your resting heart rate, the number of beats of the heart per minute while

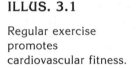

ILLUS. 3.1

Regular exercise promotes cardiovascular fitness.

at rest. The accurate measurement of heart rate is essential in determining resting heart rate and calculating target training rate.

Locating the pulse requires some practice. Any location where a pulse can be felt is satisfactory. Acceptable sites include: the radial artery, felt at the wrist on the thumb side; the brachial artery, inside the bend of the elbow toward the body side; the femoral artery in the groin; the arteries at the temple; and the carotid artery in the neck (although there is some evidence that pressure here may cause a reflexive slowing of the heart rate).

It is essential that the palpitation be done with the fingers and not the thumb, because using the thumb may lead to an error in counting. Normally, the resting heart rate should be measured after you have been sitting comfortably for 30 minutes. This time period may prove impractical in some situations and may be modified, but decreasing it to as little as 10 to 15 minutes may give invalid readings.

After obtaining your resting heart rate, subtract this from your maximal attainable heart rate (220 – age). Then multiply the result by the desired percentage of activity intensity — between 60 and 85 percent. (A sedentary individual should select 60 percent and gradually increase with time.) Finally, by adding the resting heart rate to this figure, you can calculate your "target training rate."

Example: Gayle is thirty-five years old, has a resting heart rate of 70 beats per minute (BPM), and is relatively sedentary. Her "target training rate" is found as follows:

$$220 - 35 = 185 \text{ (maximal attainable heart rate)}$$
$$185 - 70 \text{ (resting HR)} = 115$$
$$115 \times .60 \text{ (percentage of activity)} = 69$$
$$69 + 70 = 139 \text{ BPM (heartbeats per minute)}$$

Gayle's "target training rate" for cardiovascular fitness is 139 BPM.

There are few excuses for not being in good physical shape. However, there are several reasons why a person *should* be in good condition:

- it is not overly difficult;

- it doesn't take too much time;

- it costs very little;

- it has positive value for physical and emotional health.

Physical exercise renews the body and makes it strong in many ways:[10]

- New red corpuscles emerge from the bone marrow and enter the bloodstream, reviving tired blood.

- Fatty substances in the blood — cholesterol and triglycerides — are reduced, lessening the risk of arterial blockage that could lead to stroke, arteriosclerosis, and heart failure.

- New capillaries open up, increasing the effectiveness of your vascular network.

- The heart becomes more efficient, increasing the volume of blood pumped with each contraction. This is important when you realize that, weighing less than a pound and being as small as your fist, this single organ must pump 10,000 to 12,000 pints of blood through 60,000 miles of blood vessels each day.

- The brain's oxygen-carrying blood supply increases, so that you can think more clearly and quickly.

- Your overall energy level goes up, so that you can accomplish and enjoy more activities.

- The ability to obtain needed sleep is improved.

Kenneth Cooper, an expert on aerobic exercise, identifies a four-step plan for achieving physical fitness:[11]

- Have a thorough medical examination, including a physical stress test.

- Determine your target training rate for cardiovascular fitness.

- Choose an aerobic exercise you enjoy. Five good ones, in descending order for exercise value, are cross-country skiing, swimming, running (faster than nine miles per hour) or jogging (slower than nine miles per hour), outdoor cycling, and brisk walking. Other aerobic options include roller-skating, dancing, and racquet sports.

- Begin a regular program. Exercise a minimum of three times a week for approximately 40 minutes. First, warm up by stretching and loosening muscles and joints to be used. Then, engage in aerobic exercise for at least 20 minutes. Try to get your heart rate up to target training rate, but do not overexert. Signs of overexertion include pains in the chest, dizziness, nausea, severe breathlessness, and loss of muscle control. Follow the aerobic exercise by at least five minutes of cool-down activity. Finally, devote at least ten minutes to calisthenics or weight-training activities to increase muscle strength, endurance, and flexibility.

Besides physical fitness, mental fitness can be improved through exercise. Many people who exercise by cycling, running, or swimming will cram all of the problems of their day into their heads before beginning to exercise. Twenty minutes later, their minds are free, and they don't know where their problems are. Their worries are along the roadway, on the jogging path, or at the bottom of the swimming pool. Indeed, evidence from research and therapy shows that physical exercise can have positive benefits for mental health. See Figure 3.1.

Figure 3.2 presents the energy use and advantages and disadvantages of a variety of popular exercise activities.

FIGURE 3.1

**Effects of Physical Fitness Training
on Emotions, Personality, and
Self-Concept**

Study	Primary Focus	Subjects	Outcome
Hilyer and Mitchell (1979)	Self-concept	College males and females	Improved
Young (1979)	Anxiety, well-being	Male and female adults	Improved
R. S. Brown et al. (1978)	Depression	High school and university athletes	Improved
Kowal et al. (1978)	Moods, personality, self-concept	Male and female recruits	Mood improved (males)
Lynch et al. (1978)	Moods	Middle-aged males	Improved
Martinek et al. (1978)	Self-concept	Elementary age children	Improved
Morris and Husman (1978)	Well-being	College students	Improved
Tredway (1978)	Moods	Older adults	Improved
Bruya (1977)	Self-concept	Fourth graders	No change
Duke et al. (1977)	Locus of control	Children	Improved
Ismail and Young (1977)	Personality	Middle-aged males	No change
Mauser and Reynolds (1977)	Self-concept	Elementary age children	No change
Folkins (1976)	Moods	Middle-aged males at risk of coronary heart disease	Improved (anxiety)
Kowal et al. (1976)	Moods, personality, self-concept	Male and female recruits	Mood improved (males)
Young and Ismail (1976)	Personality	Middle-aged males	Some improved
Buccola and Stone (1975)	Personality	Older males	Some improved
Mayo (1975)	Personality	Seventh- and eighth-grade females	No change
J. S. Hanson and Nedde (1974)	Self-concept	Adult females	Improved

FIGURE 3.1—*continued*

Study	Primary Focus	Subjects	Outcome
McGowan et al. (1974)	Self-concept	Seventh-grade males	Improved
Ismail and Young (1973)	Personality	Middle-aged males	Some improved
Collingwood (1972)	Body and self-attitudes	Adult male rehabilitation clients	Improved
Folkins et al. (1972)	Moods, personality, work, sleep	College males and females	Improved
Folkins et al. (1972)	Personality (present adjustment)	College males and females	Improved (females)
Collingwood and Willett (1971)	Body and self-attitudes	Obese male teenagers	Improved
D. S. Hanson (1971)	Anxiety	4-year-olds	Improved
Morgan et al. (1970)	Depression	Adult males	No change
de Vries (1968)	Tension	Middle-aged males	Improved
Naughton et al. (1968)	Clinical scales	Post-coronary males	No change
Popejoy (1968)	Anxiety	Adult females	Improved
McPherson et al. (1967)	Moods	Post-coronary and healthy males	Improved
Karbe (1966)	Anxiety	College females	Improved
Werner and Gottheil (1966)	Personality	College males	No change
Tillman (1965)	Personality	High school males	No change

Source: Carlyle H. Folkins and Wesley E. Sime, "Physical Fitness Training and Mental Health," American Psychologist 36 (April 1981): 373–89. Reprinted with permission.

FIGURE 3.2

Activity Chart for Popular Exercises

Activity	Energy Use*	Advantages	Possible Disadvantages**
Walking	+ +	No cost, no equipment, no special facilities. Everyone can participate. Year-round activity	Time commitment, must walk fast for conditioning effect
Jogging (less than 5 miles per hour)	+ + +	Promotes weight loss, leg strength, cardiovascular endurance. No special facilities	May be hard on knees and other joints. Must have physical checkup, proper shoes
Running (more than 5 miles per hour)	+ + + +	Promotes weight loss, cardiovascular conditioning, and well-being	Must have physical checkup, good shoes. Can be hard on joints
Dancing (disco, other fast dances)	+ + +	Promotes weight control, total-body conditioning, especially aerobic dancing (doing cardiovascular exercises to music). Year-round activity	Must be brisk for conditioning. Requires coordination, rhythm for set dance patterns. May be hard on joints
Biking	+ + +	Good cardiovascular conditioning, promotes weight control, easier on joints than walking, jogging, running. Energy-saving transportation	Danger from autos, cost of bike, requires learned skill
Alpine skiing	+ + +	Promotes total body conditioning, especially legs. Enjoyable, apt to promote well-being	Requires learned skill, expensive equipment. Can be dangerous, especially if not in condition, from falls, cold weather, and altitude. Seasonal
Cross-country skiing	+ + + +	Excellent for cardiovascular conditioning, total body fitness. Little jar to body joints. Apt to promote well-being	Requires some learned skill, special equipment. Cold and altitude may be a negative factor. Seasonal
Swimming	+ + + +	Excellent for cardiovascular conditioning and muscle toning. No jar to joints	Requires some skill, pool, minimum cost of swimsuit

FIGURE 3.2—*continued*

Activity	Energy Use*	Advantages	Possible Disadvantages**
Racket sports (tennis, squash, racketball)	+ + +(+)	Excellent total-body conditioner if fast game is played. Promotes weight loss	Requires learned skill, special equipment and facilities. Must play at high level for conditioning effect
Golf (walk, carry own clubs)	+ +	Enjoyable and relaxing if not self-critical. Some of same benefits as walking	Requires learned skill, special equipment. Walking briskly without intermittent stops is a better conditioner
Bowling	+	Relaxing and enjoyable if not self-critical. Better than just sitting	Almost no conditioning effect. Requires learned skill and special equipment. Not recommended as treatment or preventive relaxation technique
Calisthenics	+ +	Brisk, total-body exercises have conditioning value, especially muscle toning. No cost, little or no equipment. Year-round activity	May exacerbate existing muscle problems. Tendency to overdo initially
Weight lifting	+ +	Increases strength, improves physique, and may improve self-image. Can improve cardiovascular efficiency by lifting lighter weights for greater repetitions or by circuit training	Requires special equipment. Some risk of muscular injury unless properly trained and prudently utilized

*All energy use, of course, depends on the intensity at which one pursues the activity, so only a relative rating system is used here. One "+" denotes least strenuous activity and minimal energy use, while four "+" signs denotes highest energy use.

**A possible disadvantage in most of these activities is high-level, ego-involved competition.

Source: Dorothy Dusek, *"Stress Reduction through Physical Activity," in* D. Girdano and G. Everly, Jr., eds., Controlling Stress and Tension: A Holistic Approach, *2d ed,* © *1986, 205–206. Reprinted by permission of Prentice-Hall, Inc., Englewood Cliffs, N.J.*

In summary, what kinds of exercises should adults do? How often should they do them?

Activities that emphasize large muscle groups and involve cardiorespiratory endurance are recommended. They may be incorporated in game and/or competitive situations. Rhythmic and aerobic experiences are particularly important for cardiovascular development and maintenance. Other types of activities (tennis, handball, racketball) may be incorporated into the regimen as additions, so to speak, for fun.

Healthy adults should try to participate in continuous aerobic activity for 15 to 60 minutes, depending on the intensity of the exercise. Beginning exercisers would do well to perform at low to moderate levels for relatively longer periods of time. A good criterion for determining how much exercise adults should do is sustaining a pulse rate of between 110 to 120 beats per minute or a little higher if the exerciser is already in pretty good shape.

Programs in which participation is three days a week at the intensities described above should fill the bill. Going beyond three days a week may be good or not so good, depending upon the exerciser and the exercise. Jogging and running for adults who are exercise beginners may produce orthopedic injuries when done in excess of three times per week. Swimming is not as likely to produce the same effect. Three times per week should be enough for calisthenics, stretching, and rhythmic-endurance exercises. Other game or recreational activities, such as racket sports, may be added on other days.

Combative, competitive activities such as tackle football (or even flag football) and basketball carry substantially high injury risks (particularly of the orthopedic kind) as biological age advances. It's presumptuous to identify precisely the age at which an adult should no longer pursue these kinds of experiences. Sometimes adults have difficulty disengaging from sports that have provided them a great deal of satisfaction for a long period of time. An alternative is lifetime or carryover sports, which can be continued for many years.[12]

Are you as fit as you should be to cope with the inevitable stresses of life? Are you able to deal effectively with daily physical demands without feeling fatigued? Can you handle an emergency? If not, begin today to improve. You should select an exercise program that you enjoy; do it at least three times a week, and make physical fitness a lifelong habit.

✕ 7: Relaxation

Have the equivalent of seven restful nights of sleep per week. Each person needs a different amount and interval of sleep. Some people need fewer than eight hours' sleep in twenty-four, while others need more; some rest best at night, while others spread their rest periods throughout the day. In any case, your body requires adequate rest to revitalize itself and to prepare to cope with new stress.

Typically, as you get older, the time spent in bed decreases until approximately age forty-five (17 out of 24 hours are spent in bed near birth; 8 1/2 hours at about age twelve; an average of 7 1/2 hours between the ages of twenty-five and forty-five). After age forty-five, people usually increase the amount of time they spend in bed to 8 1/2 hours but actually decrease the time spent sleeping. There is a tendency to spend more and more time in bed, with less and less time asleep. In later years, the average sleeping time is approximately 6 1/2 hours.[13]

Regardless of the amount or schedule, everyone needs two kinds of sleep — REM (rapid eye movement) and NREM (non-REM). Both are important for physical and mental health. NREM sleep serves a body-restoration function; tissue growth and repair occur during this type of sleep. Without NREM sleep, you would eventually collapse. After you have been deprived of sleep, NREM is usually made up first. Until the deficiency in NREM sleep is satisfied, you will find it difficult to carry out physical tasks. On the other hand, REM sleep serves a brain-restoration function. It helps to restore mental fitness. REM sleep helps in coping with day-to-day psychological stress. Experiments show that subjects exposed to stressful situations have a sharply increased need for REM sleep, during which time they seem to make peace with their traumatic experiences.[14]

There are two major keys to getting the rest you need:

- have a relaxing environment, including a good bed;
- understand the "chicken-and-egg" relationship between muscle tension and the reticular formation, a physiological network of nerves at the base of the brain.

The reticular formation serves as "switchperson" for the higher centers of the brain by letting in stimuli for conscious thought. Unless you relax your muscles, including the muscles of your tongue (usually busy forming words and ideas), the reticular formation will not switch off, and you will not obtain your needed rest. The "chicken-and-egg" relationship is that muscle relaxation leads to a turned-off reticular formation, which leads to muscle relaxation, which leads to rest and renewal.[15]

One relaxation technique widely used to cope with stress is meditation. Practiced during a 10-to-20-minute period once each day, or in shorter, 3-to-5-minute breaks, meditation is an excellent way to decrease muscle tension, reduce emotional strain, and provide physical rest.

Essentially, there are two types of meditation: "opening up" and "shutting down." Neither type is inherently better than the other as a relaxation technique.[16] "Opening up" concentrates on the five senses of the body: sight, sound, touch, taste, and smell. Through various opening-up exercises, one becomes more conscious of the world, resulting in physical and mental renewal. This type of meditation can be practiced while walking on the beach or lying in the sand.[17]

"Shutting down" is a different type of meditation. Instead of increasing broad sensory awareness, thoughts are blocked by concentrating on one thing. Common shutting-down exercises include:

- deep, regular breathing;
- focusing on one point, such as a flame, the navel, or a star;

- making sounds, such as religious chants;

- mentally repeating the secret, special words used in transcendental meditation (TM) or the Eastern "Ommm";

- visual concentration on one scene or person;

- movement, such as Sufi dancing (whirling dervishes) and fingering worry beads or the rosary;

- devotions, such as parables and prayers.[18]

Other relaxation techniques include scientific relaxation, the relaxation response, and hypnosis. Each of these can be effective methods to prevent and cure headaches, a common symptom of stress. Headaches can be divided into two basic types. One type is caused by contractions of blood vessels in the scalp. This is called a vascular, or migraine, headache. The other is caused by sustained muscle tension in the forehead, neck, or scalp. This is called a tension headache. Both types of disorder can be helped by using relaxation techniques.

The following are ten rules for improving the quality of your sleep and, therefore, becoming better prepared to deal with stress:

- Sleep only as much as you need to feel refreshed and healthy the next day. Oversleeping often results in fragmented and shallow rest.

- Wake up each morning at a consistent time. A standard wake-up time seems to lead to ease in falling asleep.

- Practice regular physical exercise. Regular physical activity improves sleep over a period of time; however, periodic, one-time exercise sessions do not directly influence sleep the following night.

- A quiet environment is advisable. Loud noise reduces the quality of sleep, even when you cannot remember it the next morning or do not wake up during the night.

- A moderate temperature is recommended for ideal sleep. Both excessive heat and excessive cold disturb sleep.

- A light snack such as warm milk seems to help many people. Hunger may reduce the quality of sleep.

- Avoid sleep medication. Although a sleeping pill may be helpful in some cases, the chronic use of such sleep aids is ineffective and may even be harmful.

- Reduce caffeine intake. Caffeine before sleep disturbs rest, even in people who do not seem to be affected.

- Avoid alcohol consumption. Although alcohol may help a tense person to fall asleep quickly, it results in fragmented, poor-quality sleep.

- Do not try to force sleep. If you are having difficulty falling asleep and are feeling angry, frustrated, and tense, it often helps to do something else, such as read or talk until you are relaxed.[19]

Through opening-up exercises, one becomes more conscious of the world.

To demonstrate the importance of sleep, ask yourself, Did I get enough sleep last night? If you did not, you are probably having to work much harder to read and learn than if you had. The answer: have the equivalent of seven restful nights of sleep every week. Let this be a standard part of your readiness plan to deal with the inevitable stresses of life.

= 21: Nutrition

Have the equivalent of 21 nutritious meals per week. You should get your body weight and composition to a point that pleases you and keep it there. The meals you eat should be spread out, balanced, and proportional to your body size and activity level. On the average, men need approximately 2,700 calories per day (900 per meal) and women need about 2,100 calories per day (700 per meal). A balanced diet can be achieved by following a simple rule of thumb: eat a wide variety of foods in moderation from each of the four basic food groups—fruits and vegetables, cereals and breads, dairy foods, and meat.[20]

The saying "you are what you eat" is true. Have you ever seen an ill-fed horse? Contrast this with a horse fed a proper diet. The second looks like Man o' War, and the first looks like Mr. Ed. People are no different from horses in this regard. Nutrition affects skin, teeth, and bones. You must be sure that your diet includes vitamins, minerals, carbohydrates, fats, protein, and water and that it represents a balance of the four food groups.

Figure 3.3 presents nutrients for health in a clear, easy-to-understand chart. It identifies key nutrients and explains their major physiological functions.

Fruits and vegetables are good sources of vitamin A, vitamin C, and fiber, and these help prevent some diseases, heal wounds, improve night vision, and control weight. Enriched cereals and breads, especially whole-grain products, are important sources of carbohydrates, thiamin (B_1), iron,

FIGURE 3.3

Nutrients for Health

Nutrients are chemical substances obtained from foods during digestion. They are needed to build and maintain body cells, regulate body processes, and supply energy.

About 50 nutrients, including water, are needed daily for optimum health. If one obtains the proper amount of the 10 "leader" nutrients in the daily diet, the other 40 or so nutrients will likely be consumed in amounts sufficient to meet body needs.

One's diet should include a variety of foods because no *single* food supplies all the 50 nutrients, and because many nutrients work together.

When a nutrient is added or a nutritional claim is made, nutrition labeling regulations require listing the 10 leader nutrients on food packages. These nutrients appear in the chart below with food sources and some major physiological functions.

Nutrient Leader	Important Sources of Nutrient	Some Major Physiological Functions		
		Provide Energy	Build and Maintain Body Cells	Regulate Body Processes
Protein	Meat, poultry, fish; dried beans and peas; egg; cheese; milk	Supplies 4 calories per gram	Constitutes part of the structure of every cell, such as muscle, blood, and bone; supports growth and maintains healthy body cells	Constitutes part of enzymes, some hormones and body fluids, and antibodies that increase resistance to infection
Carbohydrate	Cereal; potatoes; dried beans; corn; bread; sugar	Supplies 4 calories per gram Major source of energy for central nervous system.	Supplies energy so protein can be used for growth and maintenance of body cells	Unrefined products supply fiber—complex carbohydrates in fruits, vegetables, and whole grains—for regular elimination. Assists in fat utilization
Fat	Shortening, oil; butter, margarine; salad dressing; sausages	Supplies 9 calories per gram	Constitutes part of the structure of every cell. Supplies essential fatty acids	Provides and carries fat-soluble vitamins (A,D,E, and K)
Vitamin A (retinol)	Liver; carrots; sweet potatoes; greens; butter, margarine		Assists formation and maintenance of skin and mucous membranes that line body cavities and tracts, such as nasal passages and intestinal tract, thus increasing resistance to infection	Functions in visual processes and forms visual purple, thus promoting healthy eye tissues and eye adaptation in dim light

Nutrient	Important Sources			
Vitamin C (ascorbic acid)	Broccoli; orange; grapefruit; papaya; mango; strawberries		Forms cementing substances, such as collagen, that hold body cells together, thus strengthening blood vessels, hastening healing of wounds and bones, and increasing resistance to infection	Aids utilization of iron
Thiamin (B₁)	Lean pork; nuts; fortified cereal products	Aids in utilization of energy		Functions as part of a coenzyme to promote the utilization of carbohydrate. Promotes normal appetite. Contributes to normal functioning of nervous system.
Riboflavin (B₂)	Liver; milk; yogurt; cottage cheese	Aids in utilization of energy		Functions as part of a coenzyme in the production of energy within body cells. Promotes healthy skin, eyes, and clear vision
Niacin	Liver; meat, poultry, fish; peanuts; fortified cereal products	Aids in utilization of energy		Functions as part of a coenzyme in fat synthesis, tissue respiration, and utilization of carbohydrate. Promotes healthy skin, nerves, and digestive tract. Aids digestion and fosters normal appetite
Calcium	Milk, yogurt; cheese; sardines and salmon with bones; collard, kale, mustard, and turnip greens		Combines with other minerals within a protein framework to give structure and strength to bones and teeth	Assists in blood clotting. Functions in normal muscle contractions and relaxation, and normal nerve transmission.
Iron	Enriched farina; prune juice; liver; dried beans and peas; red meat	Aids in utilization of energy	Combines with protein to form hemoglobin, the red substance in blood that carries oxygen to and carbon dioxide from the cells. Prevents nutritional anemia and its accompanying fatigue. Increases resistance to infection	Functions as part of enzymes involved in tissue respiration

Source: Guide to Good Eating, *courtesy National Dairy Council. Reprinted with permission.*

niacin, and fiber. These foods provide energy and promote a healthy nervous system. Dairy foods, especially milk, are excellent sources of calcium, riboflavin (B_2), and protein. Milk provides for strong bones and teeth and healthy skin, and helps vision. Items in the meat group, which includes beef, pork, fish, poultry, nuts, eggs, and beans, are important sources of protein, niacin, iron, and thiamin. These foods are good for muscles, bones, blood cells, skin, and nerves.[21]

Recommended daily servings from each food group are as follows:

- fruits and vegetables—four for all ages;
- cereals and breads—four for all ages;
- dairy foods—three for children, four for teenagers, two for adults;
- meat—two for all ages.[22]

For more details as to what you should include in a good diet, refer to a high school or college health text book.

Figure 3.4 provides a helpful guide for evaluating the nutritional value of current popular fast foods in America.

Poor Nutrition Habits

It is interesting to note that, although most people acknowledge that good nutrition is important, their actions do not support their words. There are estimates that the United States pays a health bill of $30 billion per year for illness related to poor nutrition, and it is sad to note that "junk" foods account for more than 35 percent of the average family's food budget.[23] Currently, there are eight poor nutrition habits especially prevalent in America.

Caffeine Overload. Many people consume too much caffeine. It is present in much of what we eat and drink. Chocolate, colas, and tea contain the drug. In addition, caffeine is present in diet, cold, allergy, and headache medicines.

By far, the biggest culprit in caffeine consumption is coffee. Each year, Americans consume 2 1/2 billion pounds of coffee, and this accounts for 76 percent of our nearly 34-million-pound annual caffeine consumption.

On an individual level, the average American drinks three cups of coffee a day. This average is quite high when you consider that many people do not drink any at all. Someone is doing a lot of extra drinking; thus, someone is being overstimulated by caffeine.

Drinking too much coffee can be stressful. More than ten cups of coffee (1,000 milligrams of caffeine) in a day can cause toxic symptoms— mild delirium, seeing flashes of light, irregular heartbeat, muscle tension, and rapid trembling. When people "overdose" on caffeine and see lights and hear strange noises, they should know that this is not a religious experience. It may be a sign to cut back on caffeine intake.[24]

What is the solution? Consider cutting back the amount of caffeine consumed, perhaps by drinking decaffeinated beverages. You may feel discomfort for the first few days after cutting down. Caffeine is mildly addictive, so you may experience headaches and feel tired or unable to concentrate for a while. These feelings are not uncommon, and they will disappear. Remember: moderation, moderation, all things in moderation.

Too Much Sugar. Sugar and sweets offer little more than calories from a nutritional standpoint and, when you eat them in large quantities, they may take the place of foods that provide more vitamins, minerals, and protein.[25] Also, some people experience the self-inflicted symptoms of hypoglycemia by eating too much sugar.[26] They enjoy the taste of baked goods, ice creams, and candies, but they cannot afford that many calories in their diet. So they resort to going for long periods of time without eating anything at all, then consuming enormous amounts of sugar.

The solution is to cut back and space out the amount of sweets you consume. Although one piece of pie per day may be fine, a whole pie may be inappropriate.

Excess Salt. Although salt is necessary to sustain human life, too much salt can harm the system and cause undue stress.[27] Exactly how a person develops the habit of using too much salt varies, but the case of one sixty-year-old banker may offer a clue: During World War II, he was assigned to the South Pacific as a fighter pilot. The climate was hot, and he wore a heavy flight suit, so he took salt supplements. In addition, he was encouraged to put extra salt on the food he ate. Gradually, he acquired a taste for salt. After the war, his wife, wanting to please him, cooked heavily salted food, as did many spouses. To compound the problem, food companies, wanting to sell their products, began adding salt to canned goods and condiments to satisfy customers. Over time, many American families acquired a preference for a high quantity of salt in their daily diet.

In order to prevent the distress of health problems caused by consuming too much salt, cut back on the quantity you use. Instead, try seasoning with pepper or lemon juice. At least drop back to one or two shakes of the salt shaker instead of six, seven, or eight.

Empty-Calorie Foods. Many people run the risk of vitamin deficiency from consuming empty-calorie foods and having irregular mealtimes. As a solution to this problem, nothing can surpass naturally wholesome meals. As a safeguard, however, you may want to consider a daily vitamin supplement. Ask your physician's advice regarding your need for a vitamin supplement. It should be noted that taking too many of some vitamins can result in serious health problems.[28] The principle of moderation applies here, too.

See Figure 3.5 for facts on vitamins, including recommended daily allowances (RDAs), significant sources, major physiological functions, deficiency symptoms, and overconsumption symptoms.

FIGURE 3.4

Fast Food and the Basic Four Food Groups

Food Group	Milk Group	Meat Group	Fruit-Vegetable Group	Grain Group	"Others" Category
Recommended daily number of servings	3 for children 4 for teenagers 2 for adults	2 for all ages	4 for all ages	4 for all ages	None
Most important nutrients	Calcium; riboflavin (B₂); protein	Protein; niacin; iron; thiamin (B₁)	Vitamin A; vitamin C	Carbohydrate; thiamin (B₁); iron; niacin	Carbohydrate; fat
	For strong bones and teeth, healthy skin, and good vision	For muscle, bone, and blood cells, and healthy skin and nerves	To resist infections, heal wounds, and for night vision	For energy, and a healthy nervous system	These foods, low in most nutrients, are usually high in calories

Fast Food Item	Number of Calories	Milk Group	Meat Group	Fruit-Vegetable Group	Grain Group	"Others" Category
MAIN DISHES McDonald's® Big Mac®	563	Cheese	Hamburger	Onion, lettuce	Bun	Pickles, special sauce
Burger King® Whopper®	670		Hamburger	Onions, lettuce, tomato	Bun	Catsup, pickles, mayonnaise
Taco Bell® beef taco	186	Cheese	Beef	Lettuce	Taco shell	
Taco Bell® bean burrito	343	Cheese	Refried beans	Onions	Flour Tortilla	Sauce
Wendy's® chili	229		Beans, beef	Tomato sauce		
Dairy Queen® chili dog	330		Hot dog, beans	Tomato sauce	Bun	
Long John Silver's® Fish/More®	894		Fish	French fries, coleslaw	Hush puppies	

Item	Calories					
Arby's® Ham'N Cheese®	380	Cheese	Ham	Lettuce, tomato	Bun	
Kentucky Fried Chicken® dinner	767		2 pieces chicken	Mashed potatoes, coleslaw	Roll	Gravy
McDonald's® Egg McMuffin®	327	Cheese	Egg, canadian bacon		English muffin	
Pizza Hut® pork and mushroom pizza	380	Cheese	Pork	Mushrooms, tomato sauce	Crust	
DESSERTS Dairy Queen® banana split	540	Ice cream	Nuts	Banana		Whipped cream, strawberry topping, pineapple topping, chocolate syrup
Dairy Queen® ice cream cone	150	Ice cream			Cone	
Other desserts	240–250					Pies, cookies, turnovers, danish pastry
SIDE DISHES (calories)				French fries (220); coleslaw (121); corn on the cob (169); mashed potatoes (64)	Roll (61); hush puppies (153)	Onion rings (270); gravy (23)
BEVERAGES (calories)		Whole milk (150); 2% milk (120); McDonald's® chocolate shake (383)		Orange juice (80)		McDonald's® soft drinks (144); coffee (2)

Source: Fast Food, courtesy National Dairy Council. Reprinted with permission.

FIGURE 3.5

Vitamin Facts

Vitamins	U.S. RDA for Adults and Children over Four	Some Significant Sources	Some Major Physiological Functions	Some Deficiency Symptoms	Some Overconsumption Symptoms
Fat-Soluble Vitamins					
Vitamin A (retinol, provitamin carotenoids)	5000 IU	*Retinol:* liver, butter, whole milk, cheese, egg yolk. *Provitamin A:* carrots, leafy green vegetables, sweet potatoes, pumpkin, winter squash, apricots, cantaloupe, fortified margarine	Assists formation and maintenance of skin and mucous membranes, thus increasing resistance to infections. Functions in visual processes and forms visual purple. Promotes bone and tooth development	**Mild:** night-blindness, diarrhea, intestinal infections, impaired growth **Severe:** xerophthalmia	**Mild:** Nausea, irritability, blurred vision **Severe:** growth retardation, enlargement of liver and spleen, loss of hair, rheumatic pain, increased pressure in skull, dermal changes
Vitamin D (calciferol)	400 IU	Vitamin D fortified dairy products; fortified margarine; fish oils; egg yolk. Synthesized by sunlight action on skin	Promotes ossification of bones and teeth, increases intestinal absorption of calcium	Rickets in children; osteomalacia in adults, rare	**Mild:** nausea, weight loss, irritability **Severe:** mental and physical growth retardation, kidney damage, mobilization of calcium from bony tissue and deposition in soft tissues.
Vitamin E (tocopherol)	30 IU	Vegetable oil, margarine, shortening; green and leafy vegetables; wheat germ, whole grain products; egg yolk; butter, liver	Functions as antioxidant protecting vitamins A and C and fatty acids from destruction; prevents cell-membrane damage	Almost impossible to produce without starvation; possible anemia in low-birth-weight infants	Nontoxic under normal conditions
Water-Soluble Vitamins					
Vitamin C (ascorbic acid)	60 mg	Broccoli, sweet and hot peppers, collards, brussels sprouts, strawberries, orange, kale, grapefruit, papaya, potato, mango, tangerine, spinach, tomato	Forms cementing substances, such as collagen, that hold body cells together, thus strengthening blood vessels, hastening healing of wounds and bones, and increasing resistance to infection. Aids in use of iron.	**Mild:** bruise easily, bleeding gums **Severe:** scurvy	When megadose is discontinued, deficiency symptoms may briefly appear until the body adapts Newborns whose mothers took megadoses will show deficiency symptoms after birth until the body adapts
Thiamin (vitamin B₁)	1.5 mg	Pork, liver, meat; whole grains, fortified grain products; legumes; nuts	Functions as part of a coenzyme to promote carbohydrate metabolism, production of ribose, a constituent of DNA and RNA. Promotes normal appetite and normal functioning of nervous system	Impaired growth, wasting of tissues, mental confusion, low morale, edema **Severe:** beriberi	None reported

Vitamin	Amount	Function	Important Sources	Deficiency Symptoms	Megadose Effects
Riboflavin (vitamin B₂)	1.7mg	Functions as part of a coenzyme assisting cells to use oxygen for the release of energy from food. Promotes good vision and healthy skin	Liver; milk, yogurt, cottage cheese; meat; fortified grain products	Lesions of cornea, cracks at corners of mouth	None reported
Niacin (nicotinamide, nicotinic acid)	20 mg	Functions as part of a coenzyme in fat synthesis, tissue respiration, and utilization of carbohydrate for energy. Promotes healthy skin, nerves, and digestive tract. Aids digestion and fosters normal appetite	Liver, meat, poultry, fish; peanuts; fortified grain products. Synthesized from tryptophan (on the average 1 mg of niacin from 60 mg of dietary tryptophan)	Skin and gastrointestinal lesions, anorexia, weakness, irritability, vertigo. **Severe:** pellagra	None reported for nicotinamide. Flushing, headache, cramps, nausea for nicotinic acid
Folacin (folic acid)	0.4 mg	Functions as part of coenzymes in amino acid and nucleoprotein metabolism. Promotes red blood cell formation	Liver; legumes; green leafy vegetables	Red tongue, diarrhea, anemia	May obscure the existence of pernicious anemia
Vitamin B₆ (pyridoxine, pyridoxal, pyridoxamine)	2.0 mg	Functions as part of a coenzyme involved in protein metabolism, assists in conversion of tryptophan to niacin, fatty acid metabolism, and red blood cell formation	Meat, poultry, fish, shellfish; green and leafy vegetables; whole grains, legumes	Irritability, muscle twitching, dermatitis near eyes, kidney stones, hypochromic anemia	Long-term megadoses of pyridoxine may affect the peripheral nervous system, resulting in loss of sensation and coordination in extremities
Vitamin B₁₂	6.0 mcg	Functions in coenzymes involved in nucleic acid synthesis and biological methylation. Assists in development of normal red blood cells and maintenance of nerve tissue	Meat, poultry, fish, shellfish; eggs; milk and milk products	**Severe:** pernicious anemia, neurological disorders	None reported
Biotin	0.3 mg	Functions as part of a coenzyme involved in fat synthesis, amino acid metabolism, and glycogen formation	Kidney, liver; milk; egg yolk; most fresh vegetables	Fatigue, depression, nausea, dermatitis, muscular pains	None reported
Pantothenic Acid	10 mg	Functions as part of a coenzyme involved in energy metabolism	Liver, kidney, meats; milk; egg yolk; whole grains; legumes	Rare because found in most foods. Fatigue, sleep disturbances, nausea	None reported

Source: Courtesy National Dairy Council. Reprinted with permission.

Cholesterol. Cut back on bacon, eggs, butter, and other high-fat dairy and meat products. These standard items of the American diet are our primary sources of saturated fat and cholesterol. They can raise the blood's cholesterol to excessive levels, and this promotes atherosclerosis, the most common form of heart disease.

Atherosclerosis involves the buildup of plaque along the inner walls of the arteries. Plaque is composed of fat, cholesterol, calcium, and cellular debris. Plaque deposits, compounded by a buildup of scar tissue in the arterial walls (fibrosis), eventually cause the vessel walls to become so hard and thick that blood moves with difficulty through the narrowed channels, and this can cause chest pain and a heart attack.

Although the exact process by which atherosclerosis occurs is not well understood, there is no doubt that without high levels of cholesterol in the blood, it just does not occur. In Japan, where the smoking habit is as common as it is in the United States, and where high blood-pressure levels are as frequent, there are only an eighth as many heart attacks. A striking difference between the two populations is their blood cholesterol levels. Studies of Japanese who migrated to Hawaii and California and adopted American eating habits showed that their cholesterol levels increased, as did their rates of heart attack.

In 1984 the National Heart, Lung and Blood Institute released a ten-year study on cholesterol showing that if you have a high blood cholesterol level, for every 1 percent you lower it, you lower your chance of having a heart attack by 2 percent. The average American has a blood cholesterol reading of 210 to 220 mg per deciliter. According to the National Institutes of Health, adults over the age of thirty should have serum cholesterol counts under 200. Again, reduce consumption of high-cholesterol foods and turn to grains, fruits, vegetables, and other natural low-fat sources of nutrition.[29]

Weight Problems. Body composition is a problem for many people. How many snacks can you afford without becoming overweight? The answer depends on your ideal body-fat percentage. There are norms to indicate ideal body-fat percentage based on sex. You should have your body-fat percentage measured periodically. If this is not possible, Figure 3.6 will help you to determine your ideal weight. It also shows how many calories you can afford based on your activity level.

Poor Eating Style. In addition to the type and amount of food you eat, your eating style can affect your physical and psychological health and thus your ability to cope with stress. The following eating habits are recommended for enjoying food and controlling weight:[30]

- eat in the company of others;
- eat slowly, never on the run (such as while driving);
- choose foods that must be eaten slowly;
- take smaller portions;

FIGURE 3.6

What Should You Weigh?

Many people try to determine how much they should weigh by reading height-weight tables, but since these tables often indicate average weights rather than optimum weights, the figures tend to be too high. There is, however, a formula for estimating your healthiest weight.

Adult women of average build can compute their ideal weight by multiplying their height in inches by 3.5 and then subtracting 110 from the product. Thus, a woman who is five feet tall should weigh about 100 pounds (60 × 3.5 – 110 = 100). For men of average build, the formula is height in inches times four, minus 130. A six-foot man should weigh about 158.

It is reasonable to make allowances for bone structure and muscularity; even if Woody Allen and Rosie Grier were the same height, they should not weigh the same amount. But be careful that in making these allowances, you don't mistake fat for muscle. And remember that if you are 130 pounds overweight, it is unlikely that the difference is all in your bones.

Are You Overeating or Undereating?

You can use the following system for determining your calorie allowance.

Begin by rating yourself on the scale below:

13	very inactive
14	slightly inactive
15	moderately active
16	relatively active
17	frequently, strenuously active

If you are an office worker or homemaker and you rarely exercise, you should rate yourself a 13. If your physical exercise consists of occasional games of golf or an afternoon walk, you are a 14. A score of 15 means that you exercise in moderation—jogging, calisthenics, tennis. A 16 means that you are almost always on the go, seldom sitting down or standing still for long. Do not give yourself a 17 unless you engage in heavy labor and other strenuous exercise frequently. Most adult Americans rate themselves 13 or 14.

To calculate the number of calories you need to maintain your ideal weight, multiply your activity rating by your ideal weight. A 200-pound office worker, for example, needs 2,600 calories a day, while a 200-pound athlete needs 3,400 calories.

FIGURE 3.6—*continued*

To estimate how many calories you are getting now, multiply your current weight times your activity level. For example, if your weight is constant at 140 pounds and you are inactive, you are consuming about 1,820 calories a day (13 times 140).

Subtract the number of calories you need for your ideal weight from the number of calories you are consuming, and you will know the size of your energy imbalance.

Source: Reprinted with permission from Psychology Today *magazine. Copyright © 1976 American Psychological Association.*

- wait five minutes before taking seconds;
- choose foods you enjoy;
- don't use food as your only reward or pleasure;
- don't save the best for last; begin with your favorites;
- do not clean your plate as a matter of duty;
- eat only when you are hungry;
- store food out of sight;
- eat poached, broiled, or baked, instead of fried, foods;
- eat several times each day, not just once.

"Fast foods" represent the eating style of many Americans. However, such foods can be low in calcium, low in vitamins A and C, and high in calories. Figures 3.7, 3.8, and 3.9 look at three typical fast-food meals. The pros and cons of each meal are presented, and suggestions are made for improving the nutritional value of each.

Inappropriate Dieting. Many people misuse dieting. They fall into a harmful pattern of excessive weight gain and loss. Also, people go on diets that are harmful to their health. For an evaluation of widely publicized diets, including special claims and allowable foods, see Figure 3.10.

Good eating habits are important for effective stress management. You simply cannot exist on coffee, sugar, and irregular, low-nutrition meals without experiencing harmful effects. As you consider your own nutrition habits, do you see a need to improve? If the answer is yes, begin today to eat a variety of foods in proportion to your size and activity level and avoid caffeine overload, high cholesterol intake, too much sugar, excess salt, and empty-calorie foods.

In summary, it is unlikely that you, as an individual, can significantly reduce the stress caused by modern society. Also, you may not be able to reduce the stress you may be experiencing related to your job, finances, marriage, or family right this minute. However, what you can do is develop as many defenses as possible to combat the negative effects of pressure, conflict, and frustration in your life and work. Thinking positive and healthful thoughts is one way. Getting regular physical exercise is another way. Getting enough sleep is another. Following good nutrition habits is a fourth way to give you the edge against the wear and tear of inevitable stress. Weekly, you should follow the $1 \times 3 \times 7 = 21$ plan.

FIGURE 3.7

Fast-Food Meal #1

HAMBURGER, FRIES, AND SOFT DRINK (626 CALORIES)

Milk Group	Meat Group	Fruit-Vegetable Group	Grain Group	"Others" Category
	Hamburger patty (124)	French fries (220)	Bun (119)	Soft drink (144); catsup (8); mustard (11)

Note: numbers in parentheses indicate calories.

Pros: This meal contains foods from three of the four food groups. It has a moderate number of calories.

Cons: This meal does not contain any foods from the milk group. Milk provides the body with 50 or so nutrients needed for good health.

Most important, milk and other foods from the milk group are the major source of calcium in the diet. Calcium is important for developing healthy bones and teeth in children and teenagers. Adults also need calcium to keep muscles functioning and to help prevent the bone disease osteoporosis.

Add a serving from the milk group to this meal by:

- choosing milk instead of the soft drink;
- choosing a milk shake, if the shake is made with real milk and if you can afford the calories;
- choosing a cheeseburger instead of a regular hamburger, if the cheeseburger has real cheese.

Source: Fast Food, *courtesy National Dairy Council. Reprinted with permission.*

FIGURE 3.8

Fast-Food Meal #2

FISH SANDWICH AND
MILK (582 CALORIES)

Milk Group	Meat Group	Fruit-Vegetable Group	Grain Group	"Others" Category
Milk (150)	Fish (200)		Bun (119)	Tartar sauce (113)

Pros: This meal contains foods from three of the four food groups. It also has a moderate number of calories.

Cons: This meal does not contain any foods from the fruit-vegetable group. Fruits and vegetables are the major sources of vitamins A and C. Vitamin A helps form and maintain healthy skin and contributes to eye health. Vitamin C helps hold body cells together, strengthen blood vessels, and heal wounds.

Add a serving from the fruit-vegetable group to this meal by:

- choosing a fruit or vegetable from the menu;
- choosing the salad bar, if available;
- choosing french fries, if you can afford the calories.

Source: Fast Food, *courtesy National Dairy Council. Reprinted with permission.*

FIGURE 3.9

Fast-Food Meal #3

FRIED CHICKEN, MASHED POTATOES, CORN, COLESLAW, ROLL, APPLE TURNOVER, AND MILK (1431 CALORIES)

Milk Group	Meat Group	Fruit-Vegetable Group	Grain Group	"Others" Category
Milk (150)	Chicken leg and thigh (498)	Mashed potatoes (64); coleslaw (121); corn (169)	Roll (61)	Gravy (23); apple turnover (345)

Pros: This meal contains foods from all four food groups.

Cons: This meal is very high in calories. Many fast foods are fried on a grill or deep-fat fried. The fat used in frying soaks into the food and increases the calorie count.

Sauces, dressings, and gravies from the "others" category also add calories to fast-food meals. And they add few nutrients to the meal.

A steady diet of high-calorie fast foods (or high-calorie regular foods) can lead to weight gain, especially for physically inactive people.

Reduce the number of calories in this meal by:

- not choosing the gravy and apple turnover;

- choosing only one or two, instead of three, servings from the fruit-vegetable group.

Source: Fast Food, *courtesy National Dairy Council. Reprinted with permission.*

FIGURE 3.10

An Evaluation of Popular Diets

Diet	Special Claims	Allowable Foods	Evaluation
Gimmick Diets Pritikin Program	Low fat and exercise combine to produce weight loss	Whole grains, vegetables, legumes, fruit; snack on raw vegetables all day and 1 portion from dairy, grain, and fruit groups	High fiber content causes gas and diarrhea; protein is insufficient; difficult to follow; contains one-quarter normal fat intake; fairly well rounded; devoid of cholesterol, salt, and artificial sweeteners
Save Your Life Diet	Fiber in foods leads to weight loss, which increases by rapid transport of food through the digestive tract	Vegetable group emphasized, and 1 cup of bran added to six foods; meats and eggs deemphasized	Side effects may include flatulence; frequent defecation; and soft, bulky stools. Too much fiber binds to some trace minerals and may cause them to pass through the system without being absorbed
Nibbling Diet	Eating smaller portions will result in fewer calories than eating three meals per day and snacking	Low carbohydrate, high protein, and nutritious snacking	With careful calorie counting, weight loss is likely to occur, but difficult to get a balanced diet, and not easy to follow for long periods of time
Cellulite Diet	Promises removal of the "fat gone wrong" (so-called fat, water, and toxic wastes)	High in fruits and vegetables, low fat and carbohydrate intake; involves kneading the skin, massage under heat lamps to melt the fat away	No medical condition known as cellulite exists. The fat being described as cellulite cannot be eliminated by a combination of diet and massage

Diet	Theory/Claim	Foods/Method	Evaluation
Cooper's Fabulous Fructose Diet	"Fructose" (sugar from fruit) is used to help lose weight, maintain constant blood-sugar level, keep up energy, and satisfy the sweet tooth	High protein intake and 1.0 to 1.5 oz fructose supplement	Weight loss may occur from caloric deficit, not from use of a fructose supplement. Fructose does not help you consume fewer calories and contains the same number of calories as sucrose (4 per gram)
Lecithin, Vinegar, Kelp, and B₆ Diet	Grapefruit and lecithin burn off fat by regulating metabolic rate	One teaspoon of vinegar with each meal of normal foods	No one claim (grapefruit or vinegar) can be supported
The Body Clock Diet	When you eat is nearly twice as important as the number of calories you consume	Any type of food can be consumed or any diet adapted to the body clock diet	There is no convincing evidence that eating the big meals early in the day will cause significant weight loss without very close calorie counting. The somewhat hidden implication that calories don't count is inaccurate
High-Protein Diets Women Doctor's Diet for Women New You Diet Doctor's Quick Weight Loss Diet Complete Scarsdale Medical Diet Miracle Diet for Fast Weight Loss	"Specific Dynamic Action" (SDA) is the basis for some high-protein diets: extra calories burned through the process of digesting protein	Lean meats and poultry, fish, seafood, eggs, and low-fat cheese, no calorie counting	SDA has no basis. Protein calories are no more or less important than carbohydrate calories. Diets are boring; hard to follow; lacking in vitamins, minerals, and fiber; and can increase blood serum cholesterol levels; dangerous for pregnant women and a poor choice for anyone who wants weight loss to be permanent after a change in eating habits. Ketosis can be dangerous to some people
High-Fat Diets Dr. Atkins Super Energy Diet Calories Don't Count Diet	In the absence of carbohydrates, stored fat is mobilized and burned for energy. Fat-mobilizing hormone (FMH) is said to be ac-	Unlimited fatty foods: bacon, meat, mayonnaise, rich cream sauces, etc. No calorie counting and avoidance of fruits,	Carbohydrates are needed to oxidize fat completely. If in short supply, fat cannot be used completely and fatigue occurs. Ketone bodies build up in the

FIGURE 3.10—*continued*

Diet	Special Claims	Allowable Foods	Evaluation
	tivated to fuel your body with the fat stores	vegetables, sugars, starches, bread, and potatoes	blood and are excreted in the urine. The existence of a fat-mobilizing hormone has never been substantiated. The diet neglects the four food groups, is dangerous for pregnant women, and is high in cholesterol. Most weight loss is water, which is temporary
Low Carbohydrate Diets Diet of a Desperate Housewife The Drinking Man's Diet No Breakfast Diet Dr. Yudkin's Lose Weight, Feel Great Diet The Brand New Carbo-hydrate Diet	Claims are similar to those for high-protein diets: a state of ketosis provides a condition conducive to fat loss	Protein in unlimited amounts with few or no carbohydrates permitted	Most weight loss is water, and temporary fatigue results from insufficient carbohydrate intake. Ketosis is potentially dangerous over prolonged periods of time. These diets fail to provide adequate foods from the basic four food groups and are difficult to follow
One-Food Diets Grapefruit, egg, poultry, melon, banana, steak, beer, fruit, juice, yogurt, rice, etc.	Dieters must concentrate on the food they choose, use a multiple vitamin, and drink plenty of fluid	Only the one food is permissible	Impossible to obtain the proper nourishment, even with a vitamin supplement; boring and nearly impossible to follow. Fails to change eating habits, short-term approach. Potentially very dangerous because it is impossible to obtain proper nutrition from the four food groups

Pill Diets			
Appetite suppressants: Anorexiants (amphetamines, Dexedrine, Digitalis)	Appetite is depressed; metabolism is increased	Medication is designed to restrict total caloric intake. Often used in conjunction with specific diets	Anorexiants curb appetite and increase metabolic rate. Nervousness, depression, and dependence (physical and mental) are some of the possible side effects
Metabolic medication: Thyroid hormone	Increases metabolic rate and energy output to burn more calories. Promotes breakup of lipids	Used in conjunction with numerous diets	No evidence is available to support the breakup of lipids. Additional calories are burned as metabolic rate increases. Thyroid hormone induces a stage of hyperthyroidism and is dangerous to people with heart disease. It also disrupts the entire endocrine system
Diuretics: Thiazides	Excess body fluid is lost	Used in conjunction with numerous diets. Additional potassium is needed to replace that lost through fluid	Does not increase caloric expenditure. Fluid loss is unrelated to fat and permanent weight loss. Can cause dehydration, nausea, weakness, and drowsiness
Cathartics (laxatives)	Speeds food through the intestine so nutrients are not absorbed	Used in conjunction with numerous diets	May result in bowel difficulty, dehydration, and poor nutrition. Not an effective method of weight loss
Nonprescription drugs: Sugar candy	Curbs appetite when taken prior to meal	Used in conjunction with numerous diets	Only mildly effective. Claims of advertisements are not met
Benzocaine and methylcellulose	Deadens taste buds to kill hunger and provides a feeling of fullness in stomach	Used in conjunction with numerous diets	The amount that can be legally sold is not enough to be effective
Starvation and Fasting Diets			
The Zip Diet, Lockjaw, Zen Macrobiotic Diet, Liquid Protein Diet	Diets eliminate practically everything but liquids. Jaws wired shut (lockjaw diet) to aid will power. With no	Liquids and some foods	Extremely dangerous; lacking in vitamins, minerals, roughage. Anemia is likely. The Liquid Protein Diet may have caused

FIGURE 3.10—*continued*

Diet	Special Claims	Allowable Foods	Evaluation
Starvation and Fasting Diets — continued	calories from chewable foods, weight loss will occur rapidly		over 60 deaths. Weight loss is dramatic at first, then slows considerably, even though you are consuming practically no calories. Quality of weight loss is poor. Too much loss of lean muscle mass, along with fat loss, keeps you flabby
Vegetarian Diets Vegetarian	Reduction in animal fats and cholesterol and less likelihood of excess body fat and heart disease	Only foods of plant origin, including seeds, grains, nuts, fruits, and vegetables	Studies in the United States indicate that vegetarians have heart attacks 10 years later in life than meat eaters. An excellent, healthy way to lose weight and keep it off
Lacto-vegetarian		Foods of plant origin, plus foods made of milk (yogurt, cheese, and cream)	The diet is safe, providing sufficient protein, iron, calcium, and vitamin B_{12} can be consumed (an iron and B_{12} supplement may be needed)
Lacto-ovo-vegetarian		All plant foods, plus dairy products and eggs	Have your physician confirm that you do not have a peptic ulcer or other inflammation of the digestive tract. On the negative side, the new habits of cooking, purchasing, and eating are not easy to follow at first

Source: George B. Dintiman and Jerrold S. Greenberg, Health Through Discovery, 2d ed. (Reading, Mass.: Addison-Wesley Publishing Co., Inc., 1980). Reprinted by permission from Random House, Inc.

TENDER LOVING CARE

In the foregoing discussion, you have:

- learned what stress is;
- learned the relationship between stress, disease, and aging;
- identified the causes and consequences of stress at work;
- discovered how stressful your world is, and what this means regarding your health;
- learned how "little hassles" are affecting you;
- discovered how susceptible you are to stress due to your personality type;
- studied fourteen coping behaviors to deal successfully with stress;
- learned the $1 \times 3 \times 7 = 21$ plan to enable you to deal with life's inevitable stress.

The following discussion concerns a concept that is essential for the management of stress and the attainment of the highest quality of life, both on the job and in the home. "Tender loving care" (TLC), must be developed for the good of mates, children, older people, and all working people. It is important for everyone to have a high-quality relationship with at least one or two people who are nonjudgmental and who demonstrate nonpossessive caring.

Mates

The importance of helping your mate should not be underestimated if he or she is to live a happy, healthy life. Many mates join each other at the end of pressure-filled, conflict-ridden, and frustrating days and give each other additional stress. What is missing is TLC, and what results is distress, with accompanying physical and emotional sickness. Even premature aging and death can result. The major causes of this problem are:

- Insensitivity to the other person's problems (his or her pressures, conflicts, and frustrations).

- A lack of awareness of the impact of your own behavior. Your moods and the things you say and do affect the other person.

ILLUS. 3.4

There is enough stress in the world; TLC is needed at home.

- The idea that your mate must be perfect, so that you are intolerant of his or her ups and downs in life and his or her personal idiosyncrasies. The following puts this in perspective:

> The best marriages, like the best lives, are both happy and unhappy. There is even a kind of necessary tension, a certain tautness between the partners that gives the marriage strength. Like the tautness of a full sail, you go forward on it.[31]

> *Anne Morrow Lindbergh*

- The misconception that you can or should control the life and feelings of your partner. The most satisfying relationships follow the principle of the open hand. Love needs freedom to fly away. If love is true, it will return. If you grasp love too tightly, it will surely die. The words of the Lebanese poet Kahlil Gibran make this point:

> *But let there be spaces in your togetherness,*
> *And let the winds of the heavens dance*
> *between you.*
> *Love one another, but make not a bond of*
> *love:*
> *Let it rather be a moving sea between the*
> *shores of your souls.*
> *Fill each other's cup but drink not from*
> *one cup.*
> *Give one another of your bread but eat*
> *not from the same loaf.*
> *Sing and dance together and be joyous,*
> *but let each one of you be alone,*
> *Even as the strings of a lute are alone*
> *though they quiver with the same music.*
> *Give your hearts, but not into each*
> *other's keeping.*
> *For only the hand of Life can contain*
> *your hearts.*
> *And stand together yet not too near*
> *together:*
> *For the pillars of the temple stand*
> *apart,*
> *And the oak tree and the cypress grow not*
> *in each other's shadow.*[32]

- Lack of physical contact. Remember the importance of regular doses of physical affection. Research shows what common sense has always known: mates need to be touched. As the humanist Leo Buscaglia states, "Hugging can lift depression, enabling the body's immune system to become tuned up. Hugging breathes fresh life into tired bodies and makes people feel younger and more vibrant. The husband who kisses his wife before leaving in the morning lives up to five years longer than the man who does not. He has fifty percent less illness and [even] fewer car accidents." Buscaglia concludes, "For goodness' sake, do it."[33]

Children

Children are the lifeline of a healthy society, and they must be nurtured with appropriate doses of discipline and affection if they are to deal successfully with the stresses of growing up. In the words of Socrates (400 B.C.), it has never been an easy task:

> Our youths love luxury. They have bad manners and contempt for authority; they show disrespect for their elders, and love to chatter in place of exercise. Children are now tyrants, not the servants of their households. They no longer rise when their elders enter the room. They contradict their parents, chatter before company, gobble up their food, and tyrannize their teachers.

The joy of children is irrefutable, as seen in the following:

In The End It's Worth It

"Don't wake up the baby.
Come gently, my dear."

ILLUS. 3.5

As a parent, will you help moderate the stress in your child's life?

"O, mother. I've torn my new dress;
Just look here."
"I'm sorry.
I only was climbing the wall."

"And Nelly, in spelling, went up to the head."
"O, say. Can I go on the hill with my sled?"

"I've got such a toothache."
"The teacher's unfair."
"Is dinner almost ready?
I'm just like a bear."

Be patient worn mother;
They're growing up fast;
These nursery whirlwinds, not long do they last;

A still, lonely house
Would be far worse than noise;
Rejoice and be glad
In your brave girls and boys.[34]

The quality of time spent with children is at least as important as the quantity of time, and both are important to children's health and happiness; both are signs of TLC. Figure 3.11 shows the actual amount of time spent by parents in America on total child care (in average minutes per day per person).

FIGURE 3.11

How Much TLC Do We Give Them?

Parents	Average Daily Time Spent on Total Child Care (in minutes)
Married, employed men— workday	12
Married, employed men— day off	27
Married, employed women— workday	50
Married, employed women— day off	38
Housewives—workday	100
Housewives—day off	78

Source: Reprinted by permission of Pamela Roby and the Association for Childhood Education International, 11141 Georgia Avenue, Suite 200, Wheaton, Md. Copyright © 1973 by the Association.

Regarding the quality of time spent with children, consider the following advice from the *Old Farmer's Almanac*, 1982 edition:

> Why should we not try to make our children enjoy their home? They will not, unless they are made happy there. Try to avoid all unnecessary fault-finding, and especially abstain from it at mealtimes. It tends to destroy the appetite, not only of the poor offender, but the rest of the family. Give a pleasant greeting to all in the morning, and at night, and when meeting at the table. Do not be stingy of kisses. It is better to put them at interest than to hoard them.[35]

Older People

In 1776, 2 percent of the American population was sixty-five or older; in 1900, 4 percent. Today, the elderly comprise more than 11 percent of the population and will represent 12 percent by the year 2000. Somewhere around 2030, when the peak of the postwar baby boom hits the age of sixty-five, one American in five will be elderly.[36]

Older people are faced with many types of stressors—physical, economic, and social. With advanced age, many experience failing health and reduced income that pose direct threats to survival and independence. Statistics show that one out of every four Americans over the age of sixty-five lives below the poverty level.[37]

Another stressor of older age is loneliness. Many older people miss the day-to-day contacts provided by employment. Many also lose touch with their children and relatives, who may live thousands of miles away. Finally, many older people face the prospect of living the rest of their lives alone as family and friends die before they do.

The older person needs the support and love of others in order to cope with the stressors of aging. The importance of TLC to the individual is obvious, and the fact that older people have much to offer society is shown in the following:

- Laura Ingalls Wilder is best known for her *Little House Books*, which inspired the television series "Little House on the Prairie." She was sixty-five years old when she published her first book.

- General Douglas MacArthur was in his sixties when he served as supreme commander of the American occupation in Japan.

- Winston Churchill served as prime minister of Great Britain during his sixties and seventies.

- Michelangelo, who created the sculptures *David*, *Moses*, and *The Pietà*, and who painted the Sistine Chapel, continued to produce his masterpieces years after he was seventy.

- Anna Mary "Grandma" Moses, best known for her realistic scenes of rural life, was seventy-six when she began painting.

- Benjamin Franklin helped write the Declaration of Independence when he was seventy and participated in drafting the United States Constitution when he was eighty-one.

- Sophocles wrote *Oedipus at Colonus*, one of the greatest Greek tragedies, when he was nearly ninety.[38]

The Roman philosopher Cicero (age sixty-two) explains why older people have so much to offer:

> It is not by muscle, speed, or physical dexterity that great things are achieved, but by reflection, force of character, and judgment; in these qualities, old age is usually not only not poorer, but is even richer.[39]

The writer Pearl Buck, age 79, concludes:

> Would I wish to be "young" again? No, for I have learned too much to wish to lose it. It would be like failing to pass a grade in school. I have reached an honorable position in life because I am old and no longer young. I am a far more valuable person today than I was 50 years ago, or 40 years ago, or 30, 20, or even 10. I have learned so much since I was 70! I believe that I can honestly say that I have learned more in the last 10 years than I have learned in any previous decade. This, I suppose, is because I have perfected my techniques, so that I no longer waste time in learning how to do what I have to do.[40]

Working People

The world of work must be warm and supportive if it is to truly serve people. Respect and trust of employees must be the norm. People who work in adverse organizational climates frequently experience the symptoms and penalties of undue stress. When the emergency ambulance arrives to carry away yet another victim, those remaining know the reason why: the primordial jungle, with all its danger, is present still. Now, the trees are desks and machines, and the predators are other people.

On the other hand, people who work in supportive organizations with a climate of TLC are truly fortunate. Good stress, as opposed to distress, prevails in such an environment, and the quality of work is high. In a world of free choice and worker mobility, the future belongs to TLC organizations because they attract and keep the best people and help them to do their best work.

In summary, ask yourself whether you are taking positive steps to create TLC in your world. What is the nature of your relations with children, older people, your mate, and your co-workers? Is TLC the norm for your behavior, both on the job and in the home? If not, begin now to create trust and respect in all your relations.

RECOMMENDED RESOURCES

The following reading, applications, and films are suggested for greater insight into the material in Part Three:

Reading	— The Relaxation Response
Applications	— Health Behavior Assessment Scale
	Scientific Relaxation
Films	— Alcoholism: A Model of Drug Dependency
	Smoking: Games Smokers Play
	The Psychology of Eating
	What Makes Millie Run?
	Meditation: Yoga, T'ai Chi and Other Spiritual Trips
	Journey to the Outer Limits

REFERENCE NOTES

1 Daniel A. Girdano and George S. Everly, Jr., *Controlling Stress and Tension*, 2d ed. (Englewood Cliffs, N. J.: Prentice-Hall, Inc., 1986), 37–42.

2 Based on the work of Basedow, 1925, as found in Dennis Coon, *Introduction to Psychology: Exploration and Application*, 2d ed. (St. Paul: West Publishing Co., 1980), 277–78.

3 Coon, *Introduction to Psychology*, 277–78.

4 Hans Selye, *The Stress of Life*, rev. ed. (New York: McGraw-Hill, Inc., 1976), 408

5 Gordon W. Lippitt, *Quest for Dialogue* (Washington, D.C.: Development Publications, 1966), Z1.

6 Will Forpe and John McCollister, *The Sunshine Book: Expressions of Love, Hope, and Inspiration* (New York: David Publishing, Inc., 1979), 95.

7 P. O. Astrand, *Health and Fitness* (Woodbury, N. Y.: Barron's Educational Series, Inc., 1977), 58; Charles T. Kuntzleman, *Your Active Way to Weight Control*, 1980, 12–19 (Box 8644, Clinton, Iowa).

8 Kuntzleman, *Your Active Way to Weight Control*, 12–19.

9 Michael E. Gray, *What About Your Body's Fitness* (Burlington, N. C.: Carolina Biological Supply Co., 1982), 10–11.

10 Adapted from Astrand, *Health and Fitness*, 17–30; *The Better Health Handbook* (Irvine, Calif.: Plus Products, 1979), 5–13; Kuntzleman, *Your Active Way to Weight Control*, 1–8; and Bud Getchell and Wayne Anderson, *Being Fit: A Personal Guide* (New York: John Wiley & Sons, Inc. 1982), 46–48.

11 Kenneth H. Cooper, *The New Aerobics* (New York: M. Evans and Co., Inc., 1970), 9–51.

12 Jerrold S. Greenberg and David Pargman, *Physical Fitness: A Wellness Approach* (Englewood Cliffs, N. J.: Prentice-Hall, Inc., 1986), 136–41; and the National Health Clearing House.

13 *Bethesda Hospitals: Stress Management*, (St. Louis, Mo.: Department of Health Promotion, St. Louis University Medical Center), 105.

14 Peter Farb, *Humankind* (Boston: Houghton Mifflin Company, 1978), 290–99.

15 Farb, *Humankind*, 290–99; adapted from Horace Winchell Magoun, *The Waking Brain*, 2d ed. (Springfield, Ill.: Charles C Thomas, Publisher, 1963).

16 I. David Welsch, Donald C. Medirous, and George A. Tate, *Beyond Burnout* (Englewood Cliffs, N. J.: Prentice-Hall, Inc., 1982), 260–67.

17 Welsch, Medirous, and Tate, *Beyond Burnout*, 260–67.

18 Welsch, Medirous, and Tate, *Beyond Burnout*, 260–67.

19 *Bethesda Hospitals: Stress Management*, 106.

20 Kuntzelman, *Your Active Way to Weight Control*, 4–5; *Building a Better Diet*, U.S. Department of Agriculture, Food and Nutrition Service, Program Aid no. 1241, September 1979.

21 *Building a Better Diet.*

22 *Building a Better Diet.*

23 *The Better Health Handbook*, 18.

24 Lowell Ponte, "All About Caffeine," *Reader's Digest*, 123 (January 1983); 72–76.

25 *Fast Food and the Four Basic Food Groups* (Rosemont, Ill.: National Dairy Council, 1984); Edward A. Charlesworth and Ronald G. Nathan, *Stress Management: A Comprehensive Guide to Wellness* (Houston: Biobehavioral Publishers and Distributors, Inc., 1982), 443–57.

26 *Fast Food and the Four Basic Food Groups*; Charlesworth and Nathan, *Stress Management*, 443–57.

27 *Fast Food and the Four Basic Food Groups*; Charlesworth and Nathan, *Stress Management*, 443–57.

28 *Fast Food and the Four Basic Food Groups*; Charlesworth and Nathan, *Stress Management*, 443–57.

29 "Cholesterol: Latest on How to Fight It," *U.S. News and World Report* 96 (January 23, 1984), 12.

30 Henry A. Jordan and Theodore Berland, *After the Diet — Then What: 50 Rules for Staying Slim*, 1980, 15–40 (Box 8717, Clinton, Iowa).

31 Anne Morrow Lindbergh, as quoted in Forpe and McCollister, *The Sunshine Book*, 231.

32 Kahlil Gibran, *The Prophet* (New York: Alfred A. Knopf, Inc., 1976); 16–17.

33 From "Together with Leo," a public lecture by Leo Buscaglia.

34 L.D. Nichols, as quoted in Forpe and McCollister, *The Sunshine Book*, 232.

35 Forpe and McCollister, *The Sunshine Book*, 227.

36 *Centerscope: A Report to Friends of the Washington Hospital Center* (Washington, D.C.: The Washington Center, Spring/Summer 1981), 6.

37 Robert N. Butler and Myrna I. Lewis, *Aging and Mental Health: Positive Psychosocial Approaches* (St. Louis, Mo.: The C. V. Mosby Company, 1973), 10.

38 *The World Book Encyclopedia*, 1981.

39 *Centerscope*, 3.

40 *Centerscope*, 3.

STUDY QUIZ

As a test of your understanding and the extent to which you have achieved the objectives in Part Three, complete the following questions. See Appendix F for the answer key.

1. Meditation, biofeedback, and progressive relaxation are:
   a. methods to develop an external locus of control
   b. methods to develop lower perceived self-efficacy
   c. defensive coping methods
   d. methods to lower excessive bodily arousal
   e. fads that have proven ineffective in fighting long-term stress.

2. In many people, transcendental meditation produces:
   a. hypermetabolism
   b. increased anxiety
   c. a relaxation response
   d. hypertension
   e. sleeping disorders

3. A process by which people can learn to voluntarily regulate many functions such as heart rate and blood pressure, which were previously thought to be beyond conscious control, is called:
   a. transactional analysis
   b. biofeedback
   c. narrated fantasy
   d. progressive thinking
   e. none of the above

4. Most headaches result from:
   a. muscle tension
   b. allergies
   c. drug abuse
   d. breathing polluted air
   e. food additives

5. Exercise can result in:
   a. improved sleep
   b. improved self-image
   c. clearer thinking
   d. longer life
   e. all of the above

6. A regular exercise program will:

   a. raise blood pressure
   b. decrease lung capacity
   c. decrease the size of arteries
   d. improve endurance

7. Fitness is made up of all but one of the following components:

   a. cardiovascular/respiratory health
   b. sweat gland activity
   c. body flexibility
   d. muscular function — strength and endurance

8. For the average American adult, exercise specialists recommend exercising:

   a. three to five times per week
   b. twenty to thirty minutes per session
   c. within your target heart rate
   d. all of the above

9. Aerobic exercise includes all of the following *except*:

   a. weight lifting
   b. bicycling
   c. running
   d. swimming

10. Overeating and overdrinking can:

    a. be a response to stress
    b. become additional sources of stress
    c. still result in malnutrition
    d. all of the above

11. To avoid consuming too much cholesterol, you should:

    a. turn to fruits, vegetables, cereals, and grains for sources of nutrition
    b. increase use of eggs and meat
    c. eat plenty of margarines, shortening, palm oil, and coconut oil
    d. increase your intake of butter and cream

12. To lose weight, you should:

    a. decrease caloric intake of foods and beverages
    b. increase your exercise program to expend more calories
    c. lose about one pound per week by changing eating and exercise habits
    d. all of the above

13. Which of the following poor nutrition habits have been found to be prevalent in America?

a. Too much caffeine
b. Too much cholesterol
c. Overabundance of salty foods
d. Too much sugar
e. All of the above

14. An important concept for managing stress and increasing your quality of life is:

a. BYU
b. REM
c. TLC
d. G.A.S.

15. To reduce stress levels between mates, children, and the elderly, the relationship requires:

a. awareness of one's own behavior
b. sensitivity to others
c. freedom rather than control
d. tender loving care
e. all of the above

16. The 1 × 3 × 7 = 21 plan for dealing with stress means:

a. relax once a day; eat 3 good meals a day; get 7 hours of sleep a night; and exercise 21 minutes every other day
b. use meta-imagery once a day; participate in at least 3 nonwork activities; and eat 7 nutritious meals out of 21
c. think positively once a day; exercise 3 times a week; get 7 good nights of sleep a week; and eat 21 nutritious meals a week
d. once a day, think about 3 good things that happened in the last 7 hours, and repeat that daily for 21 days

17. Stress between mates is usually intensified when one tries to control the other.

a. True
b. False

18. In order to cope with the stress of aging, what does the older person need?

a. Rest
b. Support
c. Love of others
d. All of the above
e. Both b and c

19. The $1 \times 3 \times 7 = 21$ plan includes:

a. meta-imagery
b. exercise
c. psychotherapy
d. both a and b

20. Physical fitness not only improves body strength, but also enhances _____.

a. emotional health
b. world peace
c. religious faith

DISCUSSION QUESTIONS AND ACTIVITIES

The following questions and activities help personalize the subject. They are appropriate for classroom exercises and homework assignments.

1. In evaluating yourself, which elements of the $1 \times 3 \times 7 = 21$ plan do you need to improve?

   a. Do you need to think more positive thoughts?

   _____

   _____

   _____

   b. Do you need to improve your physical fitness?

   Strength _____

   _____

   _____

   Flexibility _____

   _____

   _____

   Body composition _____

   _____

   _____

   Cardiovascular fitness _____

   _____

   _____

   Endurance _____

   _____

   _____

   c. Do you need better rest and sleep habits?

   _____

   _____

   _____

   d. Do you need to improve your diet and nutrition?

   _____

   _____

   _____

2. Discuss the statement "exercise in moderation adds years to your life and adds life to your years."

_____

_____

_____

3. In the area of TLC, how are you doing? Are there people you can turn to for support and caring? Do you provide these for others?

_____

_____

_____

4. Gather into groups to discuss individual experiences with the $1 \times 3 \times 7 = 21$ formula. Who needs to think more positively to increase syntoxins? Who needs to get in shape through a good exercise program? Who needs to improve in their sleep and rest habits? Who needs to improve in their diet and nutrition?

5. Discuss the concept of TLC. What can group members do to increase TLC with (a) children; (b) older family members; (c) best friends; and (d) associates in work and personal life?

———

PART FOUR

Work-Related Stress

Learning Objectives

After completing Part Four, you will better understand:

1. the causes and consequences of occupational stress;
2. the relationship between stress levels and job performance;
3. how occupational overload and underload can result in increased stress and health problems;
4. the relationship between occupational boredom, job satisfaction, and physical health;
5. the importance of feeling in control in order to manage stress;
6. the "job burnout phenomenon";
7. your current level of job stress;
8. how to predict your life expectancy;
9. how to develop a contract to better manage stress in your life and your work.

STRESS AT WORK

Most working people spend approximately one-third of their day on the job. Occupational pressure, conflict, and frustration are important causes of physical and emotional wear and tear, and consequently disease and aging, for many of these people.

The effects of stress at work are costly and are reflected in decreased productivity and low job satisfaction. Stress can contribute to absenteeism, mistakes, turnover, and increased health costs.[1] The Aspen Institute for the Management of Stress reports that premature death of employees costs American industry $25 billion per year.[2] Currently, American industry is spending $125 billion annually on total health care for employees, a figure that has been rising by 15 percent a year.[3]

Even minor stress-related illnesses can have a substantial impact on an organization. A study conducted by one insurance company showed that the annual cost of a single employee with anxiety headaches was almost $3,400. This included loss of productivity, visits to the company medical facility, and negative psychological effects on co-workers and subordinates. One employee under stress can cause stress in others.[4]

The following are common causes of stress in the work setting.[5] See prescriptions for management (Rx) following each:

- *Schedules and deadlines.* The volume of work a person is expected to do, including travel, meetings, reports, and record keeping, may be stressful. Whether the unreasonable work load is dictated by others or initiated by the individual, continually having too many things to do, and having to do many things almost simultaneously, can result in fatigue and excessive wear and tear.

    Rx: Managers should distribute work loads evenly among the work force. Overworking some employees and underutilizing others results in high stress, low morale, and decreased productivity for all employees.

- *Fear of failure.* A major cause of stress at work is fear of failure. Such worries as, "I won't be able to do what is expected," "I might let others down," "I will probably look foolish," and "I am in over my head" wear employees down emotionally and physically.

    Rx: Managers should avoid assigning work that is beyond employees' capabilities. This can be done by matching the right person with the right job according to interest and ability levels and by being sure that employees are properly trained.

• *Inadequate support.* A common cause of stress at work is a lack of support to do the job. If there are insufficient funds, inadequate supplies, improper tools, or too little cooperation among co-workers, tension builds and energy is drained.

Rx: Managers should not make job assignments without providing the support necessary to accomplish them. Impossible assignments create stress, lower employee morale, and reduce overall productivity.

• *Problems with the boss.* The inadequacies of another person can be particularly stressful, especially if the other person has power over you. Great stress is created when an employee does not feel understood, appreciated, and supported by the supervisor. Also, if the boss is not competent in administrative or technical duties, the worker will usually experience extra stress as mistakes are made resulting in extra work. If a supervisor is incompetent and also provides inadequate support, the subordinate may really have trouble, since the inadequate supervisor may pass on the blame for personal failings when something goes wrong.

Rx: Supervisors should guard against being "stress carriers." A stress carrier doesn't feel pressure, conflict, and frustration personally; he or she passes them on to others. A good supervisor will spend the time and effort to understand subordinates, show appreciation for their work, and actively support them. A good boss will strive to be effective in technical and administrative duties so that unnecessary stress is not created for subordinates.

ILLUS. 4.1

Employee stress may be caused by feeling unappreciated or misunderstood.

- *Not knowing what is expected of you or where you stand.* Have you ever had a job in which you didn't know what your job was? Have you ever had a job in which you didn't know how well you were doing? Both of these conditions can cause anxiety and result in unnecessary stress. One university department chairman thought his job was first, to teach two courses each term; second, to advise students; and third, to develop new academic programs. After discussing his responsibilities with the dean, he learned he had the elements of the job correct, but in opposite order of priority. The chairman learned that his job was actually first, to create new academic programs; second, to advise students; and third, if he insisted, to teach a course every once in a while. The situation was stressful to both parties until they reached a common understanding about what was expected of the chairman.

  Rx: Managers should communicate job duties in order of priority. Also, managers should be sure that all employees know whether or not they are doing a good job. A good supervisor will point out in private ways to improve and give credit in public for a job well done.

Besides these common causes of stress, each job has unique pressures, conflicts, and frustrations. What are the special problems of your industry, profession, or trade?

STRESS LEVELS AND JOB PERFORMANCE — OCCUPATIONAL OVERLOAD AND UNDERLOAD

In 1908, Robert Yerkes and J. D. Dodson of Yale University showed that stress improves performance up to a maximum point, after which efficiency decreases.[6] As seen in Figure 4.1, stress is necessary for optimum job performance. If stress levels are either too low or too high, job performance is reduced.

Some occupational stress comes from overload — too much pressure, conflict, and frustration; some comes from underload — boredom, lack of meaning, and low job satisfaction. Both overload and underload are likely to result in high levels of stress, poor health, and, ultimately, poor job performance.

The following report on air traffic controllers shows the impact that occupational overloading can have on stress levels and health.

Tension in the Tower

Air traffic controllers at Chicago's O'Hare International Airport are responsible for more than 37 million passengers a year. About 666,560 takeoffs and landings occur — one every 20 seconds. Any letup from constant vigilance, a slight error in the instructions, or a switch missed can result in a fatal air crash. This intense stress is comparable to battle fatigue and has been labeled "collisionitis."

By the controllers' own estimates, there are two or three near-misses every day. These near-misses might be avoided if the controllers followed the FAA regulations that specify the minimum distance between landing aircraft: five miles apart for big jets and three miles apart for standard-sized planes. That is the theory. In practice, the controllers cannot "go by the book" because the volume of traffic is too great. The standards become the maximum, not the minimum. When peak traffic reached 220 takeoffs and landings in one hour, the controllers were commended by their supervisors; commended in part for violating the safety standards. Role confusion was then added to the stress of vigilance overload.

When the medical records of 4,000 flight controllers were compared to those of 8,000 second-class airmen, the results were startling. High blood pressure was four times as common and developed at an earlier age among the controllers. Twice as many controllers also suffered from peptic ulcers as did the airmen. These psychosomatic illnesses, as well

---

FIGURE 4.1

The Relationship Between Stress Levels and Job Performance

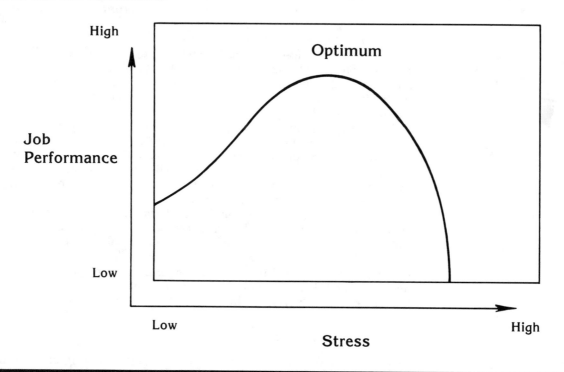

Source: Keith Davis, Human Behavior at Work *(New York: McGraw-Hill, Inc., 1981), 444. Reprinted with permission.*

as anxiety, insomnia, loss of appetite, irritability, and depression, were found to be greatest among controllers at the busiest airports. And O'Hare is the busiest one of all.[7]

Some occupations are by nature more stressful than others. Police officers, fire fighters, and bus drivers hold relatively high-stress jobs because of the amount of pressure, conflict, and frustration inherent in the work. The National Institute for Occupational Safety and Health reports that the highest stress jobs are those that place the worker in contact with the public in situations over which the worker has little personal control. Also, stress is compounded if the image of the job is negative in either the public's or the employee's eye.[8]

In contrast to overloading, some employees may be underloaded. They experience little intrinsic satisfaction and low challenge in their jobs. Their workdays are boring and dissatisfying. The following study shows the negative effect occupational underloading can have on stress levels and health.

Assembly-Line Hysteria

This strange malady affects women more than men and strikes suddenly, without warning. It spreads so quickly that an assembly line or an entire plant may have to shut down within days or even hours of the first appearance of the disorder.

Consider the experience of an electronics plant in Ohio. One morning a worker on the assembly line began to feel dizzy, light-headed, and nauseous. She complained of muscular weakness and difficulty in breathing. In a matter of minutes, some three dozen employees were being treated in the company's dispensary for the same symptoms. The illness spread. Shortly thereafter the plant had to be closed.

Investigators thought it was something in the air — some chemical, gas, virus, or other infectious agent. Physicians, toxicologists, and industrial hygienists conducted an intensive search and found nothing in the plant that could explain the disorder. The cause was assembly-line hysteria, a mass psychogenic illness that spreads by contagion and has no physical origin. It is not uncommon.

Typical symptoms of assembly-line hysteria are headaches, nausea, chills, blurred vision, muscular weakness, and difficulty in breathing. The condition seems to be related to physical and psychological stress on the job. Assembly-line hysteria is a psychological illness; there is nothing toxic in the air to produce the symptoms. Psychological stressors may be more important. Boredom seems to be the key. Monotonous, repetitive work can lead to muscle tension, job dissatisfaction, and depression.[9]

As you evaluate your own job, is yours a case of overload or underload, or are stress levels ideal for optimum job performance and personal satisfaction?

Many people do not work for wages, yet the stress in their lives can be fully as great as for those who do. The duties required in maintaining a home and raising children may result in either overload or underload, depending on the person and the situation. Those who choose to, or are forced to, hold down a job and raise a family at the same time can experience significant levels of stress with corresponding physical and emotional wear and tear. The amount of pressure they face can be intense; the amount of conflict they experience can be significant; and the amount of frustration they feel can be enormous.

OCCUPATIONAL BOREDOM, SATISFACTION, AND HEALTH

Hours worked and volume of work load often have less influence on job satisfaction than personal factors, such as having the opportunity to use one's skills and to participate in decision making. Also, as job satisfaction decreases, anxiety, depression, and psychosomatic illnesses increase. Thus, assembly-line workers report less satisfaction and experience greater stress-related disorders than do family physicians, who work an average of 55 hours per week, with many demands on their free time and great mental concentration required on the job. Figure 4.2 presents 15 occupations and their rankings according to level of satisfaction and level of boredom.

Two points should be noted:

• this study reports statistical averages and not individual cases;

ILLUS. 4.2

Job boredom is often a cause of stress.

FIGURE 4.2

Ranking of Occupational Satisfaction and Boredom

(Average Boredom: 100)

Level of Satisfaction (Highest to Lowest)	Occupation	Level of Boredom (Lowest to Highest)
1	Physician	48
2	Professor	49
3	Air traffic controller (large airport)	59
4	Police officer	63
5	Administrator	66
6	Scientist	66
7	White-collar supervisor	72
8	Electronics technician	87
9	Computer programmer	96
10	Engineer	100
11	Accountant	107
12	Monitor of continuous flow of goods	122
13	Assembler (working at own pace)	160
14	Forklift driver	170
15	Assembler (work paced by machine)	207

Source: R. D. Caplan et al., Job Demands and Worker Health: Main Effects and Occupational Differences *(Washington, D.C: National Institute for Occupational Safety and Health, 1975).*

- occupational satisfaction is a function of both the specific job assignment and the nature of the individual worker.

Thus, a person employed as an assembly worker, forklift operator, or accountant may find the job to be stimulating and satisfying and not harmful to health, while another person employed as a physician, professor, or administrator may be unchallenged and dissatisfied with the job and suffer stress-related health problems. This is called the "job rust-out" phenomenon.

THE EXECUTIVE MONKEY STUDIES

Whether yours is a high-stress field, such as law enforcement, or a low-stress profession, such as library science, and regardless of whether you are satisfied or bored with your job, if you feel the responsibility of office yet feel out of control, then the case of the "executive monkey" and related research will be of interest to you.

"Executive monkeys develop ulcers" was the conclusion of a study Joseph Brady did in 1958.[10] In this study, Brady placed pairs of monkeys in an environment where both received electric shocks. A red light signaled the shock period. However, the monkeys were not shocked if one of them operated a lever that prevented the flow of electric current.

ILLUS. 4.3

Which one is the executive?
The executive monkey is the one that must keep pressing the key to keep from getting shocked; the other monkey just gets shocked without knowing anything about the responsibility placed on the one with the key. The executive monkey will develop ulcers and die, while the other monkey, though receiving the same shocks, will remain healthy.

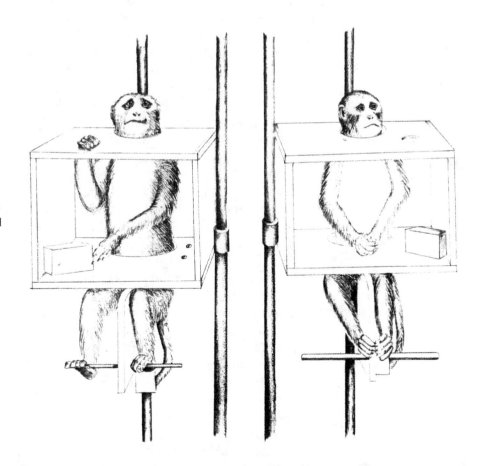

With each pair of monkeys, the "executive monkey" — the one having access to an operational lever (so named because of the analogy to human executive situations) — was able to learn the relationship between the light, the lever, and the shocks. The other, "nonexecutive" monkey had a nonoperational lever and therefore was unable to learn any way to prevent the flow of electric current. The only thing this monkey knew was that every once in a while there was a shock, but the monkey didn't know why.

In this study, the executive monkeys, who were responsible for saving their partners and themselves, developed ulcers and died, while the uninformed, nonexecutive monkeys remained healthy. The results of the study suggested that the burden of responsibility, including the need to maintain a high degree of vigilance and pressure to make decisions, was the cause of the high level of stress and the consequent ulcers resulting in death.

A follow-up study on rats conducted by Jay Weiss provided additional information as to the demise of the executive monkeys.[11] One primary difference between the Weiss study and the Brady study was that Weiss used a warning tone to signal the imminent onset of electric current. Weiss showed that the executive animals were much more able to cope with responsibility and avoid ulcers if they were given feedback on their behavior. He did this by arranging conditions so that the lever, when operated, would prevent shock and would also turn off the warning tone that preceded the shock. This provided clear evidence to the executive animal, in the form of tone cessation, that shock could be avoided, whereas Brady's executive monkeys received no such assurances.

Weiss's animals learned through feedback that they could control their situation, whereas Brady's monkeys undoubtedly felt less control. The conclusion was that pressure to perform without feeling in control results in ulcers and even death. Weiss found that the responsibility of office alone was not the cause of debilitating stress, but rather the feeling of frustration and being out of control.

In light of the executive animal studies, you may decide against assuming significant responsibilities in life (such as becoming a parent or supervisor, or having a business of your own). On the other hand, you may recognize the penalties in wear and tear that may accompany responsible positions but decide that the price is justified by the psychic, social, and economic rewards. In any case, the executive animal studies demonstrate the importance of a person being in control when he or she assumes responsbility.

Robert Karasek of Columbia University has found that people with little control over their jobs, such as assembly-line workers and cooks, have higher rates of heart disease than people who can choose the pace and method of their work. People who deal with the public but have little opportunity for independent decision making are those most negatively affected. The combination of high psychological demands and low personal control appears to raise the risk of heart disease by "about the same order of magnitude as smoking or having a high cholesterol level."[12]

If you are in a position to accept responsibility, be sure you have adequate power to control the events for which you will be held responsible. In addition, management should be sure to delegate to subordinates sufficient authority as well as responsibility to accomplish tasks. The following experiment demonstrates the importance of feeling in control — not only to manage stress, but to maximize job performance.

> Adult subjects were given complex puzzles to solve and a proofreading chore. In the background was a loud, randomly occurring distracting noise; to be specific, it was "a combination of two people speaking Spanish, one speaking Armenian, a mimeograph machine running, a desk calculator, a typewriter, and street noise — producing a composite, nondistinguishable roar. The subjects were split into two groups. Individuals in one set were just told to work at the task. Individuals in the other were provided with a button to push to turn off the noise, "a modern analog of control — the off switch." The group with the off switch solved five times the number of puzzles as their cohorts and made but a tiny fraction of the number of proofreading errors. Now for the kicker: " . . . none of the subjects in the off switch group ever used the switch. The mere knowledge that one can exert control made the difference."[13]

THE JOB BURNOUT PHENOMENON

Danger lurks in modern society, and the victim is often the dedicated and talented person. This danger is called "burnout," and it can occur both on the job and in the home. The dictionary definition of burnout is "to fail, wear out, or become exhausted due to excessive demands on one's strength, resources, and energy."

In the human sphere, burnout is what happens when a person experiences physical, psychological, and spiritual fatigue and is unable to cope. Lack of energy and low vitality are characteristics of physical fatigue. Symptoms of psychological fatigue include depression and loss of sharpness in thinking and feeling. Spiritual fatigue is characterized by lack of interest and meaning in life, often resulting in unhappiness and pessimism.[14]

Practically speaking, burnout can strike the businessperson with too many pressures and too little time, the homemaker with too much work and not enough appreciation, and the friend who is tired of being his or her "brother's keeper."[15] The following are common types of burnout victims. Do any sound familiar to you?

- "Superpeople," who want to do everything themselves because no one else can or will, and they have never let anyone down;

- "workaholics," who are driven to meet unreasonable demands placed on them (some self-incurred and some assigned by others);

- "burned-out Samaritans," who are always giving to others while receiving little help or appreciation in return;

- "mismatched people," who do their jobs well but who do not like what they are doing;
- "mid-career coasters," who may once have been high performers but whose enthusiasm is gone.[16]

Burnout is a great equalizer. It is blind to age, sex, color, and creed. It is a condition that can affect both white- and blue-collar workers as well as those who work at home. Job burnout is widespread in modern society. It is hazardous, and it can be contagious. If left unchecked, it can harm individual health, human relationships, and organization effectiveness.

In a recent study, the American Academy of Family Physicians reported the extent of job stress for five occupations. They surveyed 4,473 people working as business executives, teachers, secretaries, garment workers, and farmers, and found the number who usually or always work under stress to be high — 80 percent of the business executives, 66 percent of the teachers and secretaries, 44 percent of the garment workers, and 35 percent of the farmers.[17]

Participants in this study identified the major sources of stress to be work overload, pressure from superiors, deadlines, and low salaries. Probably the most important finding of this study was the relationship discovered between job stress and health. Individuals reporting high work stress had two to four times as many health problems, including allergies,

ILLUS 4.4

Job overload spells stress.

migraines, backaches, depression, insomnia, and other classic signs of burnout.[18]

Job burnout can be prevented and overcome. This requires self-understanding and the support of others. For a better understanding of the job burnout phenomenon, take the following test to evaluate your own status (homemakers should evaluate conditions at home).

UP IN SMOKE—ARE YOU BURNED OUT?

Directions

Rate each question on a scale of 1 to 5. (1 = never; 2 = rarely; 3 = sometimes; 4 = often; 5 = always.)

Do You:	Never	Rarely	Sometimes	Often	Always
Feel less competent or effective than you used to feel in your work?	1	2	3	4	5
Consider yourself unappreciated or "used"?	1	2	3	4	5
Dread going to work?	1	2	3	4	5
Feel overwhelmed in your work?	1	2	3	4	5
Feel your work is pointless or unimportant?	1	2	3	4	5
Watch the clock?					
Avoid conversations with others (co-workers, customers, and supervisors in the work setting; family members in the home)?	1	2	3	4	5
Rigidly apply rules without considering creative solutions?	1	2	3	4	5
Get frustrated by your work?	1	2	3	4	5
Miss work often?	1	2	3	4	5
Feel unchallenged by your work?	1	2	3	4	5
Does Your Work:					
Overload you?	1	2	3	4	5

Deny you rest periods— breaks, lunch time, sick leave, or vacation?	1	2	3	4	5
Pay too little?					
Depend on uncertain funding sources?	1	2	3	4	5
Provide inadequate support to accomplish the job (budget, equipment, tools, people, etc.)?	1	2	3	4	5
Lack clear guidelines?	1	2	3	4	5
Entail so many different tasks that you feel fragmented?	1	2	3	4	5
Require you to deal with major or rapid changes?	1	2	3	4	5
Lack access to a social or professional support group?	1	2	3	4	5
Demand coping with a negative job image or angry people?	1	2	3	4	5
Depress you?	1	2	3	4	5

Source: Reprinted with permission. Adapted from Carol Krucoff, "Careers: Confronting On-the-Job Burnout," The Washington Post, 5 August 1980, sec. B, p.5.

SCORING AND INTERPRETATION

Add up your scores for the Up in Smoke test and insert your total: _____

Scores	Category
94–110	Burnout
76–93	Flame
58–75	Smoke
40–57	Sparks
22–39	No fire

- *Burnout.* If your score is between 94 and 110, you are experiencing a very high level of stress in your work. Without some changes in yourself or your situation, your potential for stress-related illness is high. Consider seeking professional help for stress reduction and burnout prevention. Coping with stress at this level may also require help from others — supervisors, co-workers, and other associates at work, and spouse and other family members at home.

- *Flame.* If you have a score between 76 and 93, you have a high amount of work-related stress and may have begun to burn out. Mark each question that you scored 4 or above, and rank them in order of their effect on you, beginning with the ones that bother you the most. For at least your top three, evaluate what you can do to reduce the stresses involved, and act to improve your attitude or situation. If your body is reflecting the stress, get a medical checkup.

- *Smoke.* Scores between 58 and 75 represent a certain amount of stress in your work and are a sign that you have a fair chance of burning out unless you take corrective measures. For each question that you scored 4 or above, consider ways you can reduce the stresses involved. As soon as possible, take action to improve your attitude or the situation surrounding those things that trouble you must.

- *Sparks.* If your score is between 40 and 57, you have a low amount of work-related stress and are unlikely to burn out. Look over those questions that you scored 3 or above, and think about what you can do to reduce the stresses involved.

- *No fire.* People with scores of 22 through 39 are mellow in their work, with almost no job-related stress. As long as they continue at this level, they are practically burnout proof.

As mentioned in Part One, for many people, both the job and the home represent potential for high stress and burnout. For this reason, having at least one "port in a storm" is important. Ideally, if things are going badly on the job, rest and comfort can be found in the home. Similarly, if home conditions involve pressure, conflict, and frustration, having a satisfying work life helps. The person who faces problems on the job and problems in the home at the same time is fighting a war on two fronts and is a prime candidate for stress overload and burnout.

HOW LONG WILL YOU LIVE?

The following is a life expectancy quiz. It is similar to many health questionnaires now being used by doctors, medical centers, and insurance companies. It provides a more accurate picture of probable longevity than do old-fashioned actuarial tables that depend almost entirely on hereditary factors and medical history.

Current attempts to predict longevity measure risk in relation to personal data, environmental factors, and life-style behavior. Although such questionnaires are generally dependable for large groups of people, they lose precision for individual cases because of individual differences. A high salary may or may not be detrimental to a person's health. It is not how much money you earn; it is how you earn it that counts. Also, marriage or living with a mate is usually expected to increase life expectancy. However, partners may actually increase each other's stress levels if they fail to practice TLC. This is especially true for seriously embattled partners.

The Life Expectancy quiz, which follows, is included here to focus attention on the importance of effective stress management and burnout prevention. Remember that you can improve both the length and quality of your life by applying the principles and techniques discussed in this book.

LIFE EXPECTANCY QUIZ

Directions

Use a blank piece of paper. Start with the number 72 and follow these steps:

Personal Facts

If you are male, subtract 3.

If you are female, add 4.

If you live in an urban area with a population over 2 million, subtract 2.

If you live in a town with a population under 10,000 or on a farm, add 2.

If any grandparent lived to 85, add 2.

If all four grandparents lived to 80, add 6.

If either parent died of a stroke or heart attack before the age of 50, subtract 4.

If any parent, brother, or sister under 50 has (or had) cancer or a heart condition, or has had diabetes since childhood, subtract 3.

Do you earn over $50,000 a year? Subtract 2.

If you finished college, add 1. If you have a graduate or professional degree, add 2 more.

If you are 65 or over and still working, add 3.

If you live with a spouse, friend, or family, add 5. If not, subtract 1 for every ten years alone since age 25.

Life-Style Status

If you work behind a desk, subtract 3.

If your work requires regular, heavy physical labor, add 3.

If you exercise strenuously (tennis, running, swimming, etc.) three to five times a week for at least a half-hour, add 4. Two times a week, add 2.

Do you sleep more than ten hours each night? Subtract 4.

Are you intense, aggressive, easily angered? Subtract 3.

Are you easygoing and relaxed? Add 3.

Are you happy? Add 1. Unhappy? Subtract 2.

Have you had a speeding ticket in the past year? Subtract 1.

Do you smoke more than two packs of cigarettes a day? Subtract 8. One to two packs? Subtract 6. One-half to one? Subtract 3.

Do you drink the equivalent of a quart bottle of liquor a day? Subtract 1.

Are you overweight by 50 lbs. or more? Subtract 8. By 30 to 50 lbs.? Subtract 4. By 10 to 30 lbs.? Subtract 2.

If you are a man over 40 and have regular physical checkups, add 2.

If you are a woman and see a gynecologist once a year, add 2.

Age Adjustment

If you are between 30 and 40, add 2.

If you are between 40 and 50, add 3.

If you are between 50 and 70, add 4.

If you are over 70, add 5.

Source: Robert F. Allen with S. Linde, Lifegain: The Exciting New Program That Will Change Your Health — and Your Life *(Norwalk, Conn.: Appleton-Century-Crofts, 1981). Reprinted with permission.*

SCORING AND INTERPRETATION

Add up your total score on the Life Expectancy Quiz: _____.

Figure 4.3 shows how your score compares with national average life expectancies. Average life spans are 70.5 for white males, 65.3 for all other males; 78.1 for white females, 74 for all other females.[19]

FIGURE 4.3

Life Expectancy Averages

Age Now	Male	Female
0 – 10	69.8	77.2
11 – 19	70.3	77.5
20 – 29	71.2	77.8
30 – 39	71.3	77.9
40 – 49	73.5	79.4
50 – 59	76.1	79.0
60 – 69	80.2	83.6
70 – 79	85.9	87.7
80 – 89	90.0	91.1

THE STRESS MANAGEMENT CONTRACT

Directions

The following is a stress-management contract to be self written or developed with another person. It can be a useful tool to manage stress and extend your life. In the spaces provided, include the things you will do. Then, review this contract every week for at least one month to see how much progress you have made. You should make a new stress-management contract at least once every year.

Be a "B"

Coping behaviors (those behaviors necessary for you to be a "B") include:

Don't worry, take action. I will: _____

_____

_____

_____

Set priorities, following the 80/20 rule. I will: _____

_____

_____

Follow the principle "moderation, moderation, all things in moderation." I will: _____

_____

_____

Enjoy the little things in life. I will: _____

_____

_____

Go easy with criticism. I will: _____

_____

_____

Don't try to be Superwoman or Superman. I will: _____

_____

_____

Take a break. I will: _____

_____

_____

Trust in time. I will: _____

_____

_____

Talk with others. I will: _____

_____

_____

Avoid self-medication. I will: _____

_____

_____

Improve job proficiency. I will: _____

_____

_____

Use a decompression chamber technique. I will: _____

_____

_____

Keep a sense of humor. I will: _____

_____

_____

Accentuate the positive. I will: _____

_____

_____

$1 \times 3 \times 7 = 21$

A plan to help prepare for inevitable stress includes:

1: Meta-imagery. I will. _____

_____

_____

$\times$ 3: Exercise. I will: _____

_____

_____

$\times$ 7: Relaxation. I will: _____

_____

_____

= 21: Nutrition. I will: _____

_____

_____

TLC

To increase TLC, I will: _____

_____

_____

_____

_____

Signature: _____

Partner: _____

Date: _____

DISCUSSION

By taking steps to be a "B," by beginning now to follow the $1 \times 3 \times 7 = 21$ plan, and by increasing the TLC you give and receive in your dealings with others, you can prevent the burnout phenomenon—physical, psychological, and spiritual fatigue—both on the job and in the home. You can also experience a dramatic increase in the length and quality of your life. In a word, the principles and techniques of stress management will help you to succeed in your life and live to enjoy it.

RECOMMENDED RESOURCES

The following readings, case, and film are suggested for greater insight into the material in Part Four:

Readings — Death of a Salesman
The Voodoo Killer in Modern Society
Is This Trip Necessary? The Heavy Human Costs of Moving Executives Around

Case — Baton Rouge Is a Long Way from Home

Film — Transitions

REFERENCE NOTES

1 Claudia Wallis, Ruth Mehrtens Galvin, and Dick Thompson, "Stress: Can We Cope?", *Time* 121, no. 23 (June 6, 1983): 48–54.

2 Linda Standke, "The Advantages of Training People to Handle Stress," *Training/HDR* 16 (February 1979); 24.

3 Wallis, "Stress: Can We Cope?", 54.

4   James S. Manuso, "Executive Stress Management," *Personnel Administrator* 24 (November 1979): 23–26.

5   Manuso, "Executive Stress Management," 23–26; also based on the work of Robert Pearse, *What Managers Think About Their Managerial Careers* (New York: AMACOM, 1977), as it appeared in Warren H. Schmidt, "Basic Concepts of Organization Stress — Causes and Problems," in *Occupational Stress: Proceedings of the Conference on Occupational Stress*, Los Angeles, 3 November 1977 (Cincinnati: U.S. Department of Health, Education and Welfare: National Institute of Occupational Safety and Health, 1978), 5.

6   Wallis, "Stress: Can We Cope?", 54.

7   Adapted from L. Martindale, "Torment in the Tower," *Chicago* (April 1976): 96–101, as found in Philip G. Zimbardo, *Essentials of Psychology and Life*, 10th ed. (Glenview, Ill.: Scott, Foresman & Co., 1980), 366.

8   "Stress Producing Jobs" from the Editor's Notebook, *Nursing 82* 12, no. 1 (January 1982): 97.

9   Michael J. Colligan and William Stockton, "The Mystery of Assembly-Line Hysteria," *Psychology Today* 12 (June 1978): 93–99, 114, 116.

10 Joseph V. Brady, "Ulcers in Executive Monkeys," *Scientific American* 199, no. 4 (October 1958): 95–100.

11 Jay M. Weiss, "Psychological Factors in Stress and Disease," *Scientific American* 226 (June 1972): 104–113.

12 Wallis, "Stress: Can We Cope?", 52.

13 Thomas J. Peters and Robert H. Waterman, Jr., *In Search of Excellence* (New York: Harper & Row, Publishers, Inc., 1982), xxiii, xxiv.

14 Adapted from Patti Nickell, *Burnout: Could It Happen to You?* (East Jefferson, Massachusetts: East Jefferson General Hospital, 1983), 6–8, 24; Herbert J. Freudenberger, "Burn-Out: The Organizational Menace," *Training and Development* 31, no. 7 (July 1977): 26–27.

15 Nickell, *Burnout: Could It Happen to You?*, 6–8, 24; Freudenberger, "Burn-Out: The Organizational Menace," 26–27.

16 Nickell, *Burnout: Could It Happen to You?*, 6–8, 24; Freudenberger, "Burn-Out: The Organizational Menace," 26–27.

17 *Minneapolis Star*, 23 July 1979.

18 *Minneapolis Star*, 23 July 1979.

19 Robert F. Allen with S. Linde, *Lifegain: The Exciting New Program That Will Change Your Health — and Your Life* (Norwalk, Conn.: Appleton-Century-Crofts, 1981), 19–21.

STUDY QUIZ

As a test of your understanding and the extent to which you have achieved the objectives in Part Four, complete the following questions. See Appendix F for the answer key.

1. Job stress can come from either overload (too much pressure, conflict, frustration) or underload (boredom, lack of challenge, no meaning).

   a. True
   b. False

2. Job burnout is a phenomenon that is most likely to affect people who:

   a. do not perform well on the job
   b. want everyone else to do their work for them
   c. want to do all the work themselves
   d. have no drive to do any work at all

3. Types of victims of the job burnout phenomenon include:

   a. superperson
   b. mismatched worker
   c. burned-out Samaritan
   d. coaster
   e. workaholic
   f. all of the above

4. When an employee in the work setting is under stress, it can trigger stress in co-workers.

   a. True
   b. False

5. Job performance increases as a result of stress being:

   a. too high
   b. too low
   c. either too high or too low
   d. optimum

6. The "executive monkey" studies show that if you are:

   a. in a position of responsibility, be sure to control your subordinates
   b. in a responsible position, use your power to give orders
   c. not in a responsible position, use others to gain power
   d. in a position of responsibility, be sure to have adequate power to control events for which you are responsible

7. Causes of stress in the work setting include:

    a. schedules and deadlines
    b. fear of failure
    c. inadequate support
    d. not knowing what is expected of you or where you stand
    e. all of the above

8. Job burnout occurs when a person experiences physical, psychological, and spiritual fatigue and is not able to cope.

    a. True
    b. False

9. Who of the following was not a contributor to our knowledge of stress?

    a. Cannon   f. Holmes
    b. Selye   g. Lazarus
    c. Wolff   h. Friedman
    d. Jones   i. Cooper
    e. Meyer   j. Jacobson

10. Organizations that practice TLC attract and keep the best personnel.

    a. True
    b. False

11. When occupational boredom is low and job satisfaction is high, physical health tends to be:

    a. poor
    b. good
    c. unaffected

12. Key factors in predicting life expectancy include:

    a. personal data
    b. life-style status
    c. age adjustment
    d. all of the above

13. A stress-management contract can be a useful tool to manage stress and increase longevity.

    a. True
    b. False

DISCUSSION QUESTIONS AND ACTIVITIES

The following questions and activities help personalize the subject. They are appropriate for classroom exercises and homework assignments.

1. Have you witnessed or experienced the job burnout phenomenon?

   _____

   _____

   _____

2. What are the stressors you face in your work?

   _____

   _____

   _____

3. What coping skills do you use to prevent either burnout or rust-out?

   _____

   _____

   _____

4. As you evaluate your projected longevity, where do you lose points (years)? What can you do to increase the length and quality of your life?

   _____

   _____

   _____

5. In reviewing your stress-management contract, what improvements do you plan?

   _____

   _____

   _____

6. Discuss in small groups the sources of job stress for various group members—pressures? conflicts? frustrations?

7. Discuss the job burnout phenomenon. What tips and techniques can prevent job burnout? What can a company do? What can a manager do? What can an individual do?

8. Discuss the job rust-out phenomenon. What can companies, managers, and individuals do to avoid job rust-out?

———

READINGS

Anatomy of an Illness
as Perceived by the Patient

This . . . is about a serious illness that occurred in 1964. I was reluctant to write about it for many years because I was fearful of creating false hopes in others who were similarly afflicted. Moreover, I knew that a single case has small standing in the annals of medical research, having little more than "anecdotal" or "testimonial" value. However, references to the illness surfaced from time to time in the general and medical press. People wrote to ask whether it was true that I "laughed" my way out of a crippling disease that doctors believed to be irreversible. In view of those questions, I thought it useful to provide a fuller account than appeared in those early reports.

In August 1964, I flew home from a trip abroad with a slight fever. The malaise, which took the form of a general feeling of achiness, rapidly deepened. Within a week it became difficult to move my neck, arms, hands, fingers, and legs. My sedimentation rate was over 80. Of all the diagnostic tests, the "sed" rate is one of the most useful to the physician. The way it works is beautifully simple. The speed with which red blood cells settle in a test tube — measured in millimeters per hour — is generally proportionate to the severity of an inflammation or infection. A normal illness, such as grippe, might produce a sedimentation reading of, say, 30 or even 40. When the rate goes well beyond 60 or 70, however, the physician knows that he is dealing with more than a casual health problem. I was hospitalized when the sed rate hit 88. Within a week it was up to 115, generally considered to be a sign of a critical condition.

There were other tests, some of which seemed to me to be more an assertion of the clinical capability of the hospital than of concern for the well-being of the patient. I was astounded when four technicians from four different departments took four separate and substantial blood samples on the same day. That the hospital didn't take the trouble to coordinate the tests, using one blood specimen, seemed to me inexplicable and irresponsible. Taking four large slugs of blood the same day even from a healthy person is hardly to be recommended. When the technicians came the second day to fill their containers with blood for processing in separate laboratories, I turned them away and had a sign posted on my door saying that I would give just one specimen every three days and that I expected the different departments to draw from one vial for their individual needs.

I had a fast-growing conviction that a hospital is no place for a person who is seriously ill. The surprising lack of respect for basic sanitation; the rapidity with which staphylococci and other pathogenic organisms can run through an entire hospital; the extensive and sometimes promiscuous use of X-ray equipment; the seemingly indiscriminate administration of tranquilizers and powerful painkillers, sometimes more for the convenience of hospital staff in managing patients than for therapeutic needs; and the regularity with which hospital routine takes precedence over the rest requirements of the patient (slumber, when it comes for an ill person, is an uncommon blessing and is not to be wantonly interrupted) — all these and other practices seemed to me to be critical shortcomings of the modern hospital.

Perhaps the hospital's most serious failure was in the area of nutrition. It was not just that the meals were poorly balanced; what seemed inexcusable to me was the profusion of processed foods, some of which contained preservatives or harmful dyes. White bread, with its chemical softeners and bleached flour, was offered with every meal. Vegetables were often overcooked and thus deprived of much of their nutritional value. No wonder the 1969 White House Conference on Food, Nutrition, and Health made the melancholy observation that a great failure of medical schools is that they pay so little attention to the science of nutrition.

My doctor did not quarrel with my reservations about hospital procedures. I was fortunate to have as a physician a man who was able to put himself in the position of the patient. Dr. William Hitzig supported me in the measures I took to fend off the random sanguinary assaults of the hospital laboratory attendants.

We had been close friends for more than twenty years, and he knew of my own deep interest in medical matters. We had often discussed articles in the medical press, including the *New England Journal of Medicine (NEJM)*, and *Lancet*. He was candid with me about my case. He reviewed the reports of the various specialists he had called in as consultants. He said there was no agreement on a precise diagnosis. There was, however, a consensus that I was suffering from a serious collagen illness — a disease of the connective tissue. All arthritic and rheumatic diseases are in this category. Collagen is the fibrous substance that binds the cells together. In a sense, then, I was coming unstuck. I had considerable difficulty in moving my limbs and even in turning over in bed. Nodules appeared on my body, gravel-like substances under the skin, indicating the systemic nature of the disease. At the low point of my illness, my jaws were almost locked.

Dr. Hitzig called in experts from Dr. Howard Rusk's rehabilitation clinic in New York. They confirmed the general opinion, adding the more particularized diagnosis of ankylosing spondylitis, which would mean that the connective tissue in the spine was disintegrating.

I asked Dr. Hitzig about my chances for full recovery. He leveled with me, admitting that one of the specialists had told him I had one chance in five hundred. The specialist had also stated that he had not personally witnessed a recovery from this comprehensive condition.

All this gave me a great deal to think about. Up to that time, I had been more or less disposed to let the doctors worry about my condition. But now I felt a compulsion to get into the act. It seemed clear to me that if I was to be that one in five hundred I had better be something more than a passive observer.

I asked Dr. Hitzig about the possible origin of my condition. He said that it could have come from any one of a number of causes. It could have come, for example, from heavy-metal poisoning, or it could have been the aftereffect of a streptococcal infection.

I thought as hard as I could about the sequence of events immediately preceding the illness. I had gone to the Soviet Union in July 1964 as chairman of an American delegation to consider the problems of cultural exchange. The conference had been held in Leningrad, after which we went to Moscow for supplementary meetings. Our hotel was in a residential area. My room was on the second floor. Each night a procession of diesel trucks plied back and forth to a nearby housing project in the process of round-the-clock construction. It was summer, and our windows were wide open. I slept uneasily each night and felt somewhat nauseated on arising. On our last day in Moscow, at the airport, I caught the exhaust spew of a large jet at point-blank range as it swung around on the tarmac.

As I thought back on that Moscow experience, I wondered whether the exposure to the hydrocarbons from the diesel exhaust at the hotel and at the airport had anything to do with the underlying cause of the illness. If so, that might account for the speculations of the doctors concerning heavy-metal poisoning. The trouble with this theory, however, was that my wife, who had been with me on the trip, had no ill effects from the same exposure. How likely was it that only one of us would have reacted adversely?

It seemed to me, as I thought about it, that there were two possible explanations for the different reactions. One had to do with individual allergy. The second was that I could have been in a condition of adrenal exhaustion and less apt to tolerate a toxic experience than someone whose immunologic system was fully functional.

Was adrenal exhaustion a factor in my own illness?

Again, I thought carefully. The meetings in Leningrad and Moscow had not been casual. Paper work had kept me up late nights. I had ceremonial responsibilities. Our last evening in Moscow had been, at least for me, an exercise in almost total frustration. A reception had been arranged by the chairman of the Soviet delegation at his dacha, located thirty-five to forty miles outside the city. I had been asked if I could arrive an hour early so that I might tell the Soviet delegates something about the individual Americans who were coming to dinner. The Russians were eager to make the Americans feel at home, and they had thought such information would help them with the social amenities.

I was told that a car and driver from the government automobile pool in Moscow would pick me up at the hotel at 3:30 PM. This would allow ample time for me to drive to the dacha by 5:00, when all our Russian conference colleagues would be gathered for the social briefing. The rest of the American delegation would arrive at the dacha at 6:00 PM.

At 6:00, however, I found myself in open country on the wrong side of Moscow. There had been a misunderstanding in the transmission of directions to the driver, the result being that we were some eighty miles off course. We finally got our bearings and headed back to Moscow. Our chauffeur had been schooled in cautious driving; he was not disposed to make up lost time. I kept wishing for a driver with a compulsion to prove that auto racing, like baseball, originally came from the U.S.S.R.

We didn't arrive at the dacha until 9:00 PM. My host's wife looked desolate. The soup had been heated and reheated. The veal was dried out. I felt pretty wrung out myself. It was a long flight back to the States the next day. The plane was overcrowded. By the time we arrived in New York, cleared through the packed customs counters, and got rolling back to Connecticut, I could feel an uneasiness deep in my bones. A week later I was hospitalized.

As I thought back on my experience abroad, I knew that I was probably on the right track in my search for a cause of the illness. I found myself increasingly convinced, as I said a moment ago, that the reason I was hit hard by the diesel and jet pollutants, whereas my wife was not, was that I had had a case of adrenal exhaustion, lowering my resistance.

Assuming this hypothesis was true, I had to get my adrenal glands functioning properly again and to restore what Walter B. Cannon, in his famous book, *The Wisdom of the Body*, called homeostasis.

I knew that the full functioning of my endocrine system — in particular the adrenal glands — was essential for combating severe arthritis or, for that matter, any other illness. A study I had read in the medical press reported that pregnant women frequently have remissions of arthritic or other rheumatic symptoms. The reason is that the endocrine system is fully activated during pregnancy.

How was I to get my adrenal glands and my endocrine system, in general, working well again?

I remembered having read, ten years or so earlier, Hans Selye's classic book, *The Stress of Life*. With great clarity, Selye showed that adrenal exhaustion could be caused by emotional tension, such as frustration or suppressed rage. He detailed the negative effects of the negative emotions on body chemistry.

The inevitable question arose in my mind: what about the positive emotions? If negative emotions produce negative chemical changes in the body, wouldn't the positive emotions produce positive chemical changes? Is it possible that love, hope, faith, laughter, confidence, and the will to live have therapeutic value? Do chemical changes occur only on the downside?

Obviously, putting the positive emotions to work was nothing so simple as turning on a garden hose. But even a reasonable degree of control over my emotions might have a salutary physiologic effect. Just replacing anxiety with a fair degree of confidence might be helpful.

A plan began to form in my mind for systematic pursuit of the salutary emotions, and I knew that I would want to discuss it with my doctor. Two preconditions, however, seemed obvious for the experiment. The first concerned my medication. If that medication were toxic to any degree, it was doubtful whether the plan would work. The second precondition concerned the hospital. I knew I would have to find a place somewhat more conducive to a positive outlook on life.

Let's consider these preconditions separately.

First, the medication. The emphasis had been on pain-killing drugs — aspirin, phenylbutazone (butazolidine), codeine, colchicine, sleeping pills. The aspirin and phenylbutazone were antiinflammatory and thus were therapeutically justifiable. But I wasn't sure they weren't also toxic. It developed that I was hypersensitive to virtually all the medication I was receiving. The hospital had been giving me maximum dosages: twenty-six aspirin tablets and twelve phenylbutazone tablets a day. No wonder I had hives all over my body and felt as though my skin were being chewed up by millions of red ants.

It was unreasonable to expect positive chemical changes to take place so long as my body was being saturated with, and toxified by, pain-killing medications. I had one of my research assistants at the *Saturday Review* look up the pertinent references in the medical journals and found that drugs like phenylbutazone and even aspirin levy a heavy tax on the adrenal glands. I also learned that phenylbutazone is one of the most powerful drugs being manufactured. It can produce bloody stools, the result of its antagonism to fibrinogen. It can cause intolerable itching and sleeplessness. It can depress bone marrow.

Aspirin, of course, enjoys a more auspicious reputation, at least with the general public. The prevailing impression of aspirin is that it is not only the most harmless drug available but also one of the most effective. When I looked into research in the medical journals, however, I found that aspirin is quite powerful in its own right and warrants considerable care in its use. The fact that it can be bought in unlimited quantities without prescription or doctor's guidance seemed indefensible. Even in small amounts, it can cause internal bleeding. Articles in the medical press reported that the chemical composition of aspirin, like that of phenylbutazone, impairs the clotting function of platelets, disc-shaped substances in the blood.

It was a mind-boggling train of thought. Could it be, I asked myself, that aspirin, so universally accepted for so many years, was actually harmful in the treatment of collagen illness such as arthritis?

The history of medicine is replete with accounts of drugs and modes of treatment that were in use for many years before it was recognized that they did more harm than good. For centuries, for example, doctors believed that drawing blood from patients was essential for rapid recovery from virtually every illness. Then, midway through the nineteenth century, it was discovered that bleeding served only to weaken the patient. King Charles II's death is believed to have been caused in part by administered bleedings. George Washington's death was also hastened by the severe loss of blood resulting from this treatment.

Living in the second half of the twentieth century, I realized, confers no automatic protection against unwise or even dangerous drugs and methods. Each age has had to undergo its own special nostrums. Fortunately, the human body is a remarkably durable instrument and has been able to withstand all sorts of prescribed assaults over the centuries, from freezing to animal dung.

Suppose I stopped taking aspirin and phenylbutazone? What about the pain? The bones in my spine and practically every joint in my body felt as though I had been run over by a truck.

I knew that pain could be affected by attitudes. Most people become panicky about almost any pain. On all sides they have been so bombarded by advertisements about pain that they take this or that analgesic at the slightest sign of an ache. We are largely illiterate about pain and so are seldom able to deal with it rationally. Pain is part of the body's magic. It is the way the body transmits a sign to the brain that something is wrong. Leprous patients pray for the sensation of pain. What makes leprosy such a terrible disease is that the victim usually feels no pain when his extremities are being injured. He loses his fingers or toes because he receives no warning signal.

I could stand pain so long as I knew that progress was being made in meeting the basic need. That need, I felt, was to restore the body's capacity to halt the continuing breakdown of connective tissue.

There was also the problem of the severe inflammation. If we dispensed with the aspirin, how would we combat the inflammation? I recalled having read in the medical journals about the usefulness of ascorbic acid in combating a wide number of illnesses — all the way from bronchitis to some types of heart disease. Could it also combat inflammation? Did vitamin C act directly, or did it serve as a starter for the body's endocrine system — in particular, the adrenal glands? Was it possible, I asked myself, that ascorbic acid had a vital role to play in "feeding" the adrenal glands?

I had read in the medical press that vitamin C helps to oxygenate the blood. If inadequate or impaired oxygenation was a factor in collagen breakdown, couldn't this circumstance have been another argument for ascorbic acid? Also, according to some medical reports, people suffering from collagen diseases are deficient in vitamin C. Did this lack mean that the body uses up large amounts of vitamin C in the process of combating collagen breakdown?

I wanted to discuss some of these ruminations with Dr. Hitzig. He listened carefully as I told him of my speculations concerning the cause of the illness, as well as my layman's ideas for a course of action that might give me a chance to reduce the odds against my recovery.

Dr. Hitzig said it was clear to him that there was nothing undersized about my will to live. He said that what was most important was that I continue to believe in everything I had said. He shared my excitement about the possibilities of recovery and liked the idea of a partnership.

Even before we had completed arrangements for moving out of the hospital we began the part of the program calling for the full exercise of the affirmative emotions as a factor in enhancing body chemistry. It was easy enough to hope and love and have faith, but what about laughter? Nothing is less funny than being flat on your back with all the bones in your spine and joints hurting. A systematic program was indicated. A good place to begin, I thought, was with amusing movies. Allen Funt, producer of the spoofing television program "Candid Camera," sent films of some of his CC classics, along with a motion-picture projector. The nurse was instructed in its use. We were even able to get our hands on some old Marx Brothers films. We pulled down the blinds and turned on the machine.

It worked. I made the joyous discovery that ten minutes of genuine belly laughter had an anesthetic effect and would give me at least two hours of pain-free sleep. When the pain-killing effect of the laughter wore off, we would switch on the motion-picture projector again, and, not infrequently, it would lead to another pain-free sleep interval. Sometimes, the nurse read to me out of a trove of humor books. Especially useful were E. B. and Katharine White's *Subtreasury of American Humor* and Max Eastman's *The Enjoyment of Laughter*.

How scientific was it to believe that laughter — as well as the positive emotions in general — was affecting my body chemistry for the better? If laughter did in fact have a salutary effect on the body's chemistry, it seemed at least theoretically likely that it would enhance the system's ability to fight the inflammation. So we took sedimentation rate readings just before as well as several hours after the laughter episodes. Each time, there was a drop of at least five points. The drop by itself was not substantial, but it held and was cumulative. I was greatly elated by the discovery that there is a physiologic basis for the ancient theory that laughter is good medicine.

There was, however, one negative side-effect of the laughter from the standpoint of the hospital. I was disturbing other patients. But that objection didn't last very long, for the arrangements were now complete for me to move my act to a hotel room.

One of the incidental advantages of the hotel room, I was delighted to find, was that it cost only about one-third as much as the hospital. The other benefits were incalculable. I would not be awakened for a bed bath or for meals or for medication or for a change of bed sheets or for tests or for examinations by hospital interns. The sense of serenity was delicious and would, I felt certain, contribute to a general improvement.

What about ascorbic acid and its place in the general program for recovery? In discussing my speculations about vitamin C with Dr. Hitzig, I found him completely open-minded on the subject, although he told me of serious questions that had been raised by scientific studies. He also cautioned me that heavy doses of ascorbic acid carried some risk of renal damage. The main problem right then, however, was not my kidneys; it seemed to me that, on balance, the risk was worth taking. I asked Dr. Hitzig about previous recorded experience with massive doses of vitamin C. He ascertained that at the hospital there had been cases in which patients had received up to 3 grams by intramuscular injection.

As I thought about the injection procedure, some questions came to mind. Introducing the ascorbic acid directly into the bloodstream might make more effective use of the vitamin, but I wondered about the body's ability to utilize a sudden, massive infusion. I knew that one of the great advantages of vitamin C is that the body takes only the amount necessary for its purposes and excretes the rest. Again, there came to mind Cannon's phrase — the wisdom of the body.

Was there a coefficient of time in the utilization of ascorbic acid? The more I thought about it, the more likely it seemed to me that the body would excrete a large quantity of the vitamin because it couldn't metabolize it fast enough. I wondered whether a better procedure than injection would be to administer the ascorbic acid through slow intravenous drip over a period of three or four hours. In this way we could go far beyond 3 grams. My hope was to start at 10 grams and then increase the dose daily until we reached 25 grams.

Dr. Hitzig's eyes widened when I mentioned 25 grams. This amount was far beyond any recorded dose. He said he had to caution me about the possible effect not just on the kidneys but on the veins in the arms. Moreover, he said he knew of no data to support the assumption that the body could handle 25 grams over a four-hour period, other than by excreting it rapidly through the urine.

As before, however, it seemed to me we were playing for bigger stakes: losing some veins was not of major importance alongside the need to combat whatever was eating at my connective tissue.

To know whether we were on the right track we took a sedimentation test before the first intravenous administration of 10 grams of ascorbic acid. Four hours later, we took another sedimentation test. There was a drop of nine full points.

Seldom had I known such elation. The ascorbic acid was working. So was laughter. The combination was cutting heavily into whatever poison was attacking the connective tissue. The fever was receding, and the pulse was no longer racing.

We stepped up the dosage. On the second day we went to 12.5 grams of ascorbic acid, on the third day, 15 grams, and so on until the end of the week, when we reached 25 grams. Meanwhile, the laughter routine was in full force. I was completely off drugs and sleeping pills. Sleep — blessed, natural sleep without pain — was becoming increasingly prolonged.

At the end of the eighth day I was able to move my thumbs without pain. By this time, the sedimentation rate was somewhere in the 80s and dropping fast. I couldn't be sure, but it seemed to me that the gravel-like nodules on my neck and the backs of my hands were beginning to shrink. There was no doubt in my mind that I was going to make it back all the way. I could function, and the feeling was indescribably beautiful.

I must not make it appear that all my infirmities disappeared overnight. For many months I couldn't get my arms up far enough to reach for a book on a high shelf. My fingers weren't agile enough to do what I wanted them to do on the organ keyboard. My neck had a limited turning radius. My knees were somewhat wobbly, and off and on, I have had to wear a metal brace.

Even so, I was sufficiently recovered to go back to my job at the *Saturday Review* full time again, and this was miracle enough for me.

Is the recovery a total one? Year by year the mobility has improved. I have become pain-free, except for one shoulder and my knees, although I have been able to discard the metal braces. I no longer feel a sharp twinge in my wrists when I hit a tennis ball or golf ball, as I did for such a long time. I can ride a horse flat out and hold a camera with a steady hand. And I have recaptured my ambition to play the Toccata and Fugue in D Minor, though I find the going slower and tougher than I had hoped. My neck has a full turning radius again, despite the statement of specialists as recently as 1971 that the condition was degenerative and that I would have to adjust to a quarter turn.

It was seven years after the onset of the illness before I had scientific confirmation about the dangers of using aspirin in the treatment of collagen diseases. In its May 8, 1971 issue, *Lancet* published a study by Drs. M. A. Sahud and R. J. Cohen showing that aspirin can be antagonistic to the retention of vitamin C in the body. The authors said that patients with rheumatoid arthritis should take vitamin C supplements, since it has often been noted that they have low levels of the vitamin in their blood. It was no surprise, then, that I had been able to absorb such massive amounts of ascorbic acid without kidney or other complications.

What conclusions do I draw from the entire experience?

The first is that the will to live is not a theoretical abstraction, but a physiologic reality with therapeutic characteristics. The second is that I was incredibly fortunate to have as my doctor a man who knew that his biggest job was to encourage to the fullest the patient's will to live and to mobilize all the natural resources of body and mind to combat disease. Dr. Hitzig was willing to set aside the large and often hazardous armamentarium of powerful drugs available to the modern physician when he became convinced that his patient might have something better to offer. He was also wise enough to know that the art of healing is still a frontier profession. And, though I can't be sure of this point, I have a hunch he believed that my own total involvement was a major factor in my recovery.

People have asked what I thought when I was told by the specialists that my disease was progressive and incurable.

The answer is simple. Since I didn't accept the verdict, I wasn't trapped in the cycle of fear, depression, and panic that frequently accompanies a supposedly incurable illness. I must not make it seem, however, that I was unmindful of the seriousness of the problem or that I was in a festive mood throughout. Being unable to move my body was all the evidence I needed that the specialists were dealing with real concerns. But deep down, I knew I had a good chance and relished the idea of bucking the odds.

Adam Smith, in his book, *Powers of the Mind*, says he discussed my recovery with some of his doctor friends, asking them to explain why the combination of laughter and ascorbic acid worked so well. The answer he got was that neither laughter nor ascorbic acid had anything to do with it and that I probably would have recovered if nothing had been done.

Maybe so, but that was not the opinion of the specialists at the time.

Two or three doctors, reflecting on the Adam Smith account, have commented that I was probably the beneficiary of a mammoth venture in self-administered placebos.

Such a hypothesis bothers me not at all. Respectable names in the history of medicine, like Paracelsus, Holmes, and Osler, have suggested that the history of medication is far more the history of the placebo effect than of intrinsically valuable and relevant drugs. Such modalities as bleeding (in a single year, 1827, France imported 33 million leeches after its domestic supplies had been depleted); purging through emetics; physical contact with unicorn horns, bezoar stones, mandrakes, or powdered mummies — all such treatments were no doubt regarded by physicians at the time as specifics with empirical sanction. But today's medical science recognizes that whatever efficacy these treatments may have had — and the records indicate that the results were often surprisingly in line with expectations — was probably related to the power of the placebo.

Until comparatively recently, medical literature on the phenomenon of the placebo has been rather sparse. But the past two decades have seen a pronounced interest in the subject. Indeed, three medical researchers at the University of California, Los Angeles, have compiled an entire volume on a bibliography of the placebo. (J. Turner, R. Gallimore, C. Fox, *Placebo: An Annotated Bibliography.* The Neuropsychiatric Institute, University of California, Los Angeles, 1974.) Among the medical researchers who have been prominently engaged in such studies are Arthur K. Shapiro, Stewart Wolf, Henry K. Beecher, and Louis Lasagna. (Their work is discussed in the next chapter.) In connection with my own experience, I was fascinated by a report citing a study by Dr. Thomas C. Chalmers, of the Mount Sinai Medical Center in New York, which compared two groups that were being used to test the theory that ascorbic acid is a cold preventative. "The group on placebo who thought they were on ascorbic acid," says Dr. Chalmers, "had fewer colds than the group on ascorbic acid who thought they were on placebo."

I was absolutely convinced, at the time I was deep in my illness, that intravenous doses of ascorbic acid could be beneficial—and they were. It is quite possible that this treatment—like everything else I did—was a demonstration of the placebo effect.

At this point, of course, we are opening a very wide door, perhaps even a Pandora's box. The vaunted "miracle cures" that abound in the literature of all the great religions all say something about the ability of the patient, properly motivated or stimulated, to participate actively in extraordinary reversals of disease and disability. It is all too easy, of course, to raise these possibilities and speculations to a monopoly status—in which case the entire edifice of modern medicine would be reduced to little more than the hut of an African witch doctor. But we can at least reflect on William Halse Rivers' statement, as quoted by Shapiro, that "the salient feature of the medicine of today is that these psychical factors are no longer allowed to play their part unwittingly, but are themselves becoming the subject of study, so that the present age is serving the growth of a rational system of psychotherapeutics."

What we are talking about essentially, I suppose, is the chemistry of the will to live. In Bucharest in 1972, I visited the clinic of Ana Aslan, described to me as one of Romania's leading endocrinologists. She spoke of her belief that there is a direct connection between a robust will to live and the chemical balances in the brain. She is convinced that creativity—one aspect of the will to live—produces the vital brain impulses that stimulate the pituitary gland, triggering effects on the pineal gland and the whole of the endocrine system. Is it possible that placebos have a key role in this process? Shouldn't this entire area be worth serious and sustained attention?

If I had to guess, I would say that the principal contribution made by my doctor to the taming, and possibly the conquest, of my illness was that he encouraged me to believe I was a respected partner with him in the total undertaking. He fully engaged my subjective energies. He may not have been able to define or diagnose the process through which self-confidence (wild hunches securely believed) was somehow picked up by the body's immunologic mechanisms and translated into antimorbid effects, but he was acting, I believe, in the best tradition of medicine in recognizing that he had to reach out in my case beyond the usual verifiable modalities. In so doing, he was faithful to the first dictum in his medical education: above all, do not harm.

Something else I have learned. I have learned never to underestimate the capacity of the human mind and body to regenerate—even when the prospects seem most wretched. The life-force may be the least understood force on earth. William James said that human beings tend to live too far within self-imposed limits. It is possible that these limits will recede when we respect more fully the natural drive of the human mind and body toward perfectibility and regeneration. Protecting and cherishing that natural drive may well represent the finest exercise of human freedom.

QUESTIONS

1. If you were to become ill, would you turn to humor to help make you well? What forms and types of humor would you use?

   _____

   _____

   _____

2. Have you ever witnessed the phenomenon of mind over body? Discuss.

   _____

   _____

   _____

Mr. A and the Stranger:
A Parable

There was once a man named Mr. A who lived in Organizationville—a neat place, of course, where everything was quite orderly.

And so was he.

Orderliness, thought Mr. A, was good—or anyway, dependable, or at least orderly. And, besides, you didn't have to spend much time thinking about it, so you had lots of time to think about other things.

Most other people in Organizationville believed that also, or anyway seemed to, or at least didn't spend much time questioning it. So they had lots of time to think about other things, too.

Mainly, the other things that Mr. A thought about were what he ought to do and what he ought to say. Sometimes he thought about what he ought to think and even feel, too.

It was one way to spend time, of course, and since Mr. A had been doing it for a long while—ever since he was a little boy, in fact—he had built up quite a large catalogue.

For instance: One thing Mr. A thought he ought to do was to smile at his secretary every morning when he arrived at work.

And another was to look efficient and confident when he met with his assistant.

And another was to act interested and alert when he met with his boss. Mr. A also knew what he ought to say (and ought not to say). So he said, "That's a damn fine idea," to the people in the engineering department. And he said, "Your costs are too high," to the people in the manufacturing department. And, "Let's take it under advisement," to almost anybody who brought him a new idea.

What Mr. A usually thought about his thoughts, when he thought about them, was mostly that they ought to be positive.

He thought: I ought to think Organizationville is the best of all possible places to be.

And, I ought to become an even more important man in Organizationville than I am now.

And, I ought to treat all of my employees with patience, objectivity, and politeness.

Source: *S. Herman and M. Korenick,* Authentic Management: A Gestalt Orientation to Organizations and Their Development *(Reading, Mass.: Addison-Wesley Publishing Co., Inc.,* © *1977) 18–22. Reprinted with permission.*

Now, as to his thoughts about his feelings, it is more difficult to say, for Mr. A didn't think about his feelings often and, in fact, he seldom noticed that he had feelings at all.

However, if one had asked him what he thought his feelings ought to be (no one ever did), Mr. A would likely have said: "My feelings ought to be self-assured, constructive, helpful to others, and above all, controlled."

In fact, if anyone had ever asked Mr. A about feelings like love and hate and sadness and joy and anger and envy and lust, he would have been shocked or at least uncomfortable and certainly would have considered them inappropriate indeed.

By and large, Mr. A's lifestyle was a satisfactory arrangement, or at least not unsatisfactory. Until one night trouble and turbulence came to Mr. A. As he lay in his bed he could not sleep—instead, he felt.

It was very disturbing indeed. No matter how hard he tried to keep them away, strange and uncontrollable feelings kept pushing their way into his head. Instead of feeling positive, he felt negative. Instead of feeling self-assured, he felt anxious.

As nights and days went by, Mr. A's discomfort grew worse and worse. After a while, the strange and uncontrollable feelings troubled him by day as well as night. Not only did he feel negative and anxious, but also angry and depressed. He worked mightily to force these unwelcome visitors from him. Soon he was spending most of his time and strength in trying to push them away.

Mr. A grew tired and pale. It became difficult for him to do what he thought he ought to do, and say what he thought he ought to say, and even think what he thought he ought to think. His life grew very troubled.

Others noticed and would say (though not to Mr. A himself, of course): "Mr. A looks tired and pale"; or, "Yes, Mr. A certainly doesn't seem to be his old self. Too bad." And then they would go about their own business, which was mostly doing what they thought they ought to do.

Then one day when his life had grown so confused and difficult that he could hardly bear it any longer, a strange man came to Organization-ville, a man no one had ever seen before.

He was short and stubby, and had a large nose and a wrinkled face and a bushy beard and an unruly fringe of shaggy hair that circled his head like a slipped halo. (For those unfamiliar with the world of psychotherapy, an extra hint: the stranger's description sounds a lot like Fritz Perls.)

"Nyeh," said the strange man to Mr. A, "You look lousy" (which no one had ever said to Mr. A before).

"I guess you're right," replied Mr. A, who was too upset to remember that he thought he ought to be more reserved with strangers, especially such unusual-looking strangers.

"Nyeh," said the stranger. "What's the matter with you?"

"I am very worried and upset," Mr. A murmured in a low tone, for he was embarrassed and ashamed of his condition, as well as worried and upset. "I don't seem to be able to do what I think I ought to do, or say what I think I ought to say or even think what I think I ought to think. I just don't feel too well."

"Exactly!" exclaimed the stranger, then added, "Nyeh."

"What do you mean?" asked Mr. A, who somehow found himself interested.

"Just what I said," said the stranger. "I always mean what I say. There are no hidden meanings." He tugged his fuzzy beard. "And furthermore, you meant what you said as well. You just don't feel too well. If you felt better, you'd feel better."

"I'm confused," said Mr. A, fighting his confusion.

"OK," said the stranger, "then be confused."

So Mr. A sat and allowed himself to be confused and for once didn't fight it or tell himself that he ought not be confused. And in a little while his confusion passed by itself and he felt a little better than he had for some while. When he looked back to the stranger he saw that he was writing something on the large blackboard. He read:

> Be
> As you are
> And so see
> Who you are
> And how you are
> Let go
> For a moment or two
> Of what you ought to do
> And discover what you do do
>
> Risk a little if you can
> Feel your own feelings
> Say your own words
> Think your own thoughts
> Be your own self
>
> Discover
> Let the plan for you
> Grow from within you

Mr. A read the words (which he noted were not written in a very orderly fashion), then he read them again. "I think I know what you mean," said Mr. A.

"Nyeh," said the stranger, and he turned and in a moment was gone. Mr. A never saw him again, but he thought of him frequently and did not erase the stranger's words from his blackboard. Though he considered for a while asking his assistant to have them typed more neatly on a five-by-seven card, he decided against it and instead just drew a line around them and printed "SAVE" above it so that the janitor wouldn't erase the board.

In this way, Mr. A found himself looking at the stranger's words every day and soon began to try them out. It wasn't easy. At first it was hard to even figure out what he really did think and feel and want to say and do. But gradually those things became clearer.

Then there was the problem of being scared. Sometimes, even though he knew what he wanted to say or do, Mr. A was afraid of hurting other people's feelings and afraid that they might not like him, or afraid he would look foolish, or ignorant, or just not quite right.

What he did about that was to take risks, a little at a time. First he would say what he really meant only to people he knew very well, and only sometimes. Then, gradually, he grew more bold, until he was saying things that he really meant even to strangers. It was fun, and once he was surprised and pleased to overhear two people in the corridor saying, "One thing you can say about Mr. A is he certainly says what he means nowadays."

There was another problem, too. Every so often Mr. A would slip back into his old ways and find himself saying or thinking or doing what he thought he ought to do. Then he would tell himself he ought not to do that. But then he would realize that telling himself what he ought not to do was just the same as telling himself what he ought to do. For a while, he would be puzzled, but then he would just grin and relax and do whatever he felt like doing (including doing what he thought he ought to do). And in a while things would straighten themselves out without his worrying too much about it.

In his new style, Mr. A discovered a lot of new things.

For instance: some mornings he felt like smiling at his secretary, and some mornings he didn't. And she felt the same way.

Sometimes he was efficient and confident with his assistant, and other times he was unsure. And when he was unsure, sometimes his assistant had a good idea or two that helped. Other times they were unsure together, and Mr. A found it was nice to have company.

Most of the time Mr. A found he was interested in what his boss was doing, and he said so. Now and again, he wasn't interested; but because it was a favorite project of his boss, Mr. A faked it (but not always).

Mr. A also found out that he thought and felt different ways about things at different times. Sometimes he didn't think positively. He found out that he really didn't want to be president of Organizationville — it would take too much of his time and he would rather spend that time painting pictures of seagulls near the ocean. And he found out that at times when he felt angry or impatient with his employees he could let his anger or impatience come out and his employees did not wither. In fact, some argued back — and Mr. A found he liked that too.

And so, as time passed in Organizationville, Mr. A's particular place seemed slowly, almost imperceptibly, to become a little less orderly than most, and also a little more comfortable. Over the years, many Organizationville people came to visit, and, though he never saw the stranger again,

Mr. A spoke of him in warm and mellow tones. As for his life, often Mr. A felt good and sometimes he felt bad; but one thing for sure, he always felt what he felt. And he lived happily ever after.

QUESTIONS

1. What does this parable mean to you?

   _____

   _____

   _____

2. What do you think are the stresses of not being open and honest in your human relations?

   _____

   _____

   _____

The Relaxation Response

The case for the use of the Relaxation Response by healthy but harassed individuals is straightforward. It can act as a built-in method of counteracting the stresses of everyday living which bring forth the fight-or-flight response. We have also shown how the Relaxation Response may be used as a new approach to aid in the treatment and perhaps prevention of diseases such as hypertension. In this chapter, we will review the components necessary to evoke the Relaxation Response and present a specific technique that we have developed at Harvard's Thorndike Memorial Laboratory and Boston's Beth Israel Hospital. We again emphasize that, for those who may suffer from any disease state, the potential therapeutic use of the Relaxation Response should be practiced only under the care and supervision of a physician.

HOW TO BRING FORTH THE RELAXATION RESPONSE

. . . we reviewed the Eastern and Western religious, cultic, and lay practices that led to the Relaxation Response. From those age-old techniques we have extracted four basic components necessary to bring forth that response:

(1) *A Quiet Environment*
Ideally, you should choose a quiet, calm environment with as few distractions as possible. A quiet room is suitable, as is a place of worship. The quiet environment contributes to the effectiveness of the repeated word or phrase by making it easier to eliminate distracting thoughts.

(2) *A Mental Device*
To shift the mind from logical, externally oriented thought, there should be a constant stimulus: a sound, word, or phrase repeated silently or aloud; or fixed gazing at an object. Since one of the major difficulties in the elicitation of the Relaxation Response is "mind wandering," the repetition of the word or phrase is a way to help break the train of distracting thoughts. Your eyes are usually closed if you

Source: Chapter 7 in The Relaxation Response *by Herbert Benson, M.D., with Miriam Z. Klipper. Copyright © by William Morrow and Company, Inc. By permission of the publisher.*

are using a repeated sound or word; of course, your eyes are open if you are gazing. Attention to the normal rhythm of breathing is also useful and enhances the repetition of the sound or word.

(3) *A Passive Attitude*

When distracting thoughts occur, they are to be disregarded and attention redirected to the repetition or gazing; *you should not worry about how well you are performing the technique,* because this may well prevent the Relaxation Response from occurring. Adopt a "let it happen" attitude. *The passive attitude is perhaps the most important element in eliciting the Relaxation Response. Distracting thoughts will occur. Do not worry about them. When these thoughts do present themselves and you become aware of them, simply return to the repetition of the mental device. These other thoughts do not mean you are performing the technique incorrectly. They are to be expected.*

(4) *A Comfortable Position*

A comfortable posture is important so that there is no undue muscular tension. Some methods call for a sitting position. A few practitioners use the cross-legged "lotus" position of the Yogi. If you are lying down, there is a tendency to fall asleep. As we have noted previously, the various postures of kneeling, swaying, or sitting in a cross-legged position are believed to have evolved to prevent falling asleep. You should be comfortable and relaxed.

It is important to remember that there is not a single method that is unique in eliciting the Relaxation Response. For example, Transcendental Meditation is one of the many techniques that incorporate these components. However, we believe it is not necessary to use the specific method and specific *secret*, personal sound taught by Transcendental Meditation. *Tests at the Thorndike Memorial Laboratory of Harvard have shown that a similar technique used with any sound or phrase or mantra brings forth the same physiologic changes noted during Transcendental Meditation:* decreased oxygen consumption; decreased carbon-dioxide elimination; decreased rate of breathing. In other words using the basic necessary components, any one of the age-old or the newly derived techniques produces the same physiologic results regardless of the mental device used. The following set of instructions, used to elicit the Relaxation Response, was developed by our group at Harvard's Thorndike Memorial Laboratory and was found to produce the same physiologic changes we had observed during the practice of Transcendental Meditation. This technique is now being used to lower blood pressure in certain patients. A noncultic technique, it is drawn with little embellishment from the four basic components found in the myriad of historical methods. We claim no innovation but simply a scientific validation of age-old wisdom. The technique is our current method of eliciting the Relaxation Response in our continuing studies at the Beth Israel Hospital of Boston.

(1) *Sit quietly in a comfortable position.*
(2) *Close your eyes.*

(3) *Deeply relax all your muscles, beginning at your feet and progressing up to your face. Keep them relaxed.*

(4) *Breathe through your nose. Become aware of your breathing. As you breathe out, say the word, "ONE," silently to yourself. For example, breathe IN . . . OUT, "ONE"; IN . . . OUT, "ONE"; etc. Breathe easily and naturally.*

(5) *Continue for 10 to 20 minutes. You may open your eyes to check the time, but do not use an alarm. When you finish, sit quietly for several minutes, at first with your eyes closed and later with your eyes opened. Do not stand up for a few minutes.*

(6) *Do not worry about whether you are successful in achieving a deep level of relaxation. Maintain a passive attitude and permit relaxation to occur at its own pace. When distracting thoughts occur, try to ignore them by not dwelling upon them and return to repeating "ONE." With practice, the response should come with little effort. Practice the technique once or twice daily, but not within two hours after any meal, since the digestive processes seem to interfere with the elicitation of the Relaxation Response.*

The subjective feelings that accompany the elicitation of the Relaxation Response vary among individuals. The majority of people feel a sense of calm and feel very relaxed. A small percentage of people immediately experience ecstatic feelings. Other descriptions that have been related to us involve feelings of pleasure, refreshment, and well-being. Still others have noted relatively little change on a subjective level. Regardless of the subjective feelings described by our subjects, we have found that the physiologic changes such as decreased oxygen consumption are taking place.

There is no educational requirement or aptitude necessary to experience the Relaxation Response. Just as each of us experiences anger, contentment, and excitement, each has the capacity to experience the Relaxation Response. It is an innate response within us. Again, there are many ways in which people bring forth the Relaxation Response, and your own individual considerations may be applied to the four components involved. You may wish to use the technique we have presented but with a different mental device. You may use a syllable or phrase that may be easily repeated and sounds natural to you.

Another technique you may wish to use is a prayer from your religious tradition. Choose a prayer that incorporates the four elements necessary to bring forth the Relaxation Response. We believe every religion has such prayers. We would reemphasize that we do not view religion in a mechanistic fashion simply because a religious prayer brings forth this desired physiologic response. Rather, we believe, as did William James, that these age-old prayers are one way to remedy an inner incompleteness and to reduce inner discord. Obviously, there are many other aspects to religious beliefs and practices which have little to do with the Relaxation Response. However, there is little reason not to make use of an appropriate prayer within the framework of your own beliefs if you are most comfortable with it.

Your individual considerations of a particular technique may place different emphasis upon the components necessary to elicit the Relaxation Response and also may incorporate various practices into the use of the technique. For example, for some a quiet environment with little distraction is crucial. However, others prefer to practice the Relaxation Response in subways or trains. Some people choose always to practice the Relaxation Response in the same place and at a regular time.

Since the daily use of the Relaxation Response necessitates a slight change in life-style, some find it difficult at first to keep track of the regularity with which they evoke the Response. In our investigations of the Relaxation Response, patients should use a calendar. Each time they practice the Relaxation Response, they make a check on the appropriate date.

It may be said, as an aside, that many people have told us that they use our technique for evoking the Relaxation Response while lying in bed to help them fall asleep. Some have even given up sleeping pills as a result. It should be noted, however, that when you fall asleep using the technique, you are not experiencing the Relaxation Response, you are asleep. As we have shown, the Relaxation Response is different from sleep.

PERSONAL EXPERIENCES WITH THE RELAXATION RESPONSE

Several illustrations of how people include the practice of the Relaxation Response in their daily lives should answer the question that you may now be posing: "How do I find the time?" One businessman evokes the Relaxation Response late in the morning for ten or fifteen minutes in his office. He tells his secretary that he's "in conference" and not to let in any calls. Traveling quite a bit, he often uses the Relaxation Response while on the airplane. A housewife practices the Relaxation Response after her husband and children have left for the day. In the late afternoon, before her husband comes home, she again evokes the Response, telling her children not to disturb her for twenty minutes. Another woman, a researcher, usually awakes ten or twenty minutes earlier in the morning in order to elicit the Relaxation Response before breakfast. If she wakes up too late, she tries to take a "relaxation break" rather than a coffee break at work. She finds a quiet spot and a comfortable chair while her co-workers are out getting coffee. On the subway, a factory worker practices the Relaxation Response while commuting to and from work. He claims he has not yet missed his stop. A student uses the Relaxation Response between classes. Arriving fifteen minutes early, he uses the empty classroom and says he is not bothered by other students entering the room. If the classroom is in use, he simply practices the response sitting in the corridor.

The regular use of the Relaxation Response has helped these people to be more effective in their day-to-day living. The businessman feels he is "clearing the cobwebs" that have accumulated during the morning. He also states he often gets new perspectives on perplexing business problems. The housewife, before regularly eliciting the Relaxation Response, found it very difficult to face the prospects of preparing dinner and getting the family organized for another day. She now feels more energetic and enjoys her family more. The researcher no longer requires two cups of coffee in the morning to get started at work, and the factory worker notes he "unwinds" going home. The student says he is more attentive and hardly ever falls asleep during lectures. He even attributes better grades to his regular elicitation of the Relaxation Response.

The examples of when people practice the Relaxation Response are numerous. You must consider not only what times are practical but also when you feel the use of the Relaxation Response is most effective. We believe the regular use of the Relaxation Response will help you better deal with the distressing aspects of modern life by lessening the effects of too much sympathetic nervous system activation. By this increased control of your bodily reactions, you should become more able to cope with your uncertainties and frustrations.

The following two descriptions of people who have regularly used the Relaxation Response for specific problems show how they feel the Relaxation Response has been of help to them. A young man, who suffered from severe anxiety attacks, reports that he often felt fearful, nervous and shaky, tense and worried. After practicing the Relaxation Response for two months, he rarely suffered from attacks of anxiety. He felt considerably more calm and relaxed. Usually, he practiced the technique regularly twice a day, but he would also practice it when he began to feel anxious. By applying the technique in such a manner he found he could alleviate these oncoming feelings. In short, he felt that the practice of the Relaxation Response had significantly improved his life.

Our second illustration is from a woman with moderate hypertension. She has a strong family history of high blood pressure, and the regular practice of the Relaxation Response has lowered her blood pressure. She has been practicing the technique using the word "ONE" for over fourteen months. Her own words best convey what the response has meant to her.

> The Relaxation Response has contributed to many changes in my life. Not only has it made me more relaxed physically and mentally, but also it has contributed to changes in my personality and way of life. I seem to have become calmer, more open and receptive especially to ideas which either have been unknown to me or very different from my past way of life. I like the way I am becoming; more patient, overcoming some fears especially around my physical health and stamina. I feel stronger physically and mentally. I take better care of myself. I am more committed to my daily exercise and see it as an integral part of my life. I really enjoy it, too! I drink less alcohol, take less medicine. The positive feedback which I experience as a result of the Relaxation Response and

the lowered blood pressure readings make me feel I am attempting to transcend a family history replete with hypertensive heart disease.

I feel happier, content, and generally well when I use the Relaxation Response. There is a noticeable difference in attitude and energy during those occasional days in which I have had to miss the Relaxation Response.

Intellectually and spiritually, good things happen to me during the Relaxation Response. Sometimes I get insights into situations or problems which have been with me for a long time and about which I am not consciously thinking. Creative ideas come to me either during or as a direct result of the Relaxation Response. I look forward to the Relaxation Response twice and sometimes three times a day. I am hooked on it and love my addiction.

We should also comment about the side effects of the Relaxation Response. Any technique used to evoke the Relaxation Response trains you to let go of meaningful thoughts when they present themselves and to return to the repetition of the sound, the prayer, the word "ONE," or the mantra. Traditional psychoanalytic practice, on the other hand, trains you to hold on to free-association thoughts as working tools to open up your subconscious. Thus, there is a conflict between the methods of the Relaxation Response and those used in psychoanalysis. Persons undergoing psychoanalysis may have difficulty in disregarding distracting thoughts and assuming a passive attitude, and it may therefore be more difficult for them to elicit the Relaxation Response.

A basic teaching of many meditational organizations is that if a little meditation is good, a lot would be even better. This argument encourages followers to meditate for prolonged periods of time. From our personal observations, many people who meditate for several hours every day for weeks at a time tend to hallucinate. It is difficult, however, to draw a direct association between the Relaxation Response and this undesirable side effect because we do not know whether the people experiencing these side effects were predisposed to such problems to start with. For example, proponents of some meditative techniques evangelistically promise relief from all mental and physical suffering and tend to attract people who have emotional problems. There may be a preselection of people who come to learn these techniques because they already have emotional disturbances. Furthermore, the excessive daily elicitation of the Relaxation Response for many weeks may lead to hallucinations as a result of sensory deprivation. *We have not noted any of the above side effects in people who bring forth the Relaxation Response once or twice daily for ten to twenty minutes a day.*

One should not use the Relaxation Response in an effort to shield oneself or withdraw from the pressures of the outside world which are necessary for everyday functioning. *The fight-or-flight response is often appropriate and should not be thought of as always harmful. It is a necessary part of our physiologic and psychological makeup, a useful reaction to many situations in our current world.* Modern society has forced us to evoke the fight-or-flight response repeatedly. We are not using it as we believe our ancestors used it. That is, we do not always run, nor do we fight when it is elicited. However, our body is being prepared for running or for fighting, and since this preparation is not always utilized, we believe anxieties, hypertension and its related diseases ensue. The Relaxation Response offers a natural balance to counteract the undesirable manifestations of the fight-or-flight response. We do not believe that you will become a passive and withdrawn person and less able to function and compete in our world because you regularly elicit the Relaxation Response. Rather, it has been our experience that people who regularly evoke the Relaxation Response claim they are more effective in dealing with situations that probably bring forth the fight-or-flight response. We believe you will be able to cope better with difficult situations by regularly allowing your body to achieve a more balanced state through the physiologic effects of the Relaxation Response. You can expect this balanced state to last as long as you regularly bring forth the response. Within several days after stopping its regular use, we believe, you will cease to benefit from its effects, *regardless* of the technique employed, be it prayer, Transcendental Meditation or the method proposed in this book.

QUESTIONS

1. Have there been times and circumstances in your life when you could use the relaxation response? Discuss.

_____

_____

_____

2. Have you experienced physical, psychological, or behavioral signs of stress that could be relieved by the relaxation response? Discuss.

_____

_____

_____

Death of a Salesman

. . . From the right, Willy Loman, the Salesman, enters, carrying two large sample cases. The flute plays on. He hears but is not aware of it. He is past sixty years of age, dressed quietly. Even as he crosses the stage to the doorway of the house, his exhaustion is apparent. He unlocks the door, comes into the kitchen, and thankfully lets his burden down, feeling the soreness of his palms. A word-sigh escapes his lips — it might be "Oh, boy, oh, boy." He closes the door, then carries his cases out into the living-room, through the draped kitchen doorway.

Linda, his wife, has stirred in her bed at the right. She gets out and puts on a robe, listening. Most often jovial, she has developed an iron repression of her exceptions to Willy's behavior — she more than loves him, she admires him, as though his mercurial nature, his temper, his massive dreams and little cruelties, served her only as sharp reminders of the turbulent longings within him, longings which she shares but lacks the temperament to utter and follow to their end.

LINDA, *hearing Willy outside the bedroom, calls with some trepidation:* Willy!

WILLY: It's all right. I came back.

LINDA: Why? What happened? *Slight pause.* Did something happen, Willy?

WILLY: No, nothing happened.

LINDA: You didn't smash the car, did you?

WILLY, *With casual irritation:* I said nothing happened. Didn't you hear me?

> *(Editor's note: The conversation continues with a discussion of Willy's state of mind.)*

LINDA: But you didn't rest your mind. Your mind is overactive, and the mind is what counts, dear.

WILLY: I'll start out in the morning. Maybe I'll feel better in the morning. *She is taking off his shoes.* These . . . arch supports are killing me.

LINDA: Take an aspirin. Should I get you an aspirin? It'll soothe you.

WILLY, *with wonder:* I was driving along, you understand? And I was

Source: From Death of a Salesman, *by Arthur Miller. Copyright © 1949, copyright renewed © 1977 by Arthur Miller. Reprinted by permission of Viking Penguin, Inc.*

fine. I was even observing the scenery. You can imagine, me looking at scenery, on the road every week of my life. But it's so beautiful up there, Linda, the trees are so thick, and the sun is warm. I opened the windshield and just let the warm air bathe over me. And then all of a sudden I'm goin' off the road! I'm tellin' ya, I absolutely forgot I was driving. If I'd've gone the other way over the white line I might've killed somebody. So I went on again—and five minutes later I'm dreamin' again, and I nearly—*He presses two fingers against his eyes.* I have such thoughts, I have such strange thoughts.

LINDA: Willy, dear. Talk to them again. There's no reason why you can't work in New York.

WILLY: They don't need me in New York. I'm the New England man. I'm vital in New England.

LINDA: But you're sixty years old. They can't expect you to keep traveling every week.

WILLY: I'll have to send a wire to Portland. I'm supposed to see Brown and Morrison tomorrow morning at ten o'clock to show the line. . . . I could sell them! *He starts putting on his jacket.*

LINDA, *taking the jacket from him:* Why don't you go down to the place tomorrow and tell Howard you've simply got to work in New York? You're too accommodating, dear.

WILLY: If old man Wagner was alive I'd a been in charge of New York now! That man was a prince, he was a masterful man. But that boy of his, that Howard, he don't appreciate. When I went north the first time, the Wagner Company didn't know where New England was!

LINDA: Why don't you tell those things to Howard, dear?

WILLY, *encouraged:* I will, I definitely will. Is there any cheese?

LINDA: I'll make you a sandwich.

WILLY: No, go to sleep. I'll take some milk. I'll be up right away. . . .

> (*Editor's note: The scene shifts to Howard Wagner's office the following day.*)

WILLY: Pst! Pst!

HOWARD: Hello, Willy, come in.

WILLY: Like to have a little talk with you, Howard.

HOWARD: Sorry to keep you waiting. I'll be with you in a minute.

WILLY: What's that, Howard?

HOWARD: Didn't you ever see one of these? Wire recorder.

WILLY: Oh. Can we talk a minute?

HOWARD: Records things. Just got delivery yesterday. Been driving me crazy, the most terrific machine I ever saw in my life. I was up all night with it.

WILLY: What do you do with it?

HOWARD: I bought it for dictation, but you can do anything with it. Listen to this. I had it home last night. Listen to what I picked up. The first one is my daughter. Get this. *He flicks the switch and "Roll out the Barrel" is heard being whistled.* Listen to that kid whistle.

WILLY: That is lifelike, isn't it?

HOWARD: Seven years old. Get that tone.

WILLY: Ts, ts. Like to ask a little favor if you . . .

The whistling breaks off, and the voice of Howard's daughter is heard.

HIS DAUGHTER: "Now you, Daddy."

HOWARD: She's crazy for me! *Again the same song is whistled.* That's me! Ha! *He winks.*

WILLY: You're very good!

The whistling breaks off again. The machine runs silent for a moment.

HOWARD: Sh! Get this now, this is my son.

HIS SON: "The capital of Alabama is Montgomery; the capital of Arizona is Phoenix; the capital of Arkansas is Little Rock; the capital of California is Sacramento . . ." *and on, and on.*

HOWARD, *holding up five fingers:* Five years old, Willy!

WILLY: He'll make an announcer some day!

HIS SON, *continuing:* "The capital . . ."

HOWARD: Get that—alphabetical order! *The machine breaks off suddenly.* Wait a minute. The maid kicked the plug out.

WILLY: It certainly is a—

HOWARD: Sh, for . . . sake!

HIS SON: "It's nine o'clock, Bulova watch time. So I have to go to sleep."

WILLY: That really is—

HOWARD: Wait a minute! The next is my wife.

They wait

HOWARD'S VOICE: "Go on, say something." *Pause.* "Well, you gonna talk?"

HIS WIFE: "I can't think of anything."

HOWARD'S VOICE: "Well, talk—it's turning."

HIS WIFE, *shyly, beaten:* "Hello." *Silence.* "Oh, Howard, I can't talk into this . . ."

HOWARD, *snapping the machine off:* That was my wife.

WILLY: That is a wonderful machine. Can we—

HOWARD: I tell you, Willy, I'm gonna take my camera, and my bandsaw, and all my hobbies, and out they go. This is the most fascinating relaxation I ever found.

WILLY: I think I'll get one myself.

HOWARD: Sure, they're only a hundred and a half. You can't do without it. Suppose you wanna hear Jack Benny, see? But you can't be at home at that hour. So you tell the maid to turn the radio on when Jack Benny comes on, and this automatically goes on with the radio . . .

WILLY: And when you come home you . . .

HOWARD: You can come home twelve o'clock, one o'clock, any time you like, and you get yourself a Coke and sit yourself down, throw the switch, and there's Jack Benny's program in the middle of the night!

WILLY: I'm definitely going to get one. Because lots of time I'm on the road, and I think to myself, what I must be missing on the radio!

HOWARD: Don't you have a radio in the car?

WILLY: Well, yeah, but who ever thinks of turning it on?

HOWARD: Say, aren't you supposed to be in Boston?

WILLY: That's what I want to talk to you about, Howard. You got a minute? *He draws a chair in from the wing.*

HOWARD: What happened? What're you doing here?

WILLY: Well . . .

HOWARD: You didn't crack up again, did you?

WILLY: Oh, no. No . . .

HOWARD: Geez, you had me worried there for a minute. What's the trouble?

WILLY: Well, tell you the truth, Howard. I've come to the decision that I'd rather not travel any more.

HOWARD: Not travel! Well, what'll you do?

WILLY: Remember, Christmas time, when you had the party here? You said you'd try to think of some spot for me here in town.

HOWARD: With us?

WILLY: Well, sure.

HOWARD: Oh, yeah, yeah. I remember. Well, I couldn't think of anything for you, Willy.

WILLY: I tell ya, Howard. The kids are all grown up, y'know. I don't need much any more. If I could take home—well, sixty-five dollars a week, I could swing it.

HOWARD: Yeah, but Willy, see I—

WILLY: I tell ya why, Howard. Speaking frankly and between the two of us, y'know—I'm just a little tired.

HOWARD: Oh, I could understand that, Willy. But you're a road man, Willy, and we do a road business. We've only got a half-dozen salesmen on the floor here.

WILLY: . . . knows, Howard, I never asked a favor of any man. But I was with the firm when your father used to carry you in here in his arms.

HOWARD: I know that, Willy, but—

WILLY: Your father came to me the day you were born and asked me what I thought of the name Howard, may he rest in peace.

HOWARD: I appreciate that, Willy, but there just is no spot here for you. If I had a spot I'd slam you right in, but I just don't have a single solitary spot.

He looks for his lighter. Willy has picked it up and gives it to him. Pause.

WILLY, *with increasing anger:* Howard, all I need to set my table is fifty dollars a week.

HOWARD: But where am I going to put you, kid?

WILLY: Look, it isn't a question of whether I can sell merchandise, is it?

HOWARD: No, but it's a business, kid, and everybody's gotta pull his own weight.

WILLY, *desperately:* Just let me tell you a story, Howard—

HOWARD: 'Cause you gotta admit, business is business.

WILLY, *angrily:* Business is definitely business, but just listen for a minute. You don't understand this. When I was a boy—eighteen, nineteen—I was already on the road. And there was a question in my mind as to whether selling had a future for me. Because in those days I had a yearning to go to Alaska. See, there were three gold strikes in one month in Alaska, and I felt like going out. Just for the ride, you might say.

HOWARD, *barely interested:* Don't say.

WILLY: Oh, yeah, my father lived many years in Alaska. He was an adventurous man. We've got quite a little streak of self-reliance in our family. I thought I'd go out with my older brother and try to locate him, and maybe settle in the North with the old man. And I was almost decided to go, when I met a salesman in the Parker House. His name was Dave Singleman. And he was eighty-four years old, and he'd drummed merchandise in thirty-one states. And old Dave, he'd go up to his room, y'understand, put on his green velvet slippers — I'll never forget — and pick up his phone and call the buyers, and without ever leaving his room, at the age of eighty-four, he made his living. And when I saw that, I realized that selling was the greatest career a man could want. 'Cause what could be more satisfying that to be able to go, at the age of eighty-four, into twenty or thirty different cities, and pick up a phone, and be remembered and loved and helped by so many different people? Do you know? When he died — and by the way he died the death of a salesman, in his green velvet slippers in the smoker of the New York, New Haven and Hartford, going into Boston — when he died, hundreds of salesmen and buyers were at his funeral. Things were sad on a lotta trains for months after that. *He stands up. Howard has not looked at him.* In those days there was personality in it, Howard. There was respect, and comradeship, and gratitude in it. Today, it's all cut and dried, and there's no chance for bringing friendship to bear — or personality. You see what I mean? They don't know me any more.

HOWARD, *moving away, to the right:* That's just the thing, Willy.

WILLY: If I had forty dollars a week — that's all I'd need. Forty dollars, Howard.

HOWARD: Kid, I can't take blood from a stone, I —

WILLY, *desperation is on him now:* Howard, the year Al Smith was nominated, your father came to me and —

HOWARD, *starting to go off:* I've got to see some people, kid.

WILLY, *stopping him:* I'm talking about your father! There were promises made across this desk! You musn't tell me you've got people to see — I put thirty-four years into this firm, Howard, and now I can't pay my insurance! You can't eat the orange and throw the peel away — a man is not a piece of fruit! *After a pause:* Now pay attention. Your father — in 1928 I had a big year. I averaged a hundred and seventy dollars a week in commissions.

HOWARD, *impatiently:* Now, Willy, you never averaged —

WILLY, *banging his hand on the desk:* I averaged a hundred and seventy dollars a week in the year of 1928! And your father came to me — or rather, I was in the office here — it was right over this desk — and he put his hand on my shoulder —

HOWARD, *getting up:* You'll have to excuse me, Willy, I gotta see some people. Pull yourself together. *Going out:* I'll be back in a little while. *On Howard's exit, the light on his chair grows very bright and strange.*

WILLY: Pull myself together! What the hell did I say to him? My . . . , I was yelling at him! How could I! *Willy breaks off, staring at the light, which occupies the chair, animating it. He approaches this chair, standing across the desk from it.* Frank, Frank, don't you remember what you told me that time? How you put your hand on my shoulder, and Frank . . . *He leans on the desk and as he speaks the dead man's name he accidentally switches on the recorder, and instantly*

HOWARD'S SON: ". . . of New York is Albany. The capital of Ohio is Cincinnati, the capital of Rhode Island is . . ." *The recitation continues.*

WILLY, *leaping away with fright, shouting:* Ha! Howard! Howard! Howard!

HOWARD, *rushing in:* What happened?

WILLY, *pointing at the machine, which continues nasally, childishly, with the capital cities:* Shut it off! Shut it off!

HOWARD, *pulling the plug out:* Look, Willy . . .

WILLY, *pressing his hands to his eyes:* I gotta get myself some coffee. I'll get some coffee . . .

Willy starts to walk out. Howard stops him.

HOWARD, *rolling up the cord:* Willy, look . . .

WILLY: I'll go to Boston.

HOWARD: Willy, you can't go to Boston for us.

WILLY: Why can't I go?

HOWARD: I don't want you to represent us. I've been meaning to tell you for a long time now.

WILLY: Howard, are you firing me?

HOWARD: I think you need a good long rest, Willy.

WILLY: Howard—

HOWARD: And when you feel better, come back, and we'll see if we can work something out.

WILLY: But I gotta earn money, Howard. I'm in no position to—

HOWARD: Where are your sons? Why don't your sons give you a hand?

WILLY: They're working on a very big deal.

HOWARD: This is no time for false pride, Willy. You go to your sons and you tell them that you're tired. You've got two great boys, haven't you?

WILLY: Oh, no question, no question, but in the meantime . . .

HOWARD: Then that's that, heh?

WILLY: All right, I'll go to Boston tomorrow.

HOWARD: No, no.

WILLY: I can't throw myself on my sons. I'm not a cripple!

HOWARD: Look, kid, I'm busy this morning.

WILLY, *grasping Howard's arm:* Howard, you've got to let me go to Boston!

HOWARD, *hard, keeping himself under control:* I've got a line of people to see this morning. Sit down, take five minutes, and pull yourself together, and then go home, will ya? I need the office, Willy. *He starts to go, turns, remembering the recorder, starts to push off the table holding the recorder.* Oh, yeah. Whenever you can this week, stop by and drop off the samples. You'll feel better, Willy, and then come back and we'll talk. Pull yourself together, kid, there's people outside. . . .

REQUIEM

(*Editor's note: Biff and Happy are Willy's sons. Charley is Willy's brother.*)

CHARLEY: It's getting dark, Linda.

Linda doesn't react. She stares at the grave.

BIFF: How about it, Mom? Better get some rest, heh? They'll be closing the gate soon.

Linda makes no move. Pause.

HAPPY,   *deeply angered:* He had no right to do that. There was no necessity for it. We would've helped him.

CHARLEY,   *grunting:* Hmmm.

BIFF: Come along, Mom.

LINDA: Why didn't anybody come?

CHARLEY: It was a very nice funeral.

LINDA: But where were all the people he knew? Maybe they blame him.

CHARLEY: Naa. It's a rough world, Linda. They wouldn't blame him.

LINDA: I can't understand it. At this time especially. First time in thirty-five years we were just about free and clear. He only needed a little salary. He was even finished with the dentist.

CHARLEY: No man only needs a little salary.

LINDA: I can't understand it.

BIFF: There were a lot of nice days. When he'd come home from a trip; or on Sundays, making the stoop; finishing the cellar; putting on the new porch; when he built the extra bathroom; and put up the garage. You know something, Charley, there's more of him in that front stoop than in all the sales he ever made.

CHARLEY: Yeah. He was a happy man with a batch of cement.

LINDA: He was so wonderful with his hands.

BIFF: He had the wrong dreams. All, all, wrong.

HAPPY,   *almost ready to fight Biff:* Don't say that!

BIFF: He never knew who he was.

CHARLEY,   *stopping Happy's movement and reply. To Biff:* Nobody dast blame this man. You don't understand: Willy was a salesman. And for a salesman, there is no rock bottom to the life. He don't put a bolt to a nut, he don't tell you the law or give you medicine. He's a man way out there in the blue, riding on a smile and a shoeshine. And when they start not smiling back—that's an earthquake. And then you get yourself a couple of spots on your hat, and you're finished. Nobody dast blame this man. A salesman is got to dream, boy. It comes with the territory.

BIFF: Charley, the man didn't know who he was.

HAPPY, *infuriated:* Don't say that!

BIFF: Why don't you come with me, Happy?

HAPPY: I'm not licked that easily. I'm staying right in this city, and I'm gonna beat this racket! *He looks at Biff, his chin set.* The Loman Brothers!

BIFF: I know who I am, kid.

HAPPY: All right, boy. I'm gonna show you and everybody else that Willy Loman did not die in vain. He had a good dream. It's the only dream you can have—to come out number-one man. He fought it out here, and this is where I'm gonna win it for him.

BIFF, *with a hopeless glance at Happy, bends toward his mother:* Let's go, Mom.

LINDA: I'll be with you in a minute. Go on, Charley. *He hesitates.* I want to, just for a minute. I never had a chance to say good-by.

Charley moves away, followed by Happy. Biff remains a slight distance up and left of Linda. She sits there, summoning herself. The flute begins, not far away, playing behind her speech.

LINDA: Forgive me, dear. I can't cry. I don't know what it is, but I can't cry. I don't understand it. Why did you ever do that? Help me, Willy, I can't cry. It seems to me that you're just on another trip. I keep expecting you. Willy, dear, I can't cry. Why did you do it? I search and search and I search, and I can't understand it, Willy. I made the last payment on the house today. Today, dear. And there'll be nobody home. *A sob rises in her throat.* We're free and clear. *Sobbing more fully, released:* We're free. *Biff comes slowly toward her.* We're free .. we're free . . .
Biff lifts her to her feet and moves out up right with her in his arms. Linda sobs quietly. Bernard and Charley come together and follow them, followed by Happy. Only the music of the flute is left on the darkening stage as over the house the hard towers of the apartment buildings rise into sharp focus, and

The Curtain Falls

QUESTIONS

1. Do you know someone who reminds you of Willy Loman?

   _____

   _____

   _____

2. What stress-coping behaviors would you suggest for Willy to try?

   _____

   _____

   _____

3. What should managers do to help employees cope with stress?

_____

_____

_____

The Voodoo Killer in Modern Society

The legendary witch doctor to whom primitive societies frequently attribute real or imagined powers over life and death has a sinister counterpart in today's complex business and industrial organizations. The voodoo priest or priestess has emerged in "civilized" society as the insensitive, bungling, or purely Machiavellian administrator. Such managers are quite capable of producing phenomena similar to the disorientation, illness, and even death that befall the victims of the village witch doctor's voodoo rites.

It has long been recognized that the organizational climate and behavior generated by administrators can have serious effects on individuals within the organization and on organizational output. Of particular consequence to individuals are the actions that affect them personally in relation to their own economic well-being, status, prestige, and rank.

We are prone to laugh at stories told about Joe so-and-so when his parking space was changed, privileges to the executive dining room were denied, or his office carpeting did not measure up to expectations. But such tales quickly lose their humor when one later observes the all-too-frequent aftereffects on the disappointed manager's mental and physical health.

Insensitive administrators are often to blame in such situations. The perceived or actual slights also are the result of organizational bumbling or ineptness. Occasionally they are the deliberate acts of a ruthless manager or administrator who will use any organizational means to gain his own ends. For the victim of these actions, however, it makes little difference who or what is the cause. The damage has been done.

The personnel director usually plays a role in these events — as a pawn, willing co-conspirator, or colleague of incompetence. On the other hand, a skillful personnel director can humanely intervene in the process, if not to alter the decision, at least to soften the socio-psychological blows.

During the recent recession, most executives and others who were laid off — fired for one reason or another — weathered the turmoil of an unhappy situation in apparently good shape. But who knows how many individuals

Source: Reprinted, by permission of the publisher, from Personnel, *May–June 1976 © 1976 American Management Association, New York. All rights reserved.*

were able to keep families together, found themselves socially disenfranchised, and all too often suffered total mental and/or physical collapse?

In primitive organizations such mental and physical upset or disintegration usually has been regarded as magically or mysteriously inspired; in complex organizations, it is usually accepted as accidental or unavoidable. In fact, the phenomenon — regardless of organization level — is neither magical and mysterious nor accidental and inevitable.

Anthropologist Barbara W. Lex's recent examination of the phenomenon of voodoo death in primitive societies stimulates the question: Do organizations in our modern society, wittingly or unwittingly, utilize a process that results, for selected members of the organized, in actual physical illness or even death not unlike the process of voodoo death?

Voodoo death is a neuro-physiological process resulting in the stimulation of competing nervous systems of the human organism beyond the threshold levels tolerable to the organism. At that stage the normal neurological and physiological responses become interactive and uncontrollable. The result is neurological and physical collapse and, at the extreme, voodoo death.

"Thus," says Lex, "the mysterious, arcane nature of voodoo death is supplanted by a physiologically based interpretation. . . . The extreme fright experienced by the individual who has been thus singled out can be as fatal as a dose of poison."

Basic to understanding the voodoo death phenomenon, says Lex, is a knowledge of the autonomic nervous system and its property of mutual antagonism and reciprocal activation of its subsystems: the sympathetic and parasympathetic. Up to certain thresholds, activation of one of these subsystems is accompanied by a simultaneous inhibition of the other. Beyond these thresholds, however, continued stimulation results in sensitization or "tuning." This tuning may be accompanied by continued stimulation of either of the subsystems.

It thus appears that the supernatural is both natural and explainable. The supernatural is an event or situation that can be effected and manipulated intentionally or unintentionally. It can occur in a primitive society, as usually described, or in a modern society, where it often goes unnoticed.

In both modern and primitive societies, an actual death or affliction may be the direct result of the voodoo process described, or of an "accident" to the victim, who has been so disabled physically and psychologically that he or she cannot cope with the normal perils of everyday life. In a primitive society, for example, the hapless individual may be slain by a predatory animal under circumstances in which a normally functioning person would survive; in a modern society, the disoriented victim may be killed while crossing a street — also a situation in which a normally functioning individual may easily escape harm.

The case examples cited below illustrate pathological effects of the voodoo process in both primitive and modern situations. The examples of the voodoo "curse" in primitive societies are taken from summaries of occurrences analyzed and reported in anthropological research. The examples illustrating the voodoo effect in modern society are accounts of situations that occurred in two corporate organizations, which, of course, cannot be identified.

CASE 1:   AGE VERSUS YOUTH

The plight of an aging shaman, who was experiencing no success in effecting cures among his villagers, is described by anthropologist Claude Levi-Strauss in *Structural Anthropology* (Basic Books, Inc., 1963). The shaman's people were losing faith in him, and he had lost confidence in himself. In a desperate bid for help, he invited a neighboring shaman, a younger man, to visit his village and help him regain his power.

The neighboring shaman arrived and accomplished a few cures. But instead of helping the old man, it only further demeaned him in his own eyes and the eyes of his people. The old shaman pleaded with the young man to tell him the secret of his power, but the visiting shaman refused. Even an appeal from the old man's daughter failed to win help for her father.

The heartsick old man and his family suddenly disappeared from the village. A year later they returned, but both the former shaman and his daughter had gone mad. Three years later he died.

CASE 2:   DEATH BY SORCERY

Among people who believe in magical influences over life and death, the powers attributed to sorcery are strong. The fate of Isoke, accused of theft and arson in a remote African village, illustrates this phenomenon.

The story, as recounted by anthropologist John Beattie *(Bunyoro, An African Kingdom*, Holt, Rinehart & Winston, 1960), tells how Yowana, a neighbor of Isoke, was victimized by a thief who stole a piece of wood that he had intended to use to make a door for his home. Yowana accused Isoke and recovered the missing wood from Isoke's home. The authorities, however, dismissed Yowana's charges against Isoke because he lacked witnesses.

Several days later, Yowana's house was destroyed in a fire. Yowana again suspected Isoke, but knowing he could not prove these charges either, he sought his own revenge. The harassed Yowana purchased from a "vendor of powerful medicines" a substance that, if smeared on the still-standing posts of his burned house, "would cause the incendiarist to suffer from dysentery and burning pains in his chest." Yowana applied the "medicine" as directed, and four days later Isoke became ill. The stricken man's brothers consulted local diviners who told them that Yowana's medicine had caused the illness.

At that point a fearful Isoke confessed. He told Yowana that it was he who had stolen the wood and set Yowana's house afire, and he promised to make restitution. Satisfied with his revenge and the promise of payment for his losses, Yowana agreed to obtain the antidote from the medicine man who had sold him the original substance. But efforts to cure Isoke failed, and he died.

Protectorate police arrested Yowana on suspicion of murder, but released him after an autopsy showed no signs of poisoning. Nevertheless, explains Beattie's report, "nobody doubted that Yowana had killed Isoke by sorcery, least of all Yowana, who was heard to boast of his prowess at beer parties."

CASE 3: MANAGEMENT'S FATAL FUMBLE

Top management in a consulting firm perceived that one division was not producing as well as expected. Thus, when the retirement of the division director provided an opportunity to make changes, the opening was filled by an outsider who received both a mandate and the authority to hire, fire, and demote where necessary.

Although many of the targeted "undesirables" had tenure and could not easily be fired, the new director moved effectively. Some adapted to the changes and brought their performance up to expectations; some moved to new positions in the firm; others resigned or retired. In one case, however, the new division chief proceeded clumsily and was maneuvered by the organization into producing a voodoo death.

The victim was Mr. X, a well-regarded and prestigious representative of the company in the area of the state where he serviced clients. However, he did not adapt easily to the company's new objectives. The firm, a consulting organization, was trying to expand from a statewide area of operations to a position of national reputation and clientele. But when the division director urged him to utilize his skills in accordance with the new national goals, he continued to concentrate on local problems, an area where he had built his status and reputation. Thus, he became a symbol of resistance to the "new movement."

The division chief began to apply direct pressure. Raises were small and evaluations explicit as to his deficiencies. Secretarial help became very difficult for Mr. X to obtain. Local clientele, normally channeled to him, were directed elsewhere. Under this pressure, Mr. X finally began to exhibit all the symptoms of phase two tuning—where activation of the autonomic nervous system blocks analytical judgment processes.

One day a top management executive pointed out that the title held by Mr. X was not commensurate with the duties he was then performing. The executive said that a newsletter prepared by Mr. X for company clients under his name and title would no longer be tolerated and that his title should be changed. The division chief swiftly abolished the publication, but delayed on the title change. After further conferences with the top administration, however, the division chief saw that he was expected to strip Mr. X of his title—and fast. So he called him in and told him what he planned to do.

Mr. X responded irrationally, publicly threatening legal and union action that he could not win. Nonetheless, the division director now felt threatened because, although he was not committed to the title change, he perceived that the whole organization was watching to see who would win the confrontation. So if he was to accomplish anything, he had to prevail, and Mr. X's title was officially changed.

One week later Mr. X fell ill. While that physiological condition was being treated, other complications arose. Within four months he was dead.

Four years later, the organization no longer needed the division chief, and his resignation was accepted without regret. But the company had won its national reputation.

CASE 4: JEALOUSY

A large advertising agency assigned Mrs. Y, a woman in her forties with a reputation for willingness to try new approaches, to head one of its national divisions. During her first three years with the agency, Mrs. Y moved her female-dominated department (it dealt with jewelry, cosmetics, and other women-oriented products) ahead quickly. But then, consistent with her readiness to try new ideas, she asked Dr. Z, a young Ph.D. in sociology, to work with her on the development of new approaches to products and their consumers.

For a time things continued to move along smoothly. Dr. Z did well and was developing national attention. But some of the women in the department were disturbed about the attention attracted by young Dr. Z and the help he received from Mrs. Y. Finally, a small group of these employees protested to a vice-president of the agency and demanded that Dr. Z be fired.

Fearful that company harmony was threatened, the vice-president called in Mrs. Y. "Dr. Z must go," he said. "All you have to do is step aside. I'll fire him." Mrs. Y refused, praising the quality of Dr. Z's work, and the next day she and Dr. Z conferred with the vice-president on the problem. It was agreed that Dr. Z would continue in his job, but the vice-president said that careful evaluations of his work would be required.

Six months later, without further discussions with Dr. Z or Mrs. Y, the vice-president sent Dr. Z a letter informing him that his services would be terminated within six months and that he would be transferred immediately to another city and another project under Mrs. Y's direction. The vice-president stated that he had "reviewed the decision and found no reason to alter it."

Within a week Dr. Z showed signs of phase-two tuning (psychosomatic disorders and psychosis). His respiration was restricted, he alternated between constipation and diarrhea, he sweated profusely at night, and he could hardly get out of bed because of constant fatigue. The symptoms continued for the entire six months of his termination period; his only relief came during short periods when Mrs. Y was able to encourage him about his work and ability to secure another job.

After Dr. Z left the firm, Mrs. Y was relieved of her administrative responsibilities, but continued to work with the firm at a good salary. She handled important accounts independent of the new department head, but began looking for another job. Dr. Z found a position at a much lower salary and began to struggle to regain his former status and salary with his new company. Without question, Dr. Z had experienced the equivalent of a voodoo curse, phase tuning, and critical health problems. Luckily, he escaped a possible voodoo death.

As illustrated in the examples reviewed above, the specifics may differ, but the phenomenon of voodoo affliction exists in both modern and primitive societies. Certain conditions not uncommon in today's complex organizations are likely to, and often do, produce illnesses and even individual demise. The ultimate destruction of Mr. X, the demoted consultant, and the unnerving pressures inflicted upon Dr. Z and Mrs. Y resulted from forces akin to those that accomplished the destruction of the old shaman and Isoke. Without questioning whether or not demotion of Consultant X or firing of Dr. Z were necessary or correct, one can easily question the methods of accomplishing ends that caused such neuro-physiological reactions.

Today's complex organizations are subject to numerous internal and external pressures that for better or worse affect changes in organizational structure and operations. These changes frequently result in, or impose the threat of, loss of status and economic rewards for some individuals. The more such individuals look to the organization for social status and economic support, the more susceptible they are to the complex organization's version of the voodoo death.

Some organizations and their administrators pursue change with relentless disregard of its effect on individual employees. However, when armed with the knowledge that change can be a curative tool or a curse upon the individual in the organization, the humanistic change-agent administrator can move toward the necessary changes while taking proper action to avoid producing the process and attendant consequences of voodoo death.

Given that organizations can benefit from change, but that some individuals may simultaneously suffer as a result of it, the administrator should recognize that:

1. Different organizations exist within a given category or within organizations.

2. The goals and reward systems of these organizations should, and do, differ.

3. Such differences are good and should be encouraged, and no one organization is completely "right" in terms of its goals and rewards.

On the basis of these understandings and the possibility of voodoo effects, the change-agent administrator should help subordinates reach an understanding of the same tenets. When personnel action is called for as a result of an approaching organizational change, the organization's change agents should:

- Identify those whose skills and/or organizational behaviors are not commensurate with the organization's new goals.
- Confer with these persons, making explicit both the organizational goals and the reasons why the individuals are no longer needed. (With a little effort, the organization may find that the individual has skills that, while unused or required infrequently in the present job, can be utilized well under the new setup.)
- Provide in-service training opportunities where possible.
- Provide some form of systematic re-evaluation and guidance (including professional help when needed). Try to help the individual see his or her own worth in terms of the multi-organizational system.

The goal of this procedure is to reach a mutual decision regarding the fate of the individual in the organization. If it is determined that such individuals must leave, the organization should:

- Help the person perceive the problem as not one of "poor" skills failing to meet the organization's needs and goals, but rather as a condition of poor fit between individual skills and the employer's needs.
- Do as much as possible to help the individual find another job with another organization. This means offering assistance in understanding and identifying specific skills, help in identifying organizations seeking such skills, and working with the individual to secure available opportunities—that is, land the job and make the move.

QUESTIONS

1. In your own words, discuss the voodoo killer phenomenon.

_____

_____

_____

2. Have you ever personally witnessed or experienced the voodoo killer phenomenon?

_____

_____

_____

3. What should managers do to prevent the voodoo killer phenomenon?

_____

_____

_____

Is This Trip Necessary?
The Heavy Human Costs
of Moving Executives Around

In the late 1960's, I wrote a book called *Men in Groups* that sought to describe how and why males controlled the powerful organizations in all human societies, and what consequences this had for themselves, for their wives and children, and for the communities themselves. Even though I began working on it long before the present controversy about male dominance surfaced, the book's entry into the world coincided with the beginnings of the female liberation movement, and it was a very controversial book indeed. I reaped a lot of letters. One in particular struck me as an extraordinarily powerful statement of the condition I would like to explore in this article.

The writer of the letter had been married for twenty-five years to an executive of a large U.S.-based chemical company. She said that she agreed with my description of how things were. However, she wanted to tell me that in the twenty-five years of her marriage she had moved seventeen times with her husband and family. Each time she moved, she said, her husband was able to work with colleagues whom he had met before, at least through correspondence or over the telephone. But she had to construct, each time, a new life and a new personal community for herself and her children. Then she made this remarkably chilling statement: "Only my husband knows and cares about my past and future."

There occurred to me the image of her husband's brain as the museum of her existence. Only her husband knew what she was like when she was newly married and how she responded to her first child. Only her husband cared about her middle age and her concern about her body. Only her husband would have a perspective within which she could expect to live with some sense of continuity. And when he died, as he would some seven or eight years before her (if the statistics applied to this couple), she would become a peculiar kind of psychologically homeless person.

Even Gypsies move in groups. The nomads of the African drought region, facing starvation, still travel in groups, with friends, with relatives, with persons who are part of the web of their lives. When ours was a new and poor continent, it is true, people homesteaded, moved as single families; many lived at a great distance from their neighbors. But the

Source: Lionel Tiger, "Is This Trip Necessary? The Heavy Human Costs of Moving Executives Around," Fortune 90, no. 3 (September 1974): 139–41, 182. Copyright © 1974 by Lionel Tiger. Reprinted by permission of International Creative Management.

wagon trains of the settlers provided a gregarious context, a community within which the complicated business of moving one's body, one's mind, one's symbols, and one's possessions could proceed.

In the rich society we boast of, however, such a commodity of friendship and familiarity may not be available to the manager of a powerful chemical company, nor to thousands upon thousands of men and women who each year are moved around, pulled around, pushed around—choose your own term. What happens to the wives and children (or, increasingly perhaps, husbands and children) of the employees who receive marching orders, however elegantly they are framed and however persuasively they are issued? And what kinds of businessmen and citizens do the managers become who live in symbolic mobile homes?

DISENCHANTING THE CHILDREN

I would like to suggest that an important consequence of the corporate commitment to moving managers around is that their wives and children are deprived of the fundamental human requirement of social continuity and personal stability; that the managers are debarred from becoming effective members of the communities in which they find themselves; and that by forcing people to adapt to the company's scheme, rather than adapting the company to the people who work in it, American business is disenchanting the sons and daughters of its own executives, and in some degree impairing the potential effectiveness of the executives themselves. Now let me examine these contentions.

Some time ago I participated in a course for up-and-coming middle managers, given at Rutgers University, where I work. During one session I raised the matter of executive mobility, and the room exploded with emotions, anecdotes, and a large amount of baffled bitterness. One man said he had made major moves every eighteen to twenty-four months. That was the only way he could be promoted, he added, because that was how his company organized itself. Another said that if he had been unwilling to move as requested, his income would be substantially lower than it was. A woman said she expected difficulty in her company because if she and her husband could not receive good transfers together, her promising career might be hindered.

Especially memorable were the words of a man who said that he had been offered a considerable improvement in his job, but that when he presented the possibility to his family, his two oldest children refused to go. The girl was seventeen and had been in no less than eleven schools; the boy was fifteen and had been in eight different schools. They had had enough, or too much. Their father pointed out to them what they could be losing should he reject the offer. But the increased income they might share and the greater sense of power and accomplishment their father might enjoy interested them not at all. That particular family stayed put.

The discussion continued in a similar vein. None of the companies involved was a bush-league operation. Each was a leader in its field; each routinely bought full-page ads to describe its commitment to the communities it served. However, their own highly valued employees, and the families of those employees, were forced to endure on a regular basis a migration uprooting them as formidably as if there had been a natural catastrophe in their towns. These most elegant and rewarded of migrants could see their lives only in terms of a procession of more or less identical suburbs designed for interchangeable people.

The loss of social continuity involves serious costs. Human beings have a great need for intimate and regular social experience. The prototypical relationship is that of child with its parents—we are creatures who require a long period of close contact and dependency between parents and children. In social terms, children are very tender creatures; the shy child hiding behind its parent as a stranger approaches is reflecting a deeply conservative conception of what the social world is like and how unpredictable it can be.

HAVE THE TUMULTS BEEN FORGOTTEN?

While it is obviously important for children to encounter new experiences and come to know a variety of people, it is also important that there be a set of social certainties and continuities, providing a definite sense of place and identity and a confidence that even if things do change, not everything changes at once. Have the managers of companies promoting their executives from one side of this continent to another forgotten the tumults of their own childhoods, when they moved to a new house or a new town? Are they unaware of the problems of children who must establish themselves in a new school, with new friends, new bullies, new teams, new loyalties, and new challenges? Are the large numbers of affluent dropouts, the children of the most privileged members of the community, rebelling in part against a special form of deprivation—the lack of continuity and stability? Are they reflecting an unwillingness to be exiles in their own country?

While children are undoubtedly the most severely affected persons in this joyless game of musical chairs—sometimes called "executive development"—wives are surely not spared from fundamental disruption. Moreover, they are to a great extent deprived of the possibility of sustained involvement in a rewarding career. Feminist pressures for long-term careers for women have exposed, and will more starkly expose, the disability suffered by talented women whose careers are dependent on their husbands' jobs. On the principle of last hired, first fired, the wife of the mobile executive is always vulnerable to adjustments in the economy. She is very unlikely to be a serious candidate for senior posts, because she will lack seniority and will be unable to provide her employers the continuity they may seek in their higher management.

AN EXPENSIVE PATTERN

There is a vicious circle here. Since husbands by and large earn more money than their wives, job choices are made in terms of male careers; and since wives must move with their husbands, they are unable to become senior enough to earn the high salaries that might alter a male-centered pattern of mobility. The circle is not only vicious, but also expensive, for it condemns thousands of well-educated women to episodic employment rather than serious careers, and must induce them to trivialize their work in their own minds and lose confidence in its economic and social meaning.

This is by no means to be taken as an argument that wives *should* enter the labor force—what I am arguing for is increased freedom and opportunity. Some wives, of course, do not want to enter the labor force. And while the matter is controversial, it is not clear that the absence of working mothers from the home is without costs to the healthy development of preschool children. The lot of the working wife herself, of course, is not always a happy one. While what has been graphically described as "the captive housewife" may suffer social and intellectual deprivation, the wife with both demanding job and demanding young family may experience an overabundance of demands on her energy and time.

Certainly, however, there is now too little opportunity for wives who do want to pursue careers. It is well to see this in perspective. From the time of the hunting-gathering phase of our evolution, through the pastoral and agricultural phases, females were involved in extra-domestic activities of considerable variety and of major significance for the prosperity and well-being of their communities. The idle heroines of John Cheever and J.P. Marquand, with nothing but golf, adultery, couture, and martinis on their minds, are decidedly not the crowning glory of female evolution, but rather a special product of the displacements of the industrial revolution and the very specialized demands of a highly mobile work force.

Another kind of perspective has to do with demographic changes. Toward the end of the last century, a woman might well die by the age of forty-five; her adult life would have been totally involved with sustaining the existence of her children and her husband. But the situation now is radically different. Women marry early, typically at twenty or twenty-one, and they have relatively few children, who in any event are absorbed in school by the time their mothers are in their early or middle thirties. And then a woman has more than half her life to lead even though the challenges of her traditional biological career have been successfully met.

"I'VE BEEN MOVED"

I would not be at all surprised if before long there is growing and effective pressure on companies to assure spouses of reasonable employment when executives are moved—or at least some respectable opportunity to acquire skills, perhaps even in the companies involved. Nor will it be altogether unexpected if women begin to demand some more formal role in decision making about executive mobility, other than to pack their bags and then smile somewhat weakly at yet another Welcome Wagon in yet another town.

Of course, it is not solely executive mobility that causes this waste of women's abilities, and perhaps it is not even the primary factor. Nonetheless, the difficulties women face as they seek productive careers are magnified in a major way by the mobility of their husbands. Even if wives are willing and able to try something more than volunteer work or sporadic employment, both their prospective employers and they themselves have to consider that once they're in position for a major job, it'll be time to call the movers once again.

This situation not only deprives women of opportunities and satisfactions, but also deprives communities of the long-run participation of educated wives of effective husbands. In this and other ways, the practice of moving executives around reduces the useful connection of business groups with the wider society.

About a year ago I was with a realtor showing me some country cottages in the Hudson Valley, north of New York City, in an area where a large I.B.M. facility had been established. In commenting on the pattern of life in the region, he recalled the bitter, oft repeated joke that I.B.M. stands for "I've Been Moved." The company's employees, he said, had little to do with the community except help cause the tax rates to increase. He appeared to perceive the company as a group of foreign creatures living off his territory, interested only in themselves, and lacking serious connection with the place where he lived. While it has become clear to multinational companies that there are great advantages, both political and functional, in having local managers as leading figures in their foreign operations, this principle has scarcely penetrated the domestic operations of U.S. companies whose executives live the mobile life.

Now, it would plainly be absurd to suggest that members of management should work only in the region in which they were born or raised — the North American pattern of education, if nothing else, would make that unlikely. But this is all a matter of degree. It seems very plausible that to the extent they move executives rapidly from place to place, businesses lose the fruits of the individual's ability to form connections and commitments in the community. They also lose what happens when the community has an opportunity to come to know business practice and particular companies through the people who work in them, and not solely through commercial interchange.

Even at the level of local politics, a high-mobility pattern among executives condemns business organizations to try to protect their interests through formal public relations and crude economic clout rather than through sets of personal friendships, allegiances, and understandings, and the involvements of their own employees in the life and politics of the community. I would scarcely wish to suggest that this lack of local and detailed social connection is the principal reason for the decline in the prestige of business as a career and the increase in suspicion of business among both consumers and public officials. Nonetheless, moods and attitudes cannot but be affected by the network of human relationships — or lack of them in this case — that in part determine an organization's stature in its environment.

A SCORCHED-EARTH POLICY

In the very simplest kind of matter, an executive's effort to convince a local planning authority that the plant his company wants to build will have no severe ecological impact will hardly be helped if experience makes it seem reasonably certain that by the time the installation is at work, this particular executive and his family will no longer be around. While perhaps it is unfair, it is not unrealistic for local people to see corporate representatives as practitioners of a scorched-earth policy: get your orders, follow them unswervingly, make your mark, collect your reward money, and let your successor live with the consequences, and the smell. While national citizenship has been accepted as an important factor in securing a reasonable climate for business operations, that is far less so when it comes to local citizenship. The complex and subtle consequences appear to be inadequately understood by proponents of the mobile organizational style.

Now let me turn briefly to what may be the higher inefficiency of that style. Certainly there are losses of various kinds when the executive who has just moved from another community must enter a new work situation with little or no experience of the people involved in it and the human problems it presents. The newcomer has to learn not only a new job but also a new social and physical environment for the job. His peers, superiors, and subordinates must likewise adapt to an unknown, or little-known, set of qualities. While the costs in time and energy of this sociological retooling are difficult to calculate, there is reason on the face of it to think the costs are considerable.

TO IDENTIFY THOSE OF STERNER STUFF

Not that all this is without apparent benefits to the organization. One important benefit is that by demanding frequent moves from young executives, the system extracts them from the social networks they create for themselves, or from their regional affinities, and links them increasingly to their professional roles rather than social preferences. It is part of the folklore of this particular group — though becoming less important as more executives rebel — that unwillingness to move for a company implies a suspicious lack of loyalty to it.

Frequent moves, then, may serve as part of a process of initiation and testing. In this model, an important function of mobility is to identify those who can take it well, those of the sterner stuff of potential higher management. The result of all the moving and shaking, all the posting and reposting, is the selection of the elite. It is almost as if all the moiling motions of the company exist to choose the chief.

An additional advantage for companies with diverse branches and units is that over time mobility of executives provides select employees with a detailed understanding of the diversity of the companies and the special character of each area. There is plainly no substitute, in the development of broad administrative perspectives, for the experience of varied places and social patterns.

VOWS OF PSYCHOLOGICAL SILENCE

Yet the question may be asked: is repeated migration the only way to achieve such a perspective? Is it impossible to develop programs of orientation and expansion-of-perspectives that do not depend on moving the body but can rely instead on the adaptability and receptivity of the human brain?

It is well worthwhile for corporations to seek answers to these questions. For apart from the effects upon wives and children, and upon the image of the corporation, mobility does subtle damage to the executives themselves.

One important consequence of their form of lucrative exile is that it becomes almost necessary to cultivate a "cool" social style. The easy informality and congeniality of American corporate life may reflect an innovative attitude and a democratic ethic, but may also mask a lack of concern with, and even isolation from, strong relationships with colleagues and friends — detachment as a matter of personal psychological survival. When one's social network will be destroyed every few years, there is little gain and considerable cost in trying to establish the complex mixture of trust, commitment, self-exposure, and freedom that is essential to serious friendships.

Almost like monks who are vowed to silence yet live in close contact with each other, mobile executives must in a sense take vows of "psychological silence" and keep their lives, fears, and enthusiasms to themselves. Perhaps only during conventions and office parties and only under the permissive influence of alcohol is the glad-handing impersonality of corporate society broken by the jagged utterances and actions of people with a private story to tell.

As they glide from Darien to Palo Alto and from Grosse Point to Princeton, the managers of business may be helping to establish themselves as a form of quasi-religious priesthood — men who are unconcerned with local political and social affairs but are devoted instead to the larger impersonal forces of the particular system of rules they have allowed to govern their actions. Like monks, they become devout proponents of a higher order of things, a more coercive plan, than concerns other men. And yet, unlike monks, who if they avoid blotting their copybooks are ensured a lifetime (and maybe more) of security and usefulness, executives bear the personal costs with few of the guarantees.

WHAT THEY TAKE FOR GRANTED

This has been an effort to look at one aspect of the tribal behavior of corporate executives, and to suggest some implications. Needless to say, I have drawn a rather angular and severe picture. I have done so in the hope of providing perspectives on a situation that might otherwise be unrecognizable to people who are actively living within it.

A research rule that anthropologists bear in mind when studying a community runs, "The most important thing to know is what they take for granted." Corporate executives take it for granted that to do their work they have to move around a lot. Perhaps they must. But it may be worthwhile for them to ask, "Is this trip necessary?" — to ask what they are leaving and where they are going, and to try to determine why the system moves their bodies instead of enhancing their skills.

QUESTIONS

1. Have you ever experienced or witnessed the stress of relocation? Discuss.

_____

_____

_____

2. If you were the president of a company, what would be your policy regarding moving employees?

_____

_____

_____

CASES

The Price of Success

"Kevin, what has happened to that unswerving drive of yours toward working your way to the top of the company?" asked his boss. "You are almost there. We have offered you a division presidency. Three years of success in that job and we might be able to bring you back to the corporate office as a Senior Vice-President of Marketing. You are big league timber, Kevin. You are destined for greatness in our company.

"Ten years ago you came to us as an eager young business administration major just out of college. What an impression you created! Eager, intelligent, and, even at age 21, with an executive aplomb about you. We grabbed you right away for our executive training program. After two years in the field as a territory salesman, you moved effortlessly into a marketing research assignment. Within one year, you became a senior market analyst. After two years of brilliance in that position, we made you a branch manager. Again, after several years of sterling performance you then became the youngest regional manager in the history of our company. We figure you are now ready for the big jump — a general management assignment where you will be operating a profit center of your own. What more can a young executive want?

"We are sticking our necks out for you. Should you fail as a 31-year-old division president, the company could look foolish. Our offer is real. You can become President of the Cosmetics Division if you will just accept the position. I hear the excuses you are making about not being experienced enough for the job, and that other people in the company are more deserving of the position, but I don't buy them. Something else is holding you back, Kevin. What is it?"

"Fred, you're pushing for a rapid answer to a major life decision. Becoming a company president isn't like buying a cabin cruiser or going on a two-week vacation to Bermuda. It's more like getting married or having triplets. It's one helluva change in your life-style. An impulsive person shouldn't even be in such an assignment."

"Am I really talking to ambitious Kevin Brady, that hard charging, good-looking Irishman who hates to lose at anything? Two years ago, if I asked you to tackle a special assignment in Venezuela, you would have been on your way to the airport before we went over all the details of

Source: Reprinted with permission from Andrew J. DuBrin, "The Price of Success," Casebook of Organizational Behavior (Elmsford, N. Y.: Pergamon Press, Inc., 1977), 58–63. Copyright © 1977, Pergamon Press.

the job. I always had the impression that if you weren't in business you would be an automobile racing driver.

"Could it be that you are acting coy because you want us to up the ante a little? As I said, the job should pay about $42,000 a year in salary plus a healthy executive bonus, depending upon the profit of your division. In a boom year you could increase your salary by one third with your bonus. Besides that, being a division president would give you a fast track to perhaps a bigger division presidency or the Senior Vice-President of Marketing slot. It is conceivable that you could be set for life financially if you accept this assignment now."

"Fred, believe me. I'm not being an ingrate. I haven't turned down this magnificent offer. Yes, the challenge of a division presidency excites me. I believe in the product line of that division. For instance, my 14-year-old niece used that facial blemish cream and it really works. The improvement in her appearance actually raised her level of self-confidence. We are marketing something solid. Our cosmetic line does contribute something aesthetic to society in its own way. I think our company performs a lot of social good, considering its record on environmental safety and equal employment opportunity.

"Yet a man contemplating becoming a president has to carefully evaluate what becoming a president will do to his life-style. In other words, what am I really letting myself in for?"

"Kevin, you're speaking in generalities. Let's get down to the specifics of what's really holding you back from jumping at this once-in-a-lifetime opportunity. Be candid with me. I'm both your boss and your friend."

"A good way to begin, Fred, is to tell you about a recent experience my wife and I had at the Sales Executive Club. An industrial psychologist was giving a talk about the problems created by successful husbands. He wasn't putting down success, and he wasn't putting down husbands. What he seemed to be saying was that being a successful career person can create a lot of problems in your personal life, particularly with your wife and children. When he finished his talk there was tension in the air. Husbands were grinning sheepishly at their wives. Most wives had a surprised expression as if this man was revealing their personal case history. One skeptic said the psychologist was way off base, that he was dramatizing a few isolated case histories of obsessed executives and their neurotic wives. That was hardly the reaction my wife or I had to the theme of the talk.

"As an aftermath to the talk, my wife and I began some serious dialogue about our relationship. She has some real concerns that if I become any more successful as an executive I might become a flop as a husband. A woman quoted at the talk said something that really hit home with my wife. Something to the effect, 'I think the husbands with the least success in their careers make the best husbands, because their wives and families are all they have.'

"Noreen thinks that I have paid progressively less attention to her as I have advanced in my career. She told me that I'm so preoccupied with business problems that I only pay surface attention to her problems. One night she told me that her gynecologist said she would need a hysterectomy. I expressed my sympathy. She retorted that this was the second time she told me about the pending hysterectomy.

"That conversation served as a springboard for an examination of many other things about our family life. Out of nowhere, she asked me to name the teachers of our three children. I struck a blank on all three. She then asked me what grade our daughter Tricia was enrolled in. I told her I thought the third grade. I was off by one grade, which she used as evidence that I'm not really participating in our children's worlds.

"Worse than that, Noreen then pointed out that I have been out of town on her last three birthdays. I feebly pointed out to her that her birthday just happens to take place during the time of our annual sales convention. My opinion is that a good many husbands who are going nowhere in their careers — even a few unemployed husbands — forget their wives' birthdays. We can't attribute all of my shortcomings to my business success. But it did make me wonder if a company president can ever remember his wife's birthday, or maybe even his own."

"Okay, Kevin, you have the standard problems at home that an executive can anticipate. Just pay a little more attention to your wife and things will straighten out on that front."

"Fred, the problem of success interfering with my personal life goes beyond my relationship with my wife. I'm also worried about my physical health. I'm not a candidate for an ulcer or a heart attack, but the attention I have been paying to my career lately has taken its toll on my physical condition. I've gained a lot of weight owing to the amount of time I spend in bars and restaurants with customers and colleagues. Those hefty business lunches add more calories than most people realize. Not only am I gaining weight, but I don't look as sharp as I did when I devoted less time to the job.

"Part of the problem, of course, is that you have less time to exercise when you're immersing yourself in your job. When I am home on weekends, I have so much catching up to do on household tasks that I get less physical exercise. I wouldn't worry so much about having gained a few pounds and looking a little pale, if I didn't see a steady deterioration of my golf game. A few years ago, I heard a statement about golf and business that passed by me at the time, but now it makes a good deal of sense. According to the fellow making this statement, if your golf score gets under 75, you have no business.

"Now I know what that character was talking about. As my income and level of responsibility have increased, so has my golf score. When I do play, I'm more erratic. My putting is ragged, I slice more than ever, and I've added about 10 points to my average score. I used to pride myself on my golf. Now I'm just a duffer who plays recreational golf. To get my game back in shape, I'll either have to sacrifice my job or my family. I know that the stereotype of a golfer as an affluent executive fits the stereotype of a duffer. My career is very important to me, but so is my golf game. It would seem unfeeling on my part to chip away at my time with my family in order to bring my game back to snuff."

"Of course, Kevin, if you don't keep raising your income you soon will not be able to afford golf. A person needs a lot of money to keep a golf game going, perhaps a few thousand a year, depending upon the particular club. If we give you a job as a clerk, your game might return to its former level, but you would have to play in public parks. You'd spend so much time waiting to tee off, golf would then interfere with your personal life."

"Fred, I'm glad you brought up the topic of money. So far, the ever-increasing amount of money I've earned hasn't had an overwhelming impact on my standard of living. In the 10 years I've been working for the company my income has tripled, but my standard of living has hardly tripled. My cost of living creeps up every year, and I need that big 10 to 15 percent salary increase just to stay even. Taxes go up at a much steeper rate than your income does.

"At times I find it both disturbing and embarrassing when I realize how little real financial security my ever-increasing income has brought me. People think that as a regional manager for a large corporation, I have no financial worries. My in-laws think I'm stashing away about $1000 per month for the kids' college and our retirement. The truth is that except for programmed saving like the company retirement system and a mutual fund plan I'm enrolled in, many months go by without my saving any cash.

"What eats away at my insides the most is that some people grossing half as much money as I do seem to live about the same. Maybe they drive an inexpensive car instead of an expensive car, but their vehicle still performs the same function. Noreen, the children, and I took a week's vacation to the Poconos last fall. We met loads of people there, such as foremen and school teachers, who make less than half my income and they had more dough to spend at the nightclub than I did. I'm beginning to wonder if the financial rewards associated with moving up in the executive ranks are real or illusory. Most of the bankruptcies I read about involve executives. Maybe there is something wrong with our system that subtly pushes up your expenses to meet your income."

"Kevin, maybe you're just having a bad day. Most of the problems you allude to are not as serious as you make them out to be. Perhaps you're over-reacting."

"I don't entirely discount that possibility, Fred, but before I take the big plunge to a presidency, there are certain things that would have to be ironed out in advance. Most important of all, what would be expected of a division president in this company? Who takes priority in my life, my company or my family? Do I get paid the same if I work 70 or 40 hours per week? What certainty do I have of that executive bonus? And how much of it will you guarantee?"

"Kevin, get hold of yourself. To succeed at the top you have to love every minute of the job. Digging in to the corporate problems should be your biggest source of kicks in life. All the concerns about the job and the little inconveniences at home are not the central issue. They are simply part of the 'price of success'."

QUESTIONS

1. If you were Fred, how would you handle Kevin's reluctance to accept a division presidency?

_____

_____

_____

2. If you were Kevin, what would you do?

_____

_____

_____

3. What guarantees about income and working conditions do you think a company should give to upper-level managers?

_____

_____

_____

How Do You Handle a Stress Carrier?

Introduction:

You are the supervisor of Mark Lewis, a mid-level manager, and Marilyn Brownlee, your administrative assistant.

Situation:

You have just visited a staff meeting conducted by Mark, during which you saw him raise important points, as well as the stress levels of a number of people in the room. The meeting was to be a freewheeling problem-solving discussion with these people reporting to him. The problem concerned how to get a 10 percent increase in production.

As usual, Mark spoke in short, staccato bursts. His agile, inquisitive mind was working well; his suggestions were concise and his verbal delivery machine-gun quick, with ends of sentences clipped and bitten off. Someone raised a question and was brushed off with impatience and a "Yes, yes, let's get on with it." Mark felt things were going too slowly and said so in no uncertain terms. His subordinates "got with it" and "accepted" Mark's "solution" without much enthusiasm or commitment. At least the meeting was over.

Mark prides himself on his ability to think quickly, get things done, and prod others into similar performance. He views his stressful pace as the price of climbing the corporate ladder, and voices the view "If you can't take the heat, you should stay out of the kitchen!"

Marilyn Brownlee is a woman on the way up. She has impressed you with her clearheadedness and effective performance under fire. Her insights are usually good. An opening has come available that Marilyn wants and for which she is qualified. The job promotion will broaden her responsibilities considerably. She is under serious consideration, but you also have serious doubts. Marilyn seems to have little patience for things or people she considers trivial or off the mark. In meetings with co-workers, she often interrupts them and is unwilling to concede a point, and she makes it clear that she has little time for life's irrelevancies. You know

Source: Adapted from the work of Frances Meritt Stern, Director, Institute for Behavioral Awareness, Springfield, N.J. Reprinted with permission.

that she has admirably high standards, but you are also aware of the tension she generates among others (also effective employees) by her lack of regard for anyone who does not meet those standards.

QUESTIONS

1. What, if anything, would you do about Mark?

   _____

   _____

   _____

2. What, if anything, would you do about Marilyn?

   _____

   _____

   _____

3. In general, how would you handle a "stress carrier"?

   _____

   _____

   _____

Baton Rouge
Is a Long Way from Home

As an electrical design engineer with Surety Electronics, I'm faced with making at least one important decision every day at work. Each decision is unique, but all follow the same format. I do what I can to clearly identify the problem in my mind, search for innovative ways to solve the problem, mull over each one of these alternatives carefully, and make a choice. Within three months I'm able to discover if I made a good or bad decision from a technical and/or business standpoint. Recently, I faced a decision relating to my work that at the time appeared much more complex than an engineering design problem. My family and my future would be touched by the outcome of this decision.

One Monday night a few months ago, I was sitting at home relaxing and watching television. The children had been tucked into bed, the bills had been paid, and no emergency repairs were necessary around the house. In fact, things seemed unusually tranquil. Suddenly, the phone rang. Terry, an old college and fraternity friend I hadn't seen or heard from in about four years, was calling from Baton Rouge, Louisiana. For the first five minutes we exchanged the usual social amenities; he asked how I was doing and I asked how he was doing. Finally, Terry got to the point of why he had phoned. He wanted to know if I might be interested in a job with his employer, Baton Rouge Enterprises, Inc.

My first reaction was that he was joking. As the conversation continued, I began to take him seriously. Terry's company needed an electrical engineer to design and develop some automated machinery to manufacture the line of home power tools they wanted to sell. The type of work was identical in many ways to the work I was presently doing and which I found satisfying. Baton Rouge Enterprises was a small company, but their line of home power tools was selling well beyond expectations. According to their analysis, the only way they could keep pace with customer demand was to install automated, faster machinery to produce the product line. Up to this point, they had no electrical engineers on the staff; they were looking for one, and I was their first candidate. For many years, I had wondered what it would be like to be the "resident electrical

Source: Reprinted with permission from Andrew J. DuBrin, "Baton Rouge Is a Long Way from Home," Casebook of Organizational Behavior. Copyright © 1977, Pergamon Press. (Note: Ronald A. Luchetti researched and wrote this case, with the exception of a few editorial changes.)

engineer" in a small, promising company. From what I had heard, that kind of situation often leads the way to a vice presidency.

Despite the appeal of the position, I told Terry I couldn't take the job because I liked my present one so well. Also, it would affect my family if we just picked up and moved to Louisiana. We would be farther from our families than we were in our present location of Indianapolis. Terry insisted that I at least consider the job. Partly out of curiosity and partly out of courtesy, I said I would give the proposition some thought and would get back to him with my requirements for salary, vacation, relocation expenses, and job security. There I was, faced with a more complex problem than almost any problem I faced at work.

My wife, Loretta, and I discussed the offer that seemed like a golden opportunity. She told me to do what I wanted, but I knew that deep down inside she was reluctant to move farther away from her parents. She finally admitted this feeling, but still insisted that I should do what I felt was best in the long run for my career and for the family. I thought about my present position with Surety Electronics and how happy I was. Here I was an electrical design engineer, doing exactly what I wanted to do.

Out of college for only four years, I had almost doubled my starting salary. I was now eligible for three weeks' annual vacation. Overtime pay was becoming quite regular. From what I could determine, the benefits package at Surety was unsurpassed in the industry. Aside from the standard benefits, I received a substantial yearly bonus. Adding up all these items amounted to almost $25,000 per year, $17,500 of which was salary.

To add to the dilemma of making the right decision, I made a good initial effort in my pursuit of an MBA at a satellite location of Purdue University. The company footed the bill for this program. My work assignments were very challenging. I loved my job and the people I worked with. My job assignments gave me ample opportunity for travel, a rarity for an engineer.

My future with my present company looked very promising. Despite all these pluses there wasn't much chance of promotion to a managerial position, though the pay was substantial and my job security was solid. The logical next step was to see what Baton Rouge Enterprises had to offer. In the back of my mind, I felt that they would reject what I would require to leave my present job. I asked for a starting salary of $22,000, three weeks' vacation, benefits commensurate with my present benefit package, relocation expenses, and a promise of a managerial position as soon as I automated their systems. I figured it would take two years to complete the automation project.

To top off my list of demands, I asked the company to take care of selling my home and finding my family a comparable one in Louisiana. It might have looked as though I were making unreasonable demands, but I was confident that my talents and experience were deserving of an unusual opportunity. I felt that a person could ask for much more in the way of a compensation package if he is asked to relocate. If Baton Rouge

Enterprises wanted me badly enough to grant all my demands, I would accept the job offer.

After reaching this tentative decision, I began to ruminate over what would happen if I left my present job, accepted the new position with Baton Rouge, and it fell through shortly after my family and I had relocated to Louisiana. My guess was that I had about a 95 percent chance of being rehired by Surety Electronics without losing anything if I came back within a year. After a year back on the job, I would regain all my seniority, vacation, bonus, and retirement benefits. Should I return *after* one year, it would be tantamount to starting as a new employee with them.

Aside from what the company policy states about rehiring people, I had to consider what the management attitude would be toward me. It would probably affect my chances for promotion adversely. Very probably, I would be considered disloyal or ungrateful.

While I waited for a reply from Baton Rouge Enterprises, I had some research conducted into the past performance of the company and its future prospects. A lawyer friend of mine with a good background in analyzing the financial situation of companies did the investigation for me. His conclusion was that the future of the company appeared uncertain. He reasoned that the company would be successful or fold within two years because it only had one product line. I assume that every fledgling company gets a similar rating from lawyers or accountants, but I had faith in this man's judgment.

To my surprise, I received an enthusiastic reply from Baton Rouge Enterprises. They were willing to guarantee me everything I requested and urged me to visit them at their expense. My wife and I took a long weekend vacation to visit the company and the city. We both liked what we saw. To make my decision even tougher, they told me they thought I could complete the automated system within two years and after that I would become an executive in the company.

The topic of relocation dominated our thoughts for an entire week. It did seem like a unique opportunity, even better than that described in the initial phone conversation with Terry. When it looked as if I was turning in the direction of accepting the position, my wife again told me she felt uneasy about relocating to Louisiana because it would substantially increase the geographic distance between us and her parents. Living in Indianapolis, we could reach her parents in three hours by automobile.

Another letter and another phone call were forthcoming from Baton Rouge Enterprises. Although they told me to take all the time I needed to make my decision, they were pressing me. Financially, the situation looked incredibly good, provided that it all worked out well once I arrived down there. If within a year I decided to return to my old job—and it was available—nothing would be lost (to the best of my knowledge). But the anguish of moving twice within a one year period might be more than my family and I could bear.

Should I accept the position, stay more than a year, and then find that the position wasn't going to work out for the long range, I would have ruined my future with Surety. Assuming the new company fell through after two years, I would be out of a job, my children would be of school age, and the job market for engineers could conceivably be quite limited. A move at that point in life would be much more difficult than at present. Should the new job fall through in a few years from now, my wife would probably want to relocate to the area where her parents live. Job opportunities for electrical engineers have never been good in Loretta's hometown.

After two more weeks of tossing the subject around with my wife and two trusted friends, I made my decision. I turned down the offer at Baton Rouge Enterprises. As I look back upon it, I guess I turned down the decision because of the risk involved and for family reasons. My wife would probably be unhappy about living so far from her parents, but then maybe she would grow more as a person if she were less dependent upon her parents. My future with Surety still looks promising, but I still cannot help wondering if I made the right decision.

QUESTIONS

1. Based on the information presented in this case, should the engineer have accepted the job offer? Discuss.

   _____

   _____

   _____

2. How much concern do you think the engineer should have given to his wife's reluctance to move so far from her parents?

   _____

   _____

   _____

3. What is your attitude about moving for job advancement?

   _____

   _____

   _____

APPLICATIONS

Health Behavior
Assessment Scale

Do you practice health promotion behaviors? The U.S. Department of Health and Human Services has developed a health behavior assessment scale to help you answer this question.

The scale has six sections: smoking, alcohol and drugs, nutrition, exercise and fitness, stress control, and safety. Complete one section at a time by circling the number corresponding to the answer that best describes your behavior. Then add the numbers you have circled to determine your score for that section. Write the score on the line provided at the end of each section. The highest score for each section is 10.

Cigarette Smoking

	Almost Always	Sometimes	Almost Never

If you never smoke, enter a score of 10 for this section and go to the next section on Alcohol and Drugs.

	Almost Always	Sometimes	Almost Never
1. I avoid smoking cigarettes.	2	1	0
2. I smoke only low tar and nicotine cigarettes *or* I smoke a pipe or cigars.	2	1	0

Smoking Score: _____

Alcohol and Drugs

	Almost Always	Sometimes	Almost Never
1. I avoid drinking alcoholic beverages *or* I drink no more than 1 or 2 drinks a day.	4	1	0
2. I avoid using alcohol or other drugs (especially illegal drugs) as a way of handling stressful situations or the problems in my life.	2	1	0
3. I am careful not to drink alcohol when taking certain medicines (for example, medicine for sleeping, pain, colds, and allergies), or when pregnant.	2	1	0
4. I read and follow the label directions when using prescribed and over-the-counter drugs.	2	1	0

Alcohol and Drugs Score: _____

Source: U.S. Department of Health and Human Services, Health Style: A Self Test *(Washington, D.C.: Public Health Service, 1981).*

Eating Habits

	Almost Always	Sometimes	Almost Never
1. I eat a variety of foods each day, such as fruits and vegetables, whole grain breads and cereals, lean meats, dairy products, dry peas and beans, and nuts and seeds.	4	1	0
2. I limit the amount of fat, saturated fat, and cholesterol I eat (including fat on meats, eggs, butter, cream, shortenings, and organ meats such as liver).	2	1	0
3. I limit the amount of salt I eat by cooking with only small amounts, not adding salt at the table, and avoiding salty snacks.	2	1	0
4. I avoid eating too much sugar (especially frequent snacks of sticky candy or soft drinks).	2	1	0

Eating Habits Score: _____

Exercise/Fitness

	Almost Always	Sometimes	Almost Never
1. I maintain a desired weight, avoiding overweight and underweight.	3	1	0
2. I do vigorous exercises for 15–30 minutes at least 3 times a week (examples include running, swimming, brisk walking).	3	1	0
3. I do exercises that enhance my muscle tone for 15–30 minutes at least 3 times a week (examples include yoga and calisthenics).	2	1	0
4. I use part of my leisure time participating in individual, family, or team activities that increase my level of fitness (such as gardening, bowling, golf, and baseball).	2	1	0

Exercise/Fitness Score: _____

Stress Control

	Almost Always	Sometimes	Almost Never
1. I have a job or do other work that I enjoy.	2	1	0
2. I find it easy to relax and express my feelings freely.	2	1	0
3. I recognize early, and prepare for, events or situations likely to be stressful for me.	2	1	0
4. I have close friends, relatives, or others whom I can talk to about personal matters and call on for help when needed.	2	1	0
5. I participate in group activities (such as church and community organizations) or hobbies that I enjoy.	2	1	0

Stress Control Score: _____

Safety

	Almost Always	Sometimes	Almost Never
1. I wear a seat belt while riding in a car.	2	1	0
2. I avoid driving while under the influence of alcohol and other drugs.	2	1	0
3. I obey traffic rules and the speed limit when driving.	2	1	0
4. I am careful when using potentially harmful products or substances (such as household cleaners, poisons, and electrical devices).	2	1	0
5. I avoid smoking in bed.	2	1	0

Safety Score: _____

SCORING

After you have obtained scores for each of the six sections, circle the number in each column below that matches your score for that section of the test.

Remember, there is no total score for this test. Consider each section separately. You are trying to identify aspects of your health behavior that you can improve in order to be healthier and in order to reduce the risk of illness.

INTERPRETATION

The following is a general interpretation of your scores for each of the six sections of the Health Behavior Assessment Scale.

Scores of 9 and 10

These are excellent scores. Your answers show that you are aware of the importance of this area of health. Also, you are putting your knowledge to work by practicing good health habits. As long as you continue to do so, this area should not present a serious health risk.

Scores of 6 to 8

Although your health practices in this area are good, there is room for improvement. Look again at the items you answered with "Sometimes" or "Almost Never." What changes can you make to improve your score? Even a small change can often result in better health.

Scores of 3 to 5

These are low scores. You should seek more information about the risks you are facing and why it is important to change these behaviors.

Scores of 0 to 2

These are very low scores, indicating unnecessary risks with your health. Perhaps you are not aware of the danger and what to do about it. You should seek the information and help you need to improve.

Scientific Relaxation

There is a time to be alert and ready for action. Without such tension we would be unable to meet the challenges of life and work. Also, there is a time for relaxation. Unless we learn to relax, we will experience accelerated wear and tear. In effect, we will be adding unnecessary mileage to our bodies. Hans Selye writes:

> Everybody is familiar with the feeling of being keyed up from nervous tension; this process is comparable to raising the key of a violin by tightening the strings. We say that our muscles limber up during exercise and that we are thrilled by great emotional experiences; all this prepares us for better peak accomplishments. On the other hand, there is the tingling sensation, the jitteriness, when we are keyed up too much. This impairs our work and even prevents us from getting a rest.[1]

The following is an exercise in scientific relaxation. It is based on the work of Edmund Jacobson. In this exercise, you will learn how to reduce muscle tension in your body. You will learn to recognize when you are in a state of tension and when you are in a state of relaxation by tensing and then relaxing various muscle groups throughout the body. In this way, you will become aware of the difference between muscular tension and relaxation. Also, as each muscle group is tensed and then relaxed, it will become more relaxed than it was before.

When the exercise is completed, you will be in a state of total relaxation. The procedure for each muscle group is first, to tighten the muscle and focus on the tense feeling in the muscle (about 5 to 10 seconds); then, to release all tension from the muscle, concentrating on the relaxed feeling in the muscle (about 10 to 20 seconds). You will do this for the following muscle groups: hands, arms, shoulders, face, neck, chest, stomach, legs, and feet.

It is advisable to go through this exercise the first time with a group leader or a partner. If you do the exercise with a partner, go through the experience by reading the instructions aloud. Remember, teaching something is an excellent way to learn it as well. You will see that this process is not complicated, and you will learn the technique of scientific relaxation very quickly. Then, you will be able to relax at any time you wish. If you do not have a partner, you may tape-record the exercise,

Source: Based on Edmund Jacobson, Progressive Relaxation *(Chicago: University of Chicago Press, 1974), 49–51, 62–63; and Edward A. Charlesworth and Ronald G. Nathan,* Stress Management: A Comprehensive Guide to Wellness *(Houston: Biobehavioral Publishers and Distributors, Inc., 1975), 49–63.*

then follow your own instructions. Before beginning the exercise, consider these points:

- Allow approximately 30 minutes for the whole procedure. After you become skilled at it, it will take less time.

- Do the exercise in a room where there are no distractions and you will not be disturbed.

- Wear loose-fitting, comfortable clothing. Take off glasses, earrings, watches, shoes.

- The best way to learn the method is to practice twice a day during periods at least two hours apart. Practice is important. Do it regularly.

- Pay close attention to the feelings in your muscles, both when tense and when relaxed.

- As you go through the exercise, breathe deeply and at a normal rate.

INSTRUCTIONS (TO BE READ ALOUD, ONE PERSON TO ANOTHER)

Be seated in a comfortable chair. Place both feet flat on the floor and slightly extended. Let your head and shoulders rest comfortably. Let your arms rest on the arms of the chair, with the palms of your hands down. Let the chair completely support your body. No muscle tension should be required to maintain your sitting position. Just relax and let the chair completely support and hold your body. Now, close your eyes and keep them closed throughout the relaxation exercise, so that you will not be distracted by light or anything around you. Breathe normally and deeply throughout the exercise.

We will begin with the hands, then the arms, then the shoulders, then move to the face, neck, chest, and stomach, and finish with the legs and feet. For each muscle group, you will experience a feeling of deep relaxation. As each muscle group is relaxed, you will keep it free of tension while moving on to the next group. In this way, you will arrive at a final state of total relaxation in all muscle groups.

Follow the instructions as accurately as you can without thinking about them as you do so. Do not fall asleep. Focus all of your attention on each muscle group as you tense, hold, then relax the muscles to achieve complete relaxation. As you practice the tensing and relaxing of each muscle group, be sure the rest of your body remains entirely comfortable and totally relaxed. As you become deeply relaxed, you may even have pleasant sensations of warmth and heaviness flowing through your muscles.

Let us begin now with your right hand. With your right hand, make a tight fist and hold it. Tense the muscles of the hand as tightly as you can and hold it. Notice how the muscles pull across the top of the hand, in the fingers, and in the forearm. Now, relax. Let your right forearm, hand, and fingers go completely loose. Pay close attention to the feeling of relaxation in these muscles. Notice how tension gives way to complete relaxation. Focus all of your attention on how complete relaxation feels. Now, once again, with this same, right hand, make a tight fist and hold it. Again, notice how the muscles tense and pull in your hand and fingers and forearm. Now, relax. Feel how the tension flows from your forearm, from your hand, and from your fingers. These become more and more relaxed, more deeply relaxed than ever before.

Now, without lifting or moving your right arm, tense the muscles in your upper right arm. Hold it. Notice how the muscles pull on top and under the arm. Now, relax. Let the relaxation flow down your arm. Your entire right arm becomes more and more relaxed. Focus on this feeling of relaxation and go on relaxing. Allow your entire right arm and hand to become deeply and totally relaxed.

With your right arm remaining completely relaxed, make a fist with your left hand. Clench it tightly so you can feel the muscles pull across the fingers and in the upper and lower parts of the forearm. Hold it — tightly. Now, relax. Release muscle tension and let relaxation take over. Pay close attention to this feeling of complete relaxation as your forearm, hand, and fingers become more and more relaxed.

Once again, make a tight fist with your left hand, and hold it. Feel the tightness in the fingers and forearm. Now, relax. Notice how it feels as you let these muscles go completely loose. Allow your forearm, hand, and fingers to continue relaxing until they are as totally relaxed as your other forearm, hand, and fingers — deeply and completely relaxed.

Now, without lifting or tensing your left forearm, tighten the muscles in your upper left arm and hold it. Feel the pull of the muscles on top and under the arm. Now, relax. Let relaxation spread throughout your right arm. Enjoy freedom from tension as you continue to let both arms and hands become more relaxed.

Now, imagine two strings coming down from the ceiling above you, each one connecting to one of your shoulders so that your shoulders could be lifted by them. With your arms still completely relaxed, raise both of your shoulders as if pulled up by these two imaginary strings. Lift your shoulders as high as you can and hold it. Feel the pull of the large muscles across the shoulders. Now, relax. Drop your shoulders as if the strings had been cut. Allow them to sag as far as they will. Let all of your shoulder muscles relax. Experience effortless, pleasant relaxation. Notice how the feeling of relaxation spreads throughout your body.

Now, tighten the muscles in your forehead and scalp by wrinkling up your forehead and raising your eyebrows at the same time. Hold it. Hold it. Now, relax. Let your brow smooth out and completely relax. Relax the muscles in your scalp. Smooth out your forehead. Relax.

Again, pull your brow down and together. Again, notice the feeling of tightness and tension. Now, relax. Let your forehead smooth out again, smoother and smoother. Observe how the tension vanishes from your forehead and scalp. Let these muscles become more and more relaxed.

Now, squint your eyes tightly and wrinkle your nose. Tighter, tighter. Notice the tension around your eyes and nose. Hold this tension. Now, relax. Let all of the muscles around your eyes and nose completely relax. Let relaxation spread over your entire face. Let your eyes be free, free of muscle tension, as you become more and more deeply and totally relaxed. Keep your eyelids lightly closed, and go on relaxing.

Now, with your mouth closed, pull back the corners of your mouth as tightly as you can. Feel tension in the cheeks and jaw muscles as you pull the corners back farther and farther. Now, relax. Notice the sensation of warmth that flows into these muscles as they become relaxed.

Now, tense your jaw muscles by biting your teeth together. Bite hard. Notice the feeling of tightness in your jaw muscles. Now, relax. Let your jaw go completely limp. Feel the surge of relief as relaxation flows in.

Now, push your tongue against the roof of your mouth, so that you can feel the tightness in the muscles under your chin and your throat. Push hard. Hold it. Now, relax. Feel relaxation flow down the sides of your face, under your chin, and into your throat.

Your whole body is becoming more and more relaxed. Again, relax all of the muscles in your forehead. Make sure there is no tension around your eyes and nose. Let your face become completely relaxed as you release all tension in your cheeks and jaws. Let your shoulders, arms, hands, and fingers relax. You are becoming thoroughly and deeply relaxed. Your eyes are lightly closed. You are breathing softly, deeply, normally.

Now, push your head back as far as it will go. Hold it. Observe the pressure in the back of your neck. Now, relax. Let your head return to its normal position.

Now, bend your head forward, touching your chin to your chest. Feel the tightness in the back of your neck. Hold it. Now, relax. Return your head to its normal, comfortable position. Once again, go on relaxing calmly and peacefully. Extra tension in the neck, shoulders, and face is the cause of many headaches and fatigue. At this point, you should be able to easily push your head from side to side with your fingers on your chin. If there is extra tension in the muscles of the neck, you will feel unnecessary resistance.

Now, take a deep breath. Fill your lungs and hold your breath. Keep holding your breath. Notice how the muscles pull across the chest. Now, exhale. Relax. Breathe out and feel the pleasurable relief throughout your chest. Continue breathing normally — in and out, regularly and easily. Allow the rest of your body to be as relaxed as possible, and fill your lungs once again. Take a deep breath and hold it. Hold it. Again, notice the increased tension. Now, relax. Just breathe in and out normally, relaxing and enjoying the soothing relief. Notice how all of the muscles of your body become more relaxed when you exhale. Go on breathing normally, easily, freely, completely relaxed. Your hands, your arms, your shoulders, your face, your neck, your chest . . . all are completely relaxed.

Now, making sure that your other muscles remain relaxed, tighten your stomach muscles. Make them hard, as if someone were about to hit you in the stomach and you are preparing for the blow. Hold these muscles tight. Now, relax. Focus on the relief and the complete comfort of relaxation. Once again, tighten your stomach muscles. Hold it. Hold it. Now, relax. Let your stomach muscles become completely relaxed. Notice the sense of well-being that comes with relaxing your stomach muscles.

Continue relaxing for a while, enjoying the calm, pleasant sensations of deep, total relaxation. Your hands and arms are free of tension. Your shoulders are resting naturally; your face muscles are relaxed and serene. Your chest and stomach muscles are free of tension. Your breathing is easy and rhythmical — in and out, in and out. No effort should be required as you completely relax.

Now, tighten the muscles in the upper thigh portions of both legs. Observe how it feels when you tighten these muscles. Hold it. Now relax. Completely relax all of the muscles in your legs, stomach, chest, face, shoulders, arms, and hands. Once again, tighten the upper thigh muscles in both legs. Hold it. Now, relax. Feel the surge of relief as tension disappears and relaxation takes over. You may even have pleasant sensations of warmth as these muscles become more and more relaxed.

Now, raise both of your legs so that only your toes are touching the floor. Notice the tightness forming in the calves of your legs. Now, relax. Lower your feet flat to the floor and relax all of the muscles of your legs and feet. Once more, raise both of your legs so that only your toes touch the floor. Pull your calves as tightly as you can. Hold it. Now, relax. Let your feet fall to the floor, and notice the relief of relaxation. Allow all of your muscles, throughout your entire body, to become more and more relaxed.

Next, push down with your toes, and arch up both of your feet. Feel the pressure, as if something were pushing up under each arch. Hold it. Now, relax. Let your arches fall, and enjoy the release and freedom from effort. Go on relaxing. Make sure there is no tightness anywhere in your body. Just let your body totally, completely relax. Enjoy the feeling of deep, complete, pleasant relaxation. Relax more and more. There is no tension in your body.

Now, continuing to breathe normally, deeply, and regularly, and continuing to keep your eyes lightly closed, you will go to each part of the body, concentrating on what it feels like to be relaxed, free of muscle tension. Begin with the feet and feel the absence of tension in your toes, arches, and ankles; now the muscles of the calves — relax; now the muscles of the thighs — feel the lack of tension; now the stomach — there is no tension in the muscles of the stomach; now the chest — breathe softly, normally; feel the lack of tension; now the muscles of the neck — your neck is free, free of muscle tension; now, the many muscles of the face — your face is relaxed, chin heavy, cheeks heavy, eyes free of tension, forehead smooth, scalp free of tension; now the shoulders — relaxed, free of tension; and last, your forearms, hands, and fingers — these are relaxed; all tension is gone.

Now, continue to relax all of the muscles of your body. Take a few minutes to feel what it is like to experience total relaxation (allow approximately three minutes).

In a few moments you will be asked to return to a state of normal wakeful tension. You will notice that you will not be as tense as you were when you started the exercise, and you will feel refreshed and ready to go about your activities in an efficient and effective way. You will return to normal alertness gradually so that you will not be startled.

I will count from one to four. On the count of one, move your feet and legs. On the count of two, move your fingers, hands, and arms. On the count of three, sit up in the chair. On the count of four, open your eyes, touch your face, and breathe deeply. When you do this, you will feel very refreshed.

Ready . . . one, move your feet and your legs . . . two, move your fingers, hands, and arms . . . three, you may sit up in the chair . . . four, open your eyes, stretch, and breathe deeply.

DISCUSSION

The following case study illustrates the value of relaxation for managing stress.[2]

Things have not been going well for Hal Plunkett this week. As president and owner of a small public-relations firm, Hal is directly affected by almost anything of consequence that happens in the firm. One major problem involves Plunkett's biggest client, Maxwell Automotive, a supplier of plastic trim parts to the auto industry. As a consequence of low business volume, Maxwell has been forced to lay off 25 percent of its work force. A cryptic letter arrived in Hal's office today stating that Maxwell plans to cut its public-relations budget by 50 percent for the coming fiscal year.

Another worrisome development relates to Plunkett's most productive account executive, Jayne. As she explained the situation to Hal late yesterday afternoon:

> I've been in industrial public relations for ten years now. For five of those years I've worked for Plunkett Associates. They've been wonderful years. You've been good to me. But, Hal, I think it's time for me to spread my wings a little. I want to see if I can make it on my own.
>
> I'm giving you 30 days' notice. I'll spend as much time as you like trying to transfer my clients to anybody else of your choosing. But I think it could get sticky trying to transfer Redwood, my biggest account. You will recall that I brought them to the firm. It's been a very personal relationship with the people at Redwood. I think they would prefer to be my client when I'm out on my own. Maybe we could work out some kind of a fee-splitting arrangement for a while.

As Hal left the office that night, he thought:

> It looks like our biggest client will be cutting way down on our services. My best account executive is leaving to go into competition with us. She'll probably take our third biggest client with her. It's messy and kind of unprofessional to try to stop a client from working with a favored consultant.

I guess I should be looking to replace Jayne, but our current business volume doesn't justify adding another professional to the staff. Besides, our new business prospects look slim right now. It feels like I'm sliding downhill. I can feel the pains in my chest starting to build up.

Still concerned with work problems, Hal found more problems confronting him at home. Instead of her usual warm greeting, Hal's wife, Suzanne, greeted him with a frown and a curt comment: "Make yourself a cocktail if you want, Hal. I know you're home later than usual, but I've had a long day myself. I'm just not up to making dinner. Maybe we should all go out to eat. It looks like we have a crisis to face. Reggie, why don't you tell your father what you told me?"

"Okay, if I have to," said Reggie. "I hate school. I want to drop out when I'm sixteen. I'm flunking English and Algebra. The coach won't even give me a chance. He told me he's kicking me off the team. He says my grades are too low. So what's the use? No grades, no sports. Why should I bother anymore?"

"It sounds like you're very upset, son. We need to talk a lot more before you make any decision like planning to drop out of school. Let's all go out to dinner and talk about this some more."

On their return home from dinner, Hal said to his wife and son:

It seems like we're making some progress with the school situation. I want to deal with it some more. But right now I have to get my head in shape. I've been hit with a freight car's worth of stress this week. I'm going into the den now. I would like to relax a little before I try to help somebody else.

After closing the door to the den, Hal entered into a progressive relaxation session.

Hal sat down comfortably in the red leather easy chair adjacent to the bay window. Slowly he exhaled a few times. He unfastened the top button of his shirt and loosened his tie. As his body sank down further into the chair, Hal began to concentrate on the muscles in his toes and feet. He felt the tingling sensation in his big toes. Slowly and gently, he relaxed the muscles in his toes.

Following the sequence of actions that had worked for him in the past, Hal allowed the relaxation technique to progress from the toes upward. Concentrating fully on his ankles, Hal experienced the ankle muscles loosening and relaxing. The sensations of relaxation moved slowly up his body. His calves felt more limp than they had all day.

Hal began to feel as if his body were immersed in a large pool of water. The pleasant sensation traveled up his body. In consecutive order, his thighs, stomach, and chest became loose and relaxed. Hal let the experience of relaxation and calmness spread to his shoulders. As his state of relaxation increased, Hal began to feel impulses coming from his body to his brain. He became more and more in touch with his bodily sensations.

Next, Hal experienced a pleasant, almost euphoric lack of tension in the muscles surrounding his heart. He hadn't felt so far removed from potential disease in weeks. By now Hal could feel a general sense of inertness overtaking his body. In turn, the muscles in the back of his neck and in his temples loosened. At this point, Hal felt the sensation of relaxation in his forehead and scalp.

Fifteen minutes of Hal's progressive relaxation session had passed. Now the depths of relaxation brought him the sought-after relief from the stress precipitated by work and family problems. Following other techniques of relaxation, Hal began to think of pleasant fantasies and images.

He thought about his first big business success — the day he signed the contract to handle the public relations for Central Utility Company. Then his mind wandered to pleasant thoughts of his early, carefree days with Suzanne. Hal gently coaxed his mind to recall their happy times together walking along the shores of Cape Cod. Searching further for pleasant thoughts, Hal reminded himself of how much his retirement account had appreciated in the past few years. The current market value of his account was $76,000 — a big chunk of money for a man who grew up in poverty. As he moved back toward a state of full consciousness, Hal thought fleetingly about the proud day when he formally opened the doors to Plunkett Associates, Inc., public-relations consultants.

"I feel good now," thought Hal to himself. "I'm ready to tackle my problems. I'll start with Reggie tonight. Tomorrow I'll deal with the problems of Plunkett Associates."

Hal opened the den door and called up the stairs: "Reggie, why don't you join me in the den? We have a lot to talk about."

Hal Plunkett used relaxation as a coping technique for dealing with stress. He is typical of many successful people who have a great deal of responsibility, yet seem confident and capable, even when dealing with difficult problems and making critical decisions. Their lives are full, yet they seem to be in control, physically fit, energetic, and vital.

REFERENCE NOTES

1. Hans Selye, *The Stress of Life*, rev. ed. (New York: McGraw-Hill, Inc., 1976).

2. Andrew J. DuBrin, *Contemporary Applied Management* (Plano, Tex.: Business Publications, Inc., 1982), 222–24.

APPENDIX A

Background Information, Teaching Suggestions, and Testing and Grading

The Human Side of Work is a series of desk books for managers, handbooks for practitioners, and workbooks for students. These are applied books that combine behavior theory with business practice. Each book teaches central concepts and skills in an important area of the world of work. The set of eight books includes stress management, communication skills, employee motivation, leadership principles, quality of work life, managing for excellence, employee participation, and the role of ethics.

Each book combines theory with practice, gives commonsense answers to real-life problems, and is easy to read and fun to use. The series may be used as a set or as stand-alone books. The subject areas are made more forceful and the impact greater by the self-evaluation questionnaires and practical exercises that are used for personal development.

AUDIENCE

The Human Side of Work is written for two audiences. One audience includes managers and professionals interested in personal and professional development on their own or within the context of a management development program. Another audience includes students in human relations, organization behavior, and other management-related courses.

The material is appropriate for use at the four-year college and university level as well as in community colleges, proprietary schools, extension programs, and management training seminars.

CONTENT AND STYLE

The difference between most organization behavior texts and *The Human Side of Work* can be compared to the difference between a lecture and a seminar. Although both are good educational vehicles, the lecture is better for conveying large amounts of information, while the seminar is better for developing skills. The good lecture is interesting and builds knowledge; the good seminar is stimulating and builds competency. *The Human Side of Work* emphasizes the interactive, seminar approach to learning.

The writing style is personal and conversational, with minimal professional jargon. True-life examples clarify points under consideration. Concepts are supported by stories and anecdotes, which are more meaningful and easy to remember than facts, figures, and lists. Each book includes learning activities to bridge the gap between classroom theory and on-the-job practice.

The Human Side of Work is more than a series of textbooks. These are "learning" books that actively involve the reader in the learning process. Our goal has been to include material that is interesting to read, relates to the reader's own concerns, and is practical to use. The following captures the spirit of our effort:

I Taught Them All

I have taught in high school for ten years. During that time, I have given assignments, among others, to a murderer, an evangelist, a pugilist, a thief, and an imbecile.

The murderer was a quiet little boy who sat on the front seat and regarded me with pale blue eyes; the evangelist, easily the most popular boy in school, had the lead in the junior class play; the pugilist lounged by the window and let loose at intervals with a raucous laugh that startled even the geraniums; the thief was a gay-hearted Lothario with a song on his lips; and the imbecile, a soft-eyed little animal seeking the shadows.

The murderer awaits death in the state penitentiary; the evangelist has lain a year in the village churchyard; the pugilist lost an eye in a brawl in Hong Kong; the thief, by standing on tiptoe, can see the windows of my room from the county jail; and the once gentle-eyed little moron beats his head against a padded wall in the state asylum.

All of these young men once sat in my room, sat and looked at me gravely across worn brown desks. I must have been a great help to those pupils — I taught them the rhyming scheme of the Elizabethan sonnet and how to diagram a complex sentence.

Naomi John White

The focus of *The Human Side of Work* is self-discovery and personal development as the reader "learns by doing." The material covered is authoritative and up to date, reflecting current theory and practices. The level of material is appropriate for all levels of expertise (new and experienced managers) and all levels of education (undergraduate and graduate).

TESTING AND REVIEW PROCESS

The Human Side of Work has been tested and refined in our classes at Northern Kentucky University. The information and activities have been used with hundreds of organizations and thousands of employees in business, industry, and government. Users include American Telephone and Telegraph Co., International Business Machines Corp., John Hancock, Marriott Corporation, Sun Oil, and Ford Motor Co. in the private sector and the Department of Transportation, the Environmental Protection Agency, the Internal Revenue Service, the National Institutes of

Health, and state governments in the public sector.
The following are sample evaluations:

Good for student participation. My students like the exercises and learning instruments, and the fact each is a stand-alone book that is bite-size. Their reaction: "Everyone should read them!"

Joseph F. Ohren, Eastern Michigan University

A comprehensive series dealing with employee development and job performance. Information is presented in an interesting and easy-to-use style. Case studies and readings help teach the topics, and applications make the material more meaningful. It is an excellent guide for the practicing manager. Ideal as desk books.

David Duncan, IBM

I am a non-traditional student. As one who has worked for over twenty years, I thoroughly enjoyed the material. An understanding of the world of work is presented in a way that is usable at any level of an organization. The books present a common sense approach to management.

Naomi Miller, Northern Kentucky University

Best I've seen on the people side of work. Helps the person. Helps the company. Good for personal and management development. Popular with participants from all backgrounds.

Charles Apple, University of Michigan

This is an easy-to-read, comprehensive series in organization behavior. It puts theory into relevant, usable terminology. Methods for identifying and solving human relations problems are pinpointed. It sets the stage for understanding how people, environment and situations interact in an organization.

David Sprouse, AT&T

TEACHING FORMATS

The Human Side of Work is versatile and can be used in many formats:

- for seminars and training programs
- as classroom texts
- as supplemental information and activities

The following is a discussion of each option.

Seminars and Training Programs

Books used for seminars and training programs should be selected to meet the objectives and needs of the participants—communication, stress, leadership, etc. Material can be mixed and matched for training programs in personal development, professional development, management development, and team building. Material in each book is appropriate for a variety of time periods: one-half day (3 to 4 hours), one full day (6 to 8 hours), and two full days (12 to 16 hours).

The books provide excellent learning activities and questionnaires to encourage participation and personalize the subject. Books then serve as "take-home" material for further reading and personal development. In this format, study quizzes are rarely used for grading, and homework assignments are seldom given. See the following table for appropriate audiences, program focus, and recommended books when using *The Human Side of Work* for seminars and training programs.

Classroom Texts

The series is appropriate for use as texts in college courses in human relations, organization behavior, and organizational psychology. The following is a sample lesson plan using the set for a one-semester course:

Week	Focus on the Person	
1	Stress	Part One, Part Two
2	Stress	Part Three, Part Four
3	Communication	Part One, Part Two
4	Communication	Part Three, Part Four
5	Human Behavior	Part One, Part Two
6	Human Behavior	Part Three
7	Ethics	Part One, Part Two
8	Ethics	Part Three, Part Four

	Focus on the Organization	
9	Morale	Part One, Part Two
10	Morale	Part Three
11	Leadership	Part One, Part Two
12	Leadership	Part Three, Part Four

USING THE HUMAN SIDE OF WORK FOR SEMINARS AND TRAINING PROGRAMS

Appropriate Audiences	Program Focus	Recommended Books
Personal and professional development	Focus on the individual	* *Stress Without Distress: Rx for Burnout* * *Communication: The Miracle of Dialogue* * *Human Behavior: Why People Do What They Do* * *Ethics at Work: Fire in a Dark World* * *Morale: Quality of Work Life* (optional) * *Performance: Managing for Excellence* (optional)
New and experienced managers	Focus on management	* *Morale: Quality of Work Life* * *Leadership: Nine Keys to Success* * *Performance: Managing for Excellence* * *Groupstrength: Quality Circles at Work* * *Stress Without Distress: Rx for Burnout* (optional) * *Communication: The Miracle of Dialogue* (optional) * *Human Behavior: Why People Do What They Do* (optional) * *Ethics at Work: Fire in a Dark World* (optional)
Employee development and team building	Focus on the organization	* *Communication: The Miracle of Dialogue* * *Morale: Quality of Work Life* * *Groupstrength: Quality Circles at Work* * *Stress Without Distress: Rx for Burnout* (optional) * *Human Behavior: Why People Do What They Do* (optional) * *Performance: Managing for Excellence* (optional)

Popular seminar and program titles with corresponding books are as follows:

Managing Change: Personal and Professional Coping Skills	* *Stress Without Distress: Rx for Burnout*
Communication: One to One; One to Many	* *Communication: The Miracle of Dialogue*
Human Relations and the Nature of Man	* *Human Behavior: Why People Do What They Do*
Business Ethics and Corporate Culture	* *Ethics at Work: Fire in a Dark World*
Quality of Work Life	* *Morale: Quality of Work Life*
The Human Side of Management	* *Leadership: Nine Keys to Success*
Managing for Productivity: People Building Skills	* *Performance: Managing for Excellence*
Employee Involvement: If Japan Can Do It, Why Can't We?	* *Groupstrength: Quality Circles at Work*

13	Performance	Part One, Part Two
14	Performance	Part Three
15	Groupstrength	Part One, Part Two
16	Groupstrength	Part Three

Related Activities and Homework Assignments

Week	Suggested Readings, Cases and Applications
1	*Anatomy of an Illness as Perceived by the Patient* (reading) *The Price of Success* (case)
2	*Death of a Salesman* (reading) *Scientific Relaxation* (application)
3	*Barriers and Gateways to Communications* (reading) *The Power of Vocabulary* (application)
4	*The Dyadic Encounter* (application) *Attitudes toward Women Working* (application)
5	*The Human Side of Enterprise* (reading) *Significant People and Critical Events* (application)
6	*Values Auction* (application) *Personal and Interpersonal Growth* (application)
7	*If Hitler Asked You to Electrocute a Stranger, Would You?* (reading) *How Could the Jonestown Holocaust Have Occurred?* (reading)
8	*Values Flag* (application) *The Kidney Machine* (application)
9	*Work* (reading) *The Joe Bailey Problem* (application)
10	*The Coffee Break* (case) *In Search of Excellence* (application)
11	*What Happened When I Gave Up the Good Life and Became President* (case) *Black, Blue, and White* (case)
12	*The Forklift Fiasco* (case) *Train the Trainers* (application)
13	*Games Mother Never Taught You* (reading) *How Will You Spend Your Life?* (application)

14	*How to Manage Your Time: Everybody's No. 1 Problem* (reading)
	Chrysler's Turnaround Strategy (case)
15	*Groupthink* (reading)
	The Dean Practices Participative Management (case)
16	*Decisions, Decisions, Decisions* (reading)
	The Bottleneck (application)

This format for a one-semester course uses selected readings, cases, and applications from all eight books. For a two-semester course, additional readings, cases, and applications are provided.

Another popular format is to use fewer books in a one-semester course, and to use these more thoroughly. The books can be selected by the instructor or the class. For example, stress, communication, morale, and leadership may be best suited for a given group.

Testing and Grading

When using *The Human Side of Work* as classroom texts, study quizzes in each book can be used to evaluate content knowledge. Although quiz scores can be used to assign formal grades, students learn best when they are also asked to apply the concepts in some personal way. Examples include a term journal, a related research paper, a small-group project, a field assignment, and/or a self-improvement project.

Grades can be assigned on the basis of test scores and term project(s). Projects can be evaluated according to the three C's: clarity, comprehensiveness, and correctness. Half the course grade could be based on study quiz scores, and the other half on the term project(s).

Supplemental Information and Activities

The books in *The Human Side of Work* can provide supplemental information and activities for various college courses. State-of-the-art questionnaires and user-friendly exercises add variety and increase student involvement. Books matched with appropriate college courses are as follows:

Recommended Books	College Courses
Stress Without Distress: Rx for Burnout	Personal Development
	Personal Health
	Human Relations
	Organization Behavior
	Organizational Psychology
	Supervisory Development

Communication: The Miracle of Dialogue	Personal Development Communications Human Relations Organization Behavior Organizational Psychology Supervisory Development
Human Behavior: Why People Do What They Do	Personal Development Human Relations Organization Behavior Organizational Psychology Supervisory Development
Ethics at Work: Fire in a Dark World	Personal Development Business Ethics Human Relations Organization Behavior Organizational Psychology Supervisory Development
Morale: Quality of Work Life	Personnel/Human Resources Human Relations Organization Behavior Organizational Psychology Supervisory Development
Leadership: Nine Keys to Success	Management Principles Human Relations Organization Behavior Organizational Psychology Supervisory Development
Performance: Managing for Excellence	Management Principles Human Relations Organization Behavior Organizational Psychology Supervisory Development
Groupstrength: Quality Circles at Work	Personnel/Human Resources Human Relations Organization Behavior Organizational Psychology Supervisory Development

When used as supplemental material, books are rarely tested for grades. The emphasis is on using the questionnaires, exercises, cases, and applications to increase interest and participation and to personalize the subject.

APPENDIX B

Additional References

ADDITIONAL REFERENCES

The following books are recommended for further reading in the area of stress physiology, coping skills, and personal fitness. Each is included because of its significance in the field, support to this text, and value for further personal development.

Barrett, Steven. *The Health Robbers*. Philadelphia: George F. Stickley Co., 1976.

Benson, Herbert. *The Relaxation Response*. New York: Avon Books, 1975.

Berland, J., and the editors of *Consumer Guide. Rating the Diets*. New York: Signet, 1980.

Brody, Jane. *Jane Brody's Nutrition Book: A Lifetime Guide to Good Eating for Better Health and Weight Control*. New York: Bantam Books, Inc., 1982.

Brown, Barbara. *New Mind, New Body*. New York: Bantam Books, Inc. 1975.

Cannon, Walter B. *Bodily Changes in Pain, Hunger, Fear and Rage*. New York: Appleton, 1929.

Cannon, Walter B. *The Wisdom of the Body*. New York: W. W. Norton & Company, Inc., 1967.

Caplan, Robert D. *Job Demands and Worker Health: Main Effects and Occupational Differences*. Washington, D.C.: U.S. Department of Health, Education and Welfare, 1975.

Christensen, Alice, and David Rankin. *The Light of Yoga Society Beginner's Manual*. New York: Simon & Schuster, Inc., 1972.

Cooper, Kenneth. *The Aerobics Program for Total Well-Being*. New York: M. Evans & Co., Inc., 1983.

Cooper, Kenneth. *The New Aerobics*. New York: M. Evans & Co., Inc., 1970.

Daniels, Victor, and Laurence J. Horowitz. *Being and Caring*. Palo Alto, Calif.: Mayfield Publishing Co., 1976.

Darden, Ellington. *Your Guide to Physical Fitness*. Philadelphia: George F. Stickley Co., 1982.

Dass, Ram. *A Journey to Awakening: A Guide to the Meditative Experience*. New York: Bantam Books, Inc., 1978.

Debakey, M., and A. Gotto. *The Living Heart*. New York: David McKay Co., Inc., 1977.

Deutsch, Ronald. *New Nuts Among the Berries*. Palo Alto, Calif.: Bull Publishing Co., 1977.

Deutsch, Ronald. *Realities of Nutrition*. Palo Alto, Calif.: Bull Publishing Co., 1976.

Fast, Howard. *The Art of Zen Meditation*. Culver City, Calif.: Peace Press, 1977.

Friedman, Meyer and R. Rosenman. *Type A Behavior and Your Heart*. New York: Alfred A. Knopf, Inc., 1974.

Getchell, Bud. *Physical Fitness: A Way of Life*. New York: John Wiley & Sons, Inc., 1983.

Girdano, Daniel A., and George S. Everly, Jr. *Controlling Stress and Tension*. Englewood Cliffs, N. J.: Prentice-Hall, Inc., 1986.

Greenberg, Jerrold S. and David Pargman. *Physical Fitness: A Wellness Approach*. Englewood Cliffs, N. J.: Prentice-Hall, Inc., 1986.

Holmes, Thomas H. *Life Change Events Research 1966–1978*. New York: Praeger Publishers, 1984.

Holmes, Thomas H., and T. Stephenson Holmes. "How Change Can Make Us Ill." *A Report from Your Blue Cross Plan: Stress* 25, no. 1 (1974).

Jacobson, Edmund. *Progressive Relaxation*. Chicago: The University of Chicago Press, 1968.

Jacobson, Edmund. *You Must Relax*. 5th ed. New York: McGraw-Hill, Inc., 1978.

Katch, Frank I., and William D. McArdle. *Nutrition, Weight Control and Exercise*. 2d ed. Philadelphia: Lea & Febiger, 1983.

Lazarus, Richard S. *Psychological Stress and the Coping Process*. New York: Columbia University Press, 1977.

Lazarus, Richard S. *Stress, Appraisal, and Coping*. New York: Springer-Verlag New York, Inc. 1984.

Lazarus, Richard S. *Stress and Coping*. New York: Springer-Verlag New York, Inc., 1984.

Levinson, D. *The Seasons of a Man's Life*. New York: Alfred A. Knopf, Inc., 1978.

Levinson, Harry. *Executive Stress*. New York: Harper & Row, Publishers, Inc., 1966.

Mayer, Jean. *A Diet for Living*. New York: Pocket Books, 1980.

Pelletier, Kenneth R. *Mind as Healer, Mind as Slayer: A Holistic Approach to Preventing Stress Disorders.* New York: Dell Publishing Co., Inc., 1977.

Selye, Hans. *Guide to Stress Research.* Vol. 1. New York: Van Nostrand Reinhold Co., Inc., 1980.

Selye, Hans. *The Stress of Life.* Rev. ed. New York: McGraw-Hill, Inc., 1976.

Selye, Hans. *Stress Without Distress.* Philadelphia: J.B. Lippincott Company, 1974.

Sheehy, G. *Passages: Predictable Crises of Adult Life.* New York: Bantam Books, Inc., 1977.

Stare, F., and E. Whelan. *Eat O.K. — Feel O.K.! Food Facts and Your Health.* Norwell, Mass.: Christopher Publishing House, 1978.

Toffler, Alvin. *Future Shock.* New York: Random House, Inc., 1970.

Welch, I. David. *Beyond Burnout.* Englewood Cliffs, N. J.: Prentice-Hall, Inc., 1982.

Wolff, Harold G. *Stress and Disease.* 2d ed. Springfield, Ill.: Charles C Thomas, Publisher, 1968.

Wolff, S., and H.G. Wolff. *Human Gastric Function.* 2d ed. New York: Oxford University Press, Inc., 1947.

Wolpe, Joseph. *The Practice of Behavior Therapy.* Maxwell House, N. Y.: Pergamon Press, Inc., 1974.

Yates, Jere E. *Managing Stress.* New York: American Management Association, 1979.

APPENDIX C

Suggested Films

The following films are excellent learning aids. These are supplementary media that can enrich a class or training program. They are ideal for small-group discussion, panel debates, and question-and-answer periods. Topics are listed in the order in which they appear in the text.

FUTURE SHOCK
(McGraw-Hill, 42 min.)

This film presents a stunning look at the collision between present and future. "Future shock," the film explains, "is sickness which comes from too much change in too short a time. . . . It's a reaction to changes that happen so fast we can't absorb them. It is premature arrival of the future—and for those who are unprepared, its effects can be devastating."

McGraw-Hill Films
Princeton Road
Highstown, New Jersey 08520

STRESS: A DISEASE OF OUR TIME
(Time-Life, 35 min.)

Different types of stress are demonstrated in experiments, and their implications are discussed.

Time-Life Films
43 West 16th Street
New York, New York 10011

STRESS
(National Film Board of Canada, 11 min.)

Hans Selye explains the General Adaptation Syndrome in this 1950s film.

National Film Board of Canada
Headquarters—U.S. Territory
1251 Avenue of the Americas
New York, New York 10020

LEARN TO LIVE WITH STRESS: PROGRAMMING THE BODY FOR HEALTH
(Document Associates, 19 min.)

Hans Selye and Herbert Benson describe the effects of stress on health, using an air traffic controller as an example. Recommended film.

Document Associates, Inc.
211 East 43rd Street
New York, New York 10017

STRESS, HEALTH AND YOU
(American Educational Films, 18 min.)

Deals with stress and its effect on our health. It discusses how stress can have both positive and negative causes. This is an important overview film that helps people analyze how their own health is modified by stressful events. Features Hans Selye and Richard Rahe.

American Education Films
3384 Peachtree Rd. N.E.
Atlanta, Georgia 30326

MANAGING STRESS
(CRM, 33 min.)

This film explores sources of stress and stress reactions (both beneficial and destructive). Various techniques for alleviating stress are discussed.

CRM Educational Films
Del Mar, California 92014

ALCOHOLISM: A MODEL OF DRUG DEPENDENCY
(CRM, 20 min.)

This is an award-winning discussion of alcoholism and its treatment.

CRM Educational Films
Del Mar, California 92014

SMOKING: GAMES SMOKERS PLAY
(Document Associates, 26 min.)

Combines facts and humor to encourage viewers to seriously consider their real reasons for smoking.

Document Associates, Inc.
211 East 43rd Street
New York, New York 10017

WHAT MAKES MILLIE RUN?
(Brigham Young University, 14 min.)

An aerobics film for women featuring Mildred Cooper, wife of Kenneth Cooper and author of *Aerobics for Women*. A film to motivate women to become physically fit.

Brigham Young University
Salt Lake City, Utah 84103

THE PSYCHOLOGY OF EATING
(Harcourt Brace Jovanovich, 29 min.)

Presents information on eating, taste preferences and aversions, and hypothalamic control of hunger and their implications for obesity and weight control. Behavioral approaches to weight control are also included.

Harcourt Brace Jovanovich, Inc.
757 Third Avenue
New York, New York 10017

TRANSITIONS
(CRM, 29 min.)

Examines the process of making major life changes and the personal, internal, and emotional adjustments required; focuses primarily on the effects such changes have within work settings.

CRM Educational Films
Del Mar, California 92014

THE TIME OF YOUR LIFE
(Calley Curtis Films, 28 min.)

This is an excellent film for teaching effective principles of time management. Short vignettes show time-management mistakes. James Whitmore stars. Award winner. Highest rating.

Calley Curtis Films
3384 Peachtree Rd. N.E.
Atlanta, Georgia 30326

MEDITATION: YOGA, T'AI CHI AND OTHER SPIRITUAL TRIPS
(Document Associates, 20 min.)

Filmed visits to various teachers and practitioners of esoteric meditative disciplines. Alan Watts is interviewed.

Document Associates, Inc.
211 East 43rd Street
New York, New York 10017

JOURNEY TO THE OUTER LIMITS
(National Geographic, 50 min.)

Documents Colorado Outward Bound School's special mountain-climbing expedition in Peru, from training in Colorado through the final climb. Nominated for an Academy Award.

Outward Bound National Office
384 Field Point Road
Greenwich, Connecticut 06830

APPENDIX D

Telephone Hot Lines for Self-Help and Emergency Aid

ABUSED OR BATTERED ADULTS

Partners Anonymous: (800) 421-0353; in California, (800) 352-0386. Available 24 hours, 7 days a week.

ABUSED OR BATTERED CHILDREN

Parents Anonymous: (800) 421-0353; in California, (800) 352-0386. Available 24 hours, 7 days a week.

AIR AMBULANCE SERVICE

Air Medic: (800) 423-2667. Provides medically equipped planes to fly patients to any airport.

AAA Air Ambulance: (800) 245-9987; in Pennsylvania, (800) 542-0377. Domestic and international air ambulance service.

ALCOHOLISM

Alcoholics Anonymous: General service office, New York City, (212) 686-1100. Hours, 9:00 a.m. – 5:00 p.m. weekdays. Gives nationwide information on AA chapters.

Al-Anon — for friends and family of alcoholics: New York City, (212) 481-6565. Hours, 8:30 a.m. – 5:00 p.m. weekdays. Gives nationwide information on Al-Anon chapters.

ANIMAL RIGHTS

Humane Society of the United States: Washington, D.C., (202) 452-1100.

Society for the Prevention of Cruelty to Animals: New York City, (212) 876-7700.

BUSINESS

Service Corps of Retired Executives (SCORE): Small-business advice; 375 offices. Check your local telephone directory under "Small Business Administration" or "SCORE."

CIVIL RIGHTS

American Civil Liberties Union: National headquarters, New York City, (212) 752-1222. Will direct you to their nearest office.

CONSUMER PRODUCTS

Consumer Product Safety Commission: (800) 638-8326.

Bureau of Consumer Protection: Washington, D.C., (202) 523-3727. Provides advice about credit problems and false advertising.

COUNSELING

Contact Teleministries: National headquarters, Pennsylvania, (717) 652-3410. Chapters in 90 cities; 24-hour hot lines available throughout the country; check your local directory.

Neurotics Anonymous: Washington, D.C., (202) 628-4379. Check your local directory for a nearby chapter.

Recovery, Inc.: National headquarters, Chicago, (312) 263-2292. Support groups for former mental patients; 1,000 chapters; will refer you to a local meeting.

DRUG ABUSE

Crisis Intervention Center: New York, N. Y., (212) 662-8630.

Drug Abuse Hotline: New York, N. Y., (800) 538-4840.

Drug Abuse Information and Referral Line, National Institute on Drug Abuse: Rockville, Md., (800) 662-4357.

Most cities have a drug hot line; check your local directory.

EDUCATIONAL GRANTS

Student Information Center: (800) 638-6700.

FAMILY PLANNING

Planned Parenthood's Family Planning: New York City, (212) 677-3040. Check your local directory under "Family Planning" or "Planned Parenthood."

GAMBLING AND DEBTORS

Debtors Anonymous: New York City only, (212) 868-3330. Check your local directory.

Gamblers Anonymous: National service office, California, (213) 386-8789. Will direct you to the nearest meeting.

HEALTH

Tel-Med: California, (714) 825-6034. Plays short tapes on over 300 medical problems; will direct you to their closest outlet; 225 offices.

Cancer Information Center: (800) 638-6694.

HOUSING

Fair Housing Commission: (800) 424-8590.

INFERTILITY

Resolve, Inc.: Massachusetts, (617) 484-2424. Will advise people around the country; hours, 9:00 a.m. – 4:00 p.m. weekdays.

JOBS FOR YOUNGSTERS

J.O.B.S.: Washington, D.C., (202) 737-9616. Gives information on federal jobs available around the country.

LEGAL

Children's Defense Fund: (800) 424-9602. Provides information on national issues and refers callers to proper government agencies for help; not a direct-service organization.

National Legal Aid and Defender Association: National headquarters, Washington, D.C., (202) 452-0620. Check your local directory under "Legal Aid."

PERSONAL GROWTH

Outward Bound, Inc.: (800) 243-8520. Personal growth challenges in the United States and abroad.

POISON

Poison Control Center: Seattle, (206) 634-5252. Gives emergency advice across the country.

RAPE

Rape Help Line: New York City only, (212) 233-3000. Service is available in most cities; check under "Rape Crisis Center" in your local directory.

RUNAWAYS

Operation Peace of Mind: (800) 231-6946; in Texas, (800) 392-3353. Available 24 hours.

National Hotline for Missing Children: Washington D.C., (800) 843-5678.

National Runaway Switchboard: (800) 621-4000; in Illinois, (800) 393-3352. Available 24 hours.

SINGLE PARENTS

National Pregnancy Hotline: Fresno, Calif., (800) 344-7211; in California, (800) 831-5811.

Parents Without Partners: National headquarters; Maryland, (301) 654-8850. Check your local directory under "Parents Without Partners" for a local chapter.

SUICIDE

The Samaritans: Boston, (617) 247-0220. Will direct you to a local chapter; available 24 hours.

National Adolescent Suicide Hotline: Chicago, (800) 621-4000. 24 hour crisis intervention for adolescents.

Suicide Prevention League: New York City, (212) 736-6191. Will refer you to a local source of help; available 24 hours.

SURGERY

Second Opinion Hot Line: (800) 638-6833; in Maryland, (800) 492-6603. Referrals for second medical opinion on elective surgery.

WEIGHT PROBLEMS

Overeaters Anonymous: California, (213) 320-7941. Will direct you to the nearest meeting; or check in your local directory.

WOMEN

National Organization for Women: Chicago, (312) 922-0025. Check your local directory under "National Organization for Women" for a local chapter.

APPENDIX E

Organizations for Specific Sports and Physical Fitness Activities

ORGANIZATIONS FOR SPECIFIC SPORTS AND PHYSICAL FITNESS ACTIVITIES

Basketball

Amateur Basketball Association of the United States of America (ABAUSA), 1750 East Boulder St., Colorado Springs, CO 80909. (303) 636-7687. The ABAUSA serves as the national governing body for the sport of basketball. They will respond to requests for information on their programs.

Bicycling

Bicycle Touring Group of America, P.O. Drawer 330976, Coconut Grove, Fl 33133. (305) 661-8846. The Bicycle Touring Group is an industry-sponsored association to promote noncompetitive recreational bicycling.

Bikecentennial, The Bicycle Travel Association, P.O. Box 8308, Missoula, MT 59807. (406) 721-1776. Bikecentennial is a national service organization for touring bicyclists. The organization's efforts are aimed at educating the public in bicycle use and safety and researching and mapping bicycle touring routes. A publications list is available and questions are answered on all aspects of bike touring.

League of American Wheelmen, P.O. Box 988, Baltimore, MD 21203. (301) 727-2022. The League answers inquiries on topics such as where to ride, what to take along, routes, how to plan and conduct bicycle events, and safety.

United States Cycling Federation, 1750 East Boulder St., Colorado Springs, CO 80909. (303) 632-5551. The governing body for amateur and professional cycling in the United States, and an organization concerned with the preservation, development, and administration of bicycle racing.

Bowling

American Bowling Congress (ABC) and Women's International Bowling Congress (WIBC), 5301 South 76th St., Greendale, WI 53129. (414) 421-6400. These two groups are the primary organizations promoting bowling for men and for women. Direct your questions on bowling to

Source: National Health Information Clearinghouse, "Selected Sources of Information on Physical Fitness and Sports," Healthfinder (Washington, D.C.: U.S. Department of Health and Human Services, Office of Disease Prevention and Health Promotion, 1983).

the public relations department of the appropriate organization (men should write to the ABC, and women should write to the WIBC).

Dancing

Aerobic Dancing, Inc., 18907 Nordhoff St., Box 6600, Northridge, CA 91328. (213) 885-0032. Aerobic dancing is a fitness program originated by Jacki Sorenson, consisting of vigorous dances designed to improve physical fitness. Contact Aerobic Dancing at the above address for a location near you, or check your local telephone directory.

Jazzercise, Inc., 2808 Roosevelt St., Carlsbad, CA 92008. (619) 434-2101. Jazzercise is a dance and fitness program of simple jazz dance movements set to a variety of music. Contact Jazzercise at the above address for classes near you.

Hiking/Backpacking

Forest Service, U.S. Department of Agriculture, Information Office, P.O. Box 2417, Washington, DC 22013. (202) 447-3957. The Information Office of the Forest Service will provide a list of Forest Service field offices and addresses. They request that inquirers contact the field offices to obtain information on recreation opportunities in the national forests.

National Campers and Hikers Association (NCHA), 7172 Transit Rd., Buffalo, NY 14221. (716) 634-5433. The NCHA will answer questions on hiking and camping. This organization is dedicated to camping fellowships, the preservation of our natural heritage, and the strengthening of family bonds through activities in the out-of-doors.

Sierra Club, 530 Bush St., San Francisco, CA 94108. (415) 981-8634. The Sierra Club is dedicated to the principles of wilderness conservation. The national office will answer inquiries on hiking, camping, backpacking, canoeing, and other outdoor activities.

Racquetball

American Amateur Racquetball Association (AARA), 815 North Weber St., Colorado Springs, CO 80903. (303) 635-5396. The AARA promotes the sport of racquetball and is a member of the U.S. Olympic Committee. They will respond to requests for information on racquetball.

Running/Jogging

American Running and Fitness Association (ARFA), 2420 K St. NW., Washington, DC 20037. (202) 965-3430. The American Running and Fitness Association serves as a clearinghouse of information on running and jogging. They promote healthful running by physically qualified people. Their Runner's Referral Service will match you with a runner of similar ability in your area. To be included in the referral service, a runner can complete an information form and file it with the ARFA.

Road Runners Club of America (RRCA), 1226 Orchard Village, Manchester, MO 63011. (314) 391-6712. The RRCA promotes long distance running on an amateur basis. They can answer requests on organizing a running club or a running competition.

Skating

Ice Skating Institute of America, 1000 Skokie Blvd., Wilmette, IL 60091. (312) 256-5060. The goals of the Ice Skating Institute are to improve the ice rink business and to increase public interest in ice skating. They can respond to requests for information on ice skating.

Roller Skating Rink Operators Association (RSROA), P.O. Box 811846, Lincoln, NE 68510. (402) 489-8811. RSROA's membership consists of almost 2,000 roller skating rinks across the country. It promotes and popularizes the sport of roller skating. Publications on skating are available, but they cannot respond to specific requests for information. These questions should be directed to your local rink.

United States Figure Skating Association, 20 First St., Colorado Springs, CO 80906. (303) 635-5200. The U.S. Figure Skating Association is the governing body for amateur figure skating in the United States. Information will be provided by mail on local clubs and on learning to ice skate.

Skiing

American Water Ski Association, P.O. Box 191, Winter Haven, FL 33880. (813) 324-4341. The American Water Ski Association promotes competitive and noncompetitive water skiing in the United States. It acts as a clearinghouse for information on water skiing.

Ski Touring Council, c/o Lewis Polak, 32 Harmony Rd., Spring Valley, NY 10976. (914) 356-9376. The Ski Touring Council is a nonprofit organization founded to promote ski touring or noncompetitive cross-country skiing. They will answer mail or telephone inquiries on cross-country skiing, but will not answer questions on snow conditions or similar subjects.

United States Ski Association (USSA), P.O.Box 100, Park City, UT 84060. (801) 649-6935. The USSA is the national governing body for organized skiing. Information services include answers to mail or telephone inquiries on cross-country skiing, alpine skiing, and ski jumping. Information on cross-country skiing for older people is also available.

Soccer

United States Soccer Federation (USSF), 350 Fifth Ave., Room 4010, New York, NY 10118. (212) 736-0915. The United States Soccer Federation is the national governing body for the sport of soccer. They serve as a clearinghouse for information, publications, and audiovisuals on soccer.

Softball

Amateur Softball Association of America, 2801 NE. 50th St., Oklahoma City, OK 73111. (405) 424-5266. The Amateur Softball Association of America develops and promotes the sport of softball on an organized basis. It will answer inquiries on all aspects of softball.

Swimming

International Amateur Swimming Federation (IASF), 200 Financial Center, Des Moines, IA 50309. (515) 244-1116. The IASF promotes and encourages the development of amateur swimming, diving, water polo, and synchronized swimming. They will respond to mail and telephone requests for information on swimming.

United States Swimming, Inc. (USS), 1750 East Boulder St., Colorado Springs, CO 80909. (303) 578-4578. The USS is the national governing body for amateur competitive swimming. They offer a variety of programs geared to all levels of swimmers. They will answer requests for information on their programs.

Tennis

United States Tennis Association Education and Research Center, 729 Alexander Rd., Princeton, NJ 08540. (609) 452-2580. The objective of the United States Tennis Association is to develop tennis as a means of healthful recreation and physical fitness. It serves as a clearinghouse for information on recreational tennis.

Volleyball

United States Volleyball Association, 1750 East Boulder St., Colorado Springs, CO 80909. (303) 632-5551, ext. 3331. The U.S. Volleyball Association is the national governing body for the sport of volleyball. It will refer inquirers to an appropriate regional director.

Walking

Walking Association, 4113 Lee Highway, Arlington, VA 22207. (703) 527-5374. The Walking Association is concerned with all matters related to walking, including its health and recreational aspects. It will respond to inquiries on walking but suggests that inquirers first check their local libraries.

ORGANIZATIONS FOR SPECIAL GROUPS

American Athletic Association for the Deaf (AAAD), 3916 Lantern Dr., Silver Spring, MD 20902. (202) 224-8637. The AAAD provides physical recreation activities for members of its clubs. The group can refer a deaf person to a local club and answer inquiries on subjects pertaining to athletics for the deaf. They also promote participation in the World Games for the Deaf.

Blind Outdoor Leisure Development, Inc. (BOLD), 533 East Main St., Aspen, CO 81611. (303) 925-2086. BOLD is dedicated to encouraging and helping blind people engage in outdoor recreation activities such as skating, swimming, and skiing. BOLD can refer the inquirer to a local club, advise individuals interested in setting up a club, and answer questions on athletics for the blind.

National Handicapped Sports and Recreation Association, Capitol Hill Station, P.O. Box 18664, Denver, CO 80218. (303) 978-0564. The National Handicapped Sports and Recreation Association promotes physical activities for handicapped persons as a means of enhancing physical and mental well-being and the overall quality of life. They will refer the inquirer to a local chapter for more information on becoming involved in a particular physical activity.

National Wheelchair Athletic Association (NWAA), 2107 Templeton Gap Rd., Suite C, Colorado Springs, CO 80907. (303) 632-0698. The NWAA establishes the rules and regulations for and governs all wheelchair sports in the United States except basketball and bowling. They will answer inquiries by telephone or mail on subjects pertaining to wheelchair sports, including archery, field events, slalom, table tennis, swimming, track, and weightlifting.

National Wheelchair Basketball Association (NWBA), 110 Seaton Bldg., University of Kentucky, Lexington, KY 40506. (606) 257-1623. The NWBA is the governing body for all teams playing in organized competition in the United States. They will respond to inquiries by telephone or mail on topics such as where a person can join a local team, rules of wheelchair basketball, and how to start a team.

North American Riding for the Handicapped Association (NARHA), P.O. Box 100, Ashburn, VA 22011. (703) 471-1621. The NARHA promotes horseback riding as therapeutic recreation for the handicapped and coordinates the activities of local programs. Local programs provide instruction in horseback riding and sponsor recreational events. They will direct inquirers to programs in their area.

Special Olympics, 1701 K St. NW., Suite 203, Washington, DC 20006. (202) 331-1346. Special Olympics is the largest international program of physical fitness, sports training, and athletic competition for mentally retarded children and adults. The international headquarters, at the address given above, will mail an information package that provides a general introduction to the Special Olympics. A list of state and U.S. territory chapters is included.

United States Association for Blind Athletes, 55 West California Ave., Beach Haven, NJ 08008. (609) 492-1017. The United States Association for Blind Athletes develops and promotes sports programs for the blind and visually impaired. The association serves as a clearinghouse of information on sports for the blind including track and field, swimming, wrestling, gymnastics, and goal ball.

OTHER ORGANIZATIONS

American Alliance for Health, Physical Education, Recreation and Dance (AAHPERD), 1900 Association Dr., Reston, VA 22091. (703) 476-3424. AAHPERD is a voluntary educational organization made up of seven national and six regional associations. Publications produced cover general physical fitness, individual sports, women's sports, safety education, recreation education, health education, and career opportunities. Materials for teaching special groups such as the handicapped and the mentally retarded are available.

American College of Sports Medicine (ACSM), 1440 Monroe St., Madison, WI 53706. (608) 262-3632. The American College of Sports Medicine is a nonprofit multidisciplinary professional and scientific society created to generate and disseminate information concerning the responses, adaptations, and clinical aspects of the human organism engaged in exercise and in recreational and competitive sports.

American Volkssport Association (AVA), Phoenix Square, Suite 203, 1001 Pat Booker Rd., Universal City, TX 78148. (512) 659-2112. The concept of volkssport involves walking, biking, swimming, and snow skiing events sponsored by clubs across the country. AVA-sanctioned events include noncompetitive family walks of distances between 6 and 12 miles. They will answer general questions and direct you to a club in your area.

National Recreation and Park Association (NRPA), 3101 Park Center Dr., Alexandria, VA 22302. (703) 820-4940. The NRPA promotes the interests of the park and recreation movement. They promote public awareness of the role of physical fitness in health, encourage recreation among the elderly, and promote recreation services for the handicapped. They maintain an information center on park and recreation interests.

President's Council on Physical Fitness and Sports, 450 5th St., NW., Room 7103, Washington, DC 20001. (202) 272-3430. The President's Council on Physical Fitness and Sports promotes physical fitness opportunities for Americans of all ages. They produce informational materials on exercise, school physical education programs, sports, and physical fitness for youth, adults, and the elderly.

Women's Sport Foundation (WSF), 195 Moulton St., San Francisco, CA 94123. (415) 563-6266, (800) 227-3988, (800) 652-1455 in CA, 12:00–5:00 p.m. weekdays. The WSF was created to encourage and support the participation of women in sports; to provide opportunities, facilities, and training for women in sports; and to educate women and the public about women's athletic capabilities and the value of sports for them. They maintain an information and resource center on all women's sports and related topics.

APPENDIX F

Parts One, Two, Three, and Four Study Quiz Answers

STUDY QUIZ ANSWERS

Part One	Part Two	Part Three	Part Four
1. d	1. b	1. d	1. a
2. a	2. c	2. c	2. c
3. c	3. a	3. b	3. f
4. b	4. d	4. a	4. a
5. a	5. d	5. e	5. d
6. c	6. c	6. d	6. d
7. a	7. c	7. b	7. e
8. c	8. a	8. d	8. a
9. a	9. a	9. a	9. d
10. e	10. a	10. d	10. a
11. b	11. a	11. a	11. b
12. b	12. g	12. d	12. d
13. d	13. a	13. e	13. a
14. b	14. b	14. c	
15. a	15. d	15. e	
16. a	16. d	16. c	
17. d		17. a	
18. b		18. d	
19. a		19. d	
20. a		20. a	
21. a			
22. d			
23. a			
24. a			
25. a			
26. a			
27. b			
28. a			
29. a			
30. a			
31. d			
32. b			
33. d			
34. a			
35. a			

APPENDIX G

The Relationship of the Quiz Questions and the Discussion and Activities to the Part Objectives

The following chart shows the relationship of the quiz questions and the discussion and activities to the part objectives:

PART ONE

Objective Number	Quiz (Q), Discussion and Activities (D&A)
1	Q: 1, 2, 3, 4, 5, 25, 31, 35 D&A: 1
2	Q: 11, 12, 13, 32, 34 D&A: 10
3	Q: 17, 33 D&A: 2
4	Q: 21, 26, 27, 28, 29, 30 D&A: 9
5	Q: 19, 22 D&A: 3, 7
6	Q: 6, 7, 8, 18, 19, 23 D&A: 4
7	Q: 6, 7, 8, 18, 19, 23 D&A: 4
8	Q: 9, 14, 15 D&A: 5
9	Q: 16, 20, 24 D&A: 6, 8

PART TWO

Objective Number	Quiz (Q), Discussion and Activities (D&A)
1	Q: 1, 2, 3, 4, 5, 7, 11, 13, 14, 16 D&A: 4
2	Q: 2, 5, 6, 8, 9, 10, 12, 15 D&A: 2, 3
3	Q: 3, 7, 11, 13, 14 D&A: 1

PART THREE

Objective Number	Quiz (Q), Discussion and Activities (D&A)
1	Q: 1, 2, 3, 4, 5, 6, 7, 8, 9, 10, 11, 12, 13, 14, 16, 19, 20 D&A: 1, 2, 4
2	Q: 15, 17, 18 D&A: 3, 5

PART FOUR

Objective Number	Quiz (Q), Discussion and Activities (D&A)
1	Q: 4, 7, 10 D&A: 2, 6
2	Q: 1, 5 D&A: 1, 7, 8
3	Q: 5 D&A: 7,8
4	Q: 11 D&A: 3, 8
5	Q: 6 D&A: 3, 7
6	Q: 2, 3, 8 D&A: 1
7	Q: 2, 3, 8 D&A: 1, 2
8	Q: 12 D&A: 4
9	Q: 13 D&A: 5